WITHIN ADOBE WALLS

WITHIN ADOBE WALLS

A Santa Fe Journal

Selections from the Charlotte White Journals

EDITED BY CORINNE P. SZE

FOREWORD BY MARC SIMMONS

THE HISTORIC SANTA FE FOUNDATION

Published by the Historic Santa Fe Foundation
P.O. Box 2535
Santa Fe, New Mexico 87504-2535
The Historic Santa Fe Foundation World Wide Web site is http://www.historicsantafe.com

To order this or other HSFF publications call (505) 983-2567 or e-mail: hsffnm@aol.com

Design and Production: Janine Lehmann Design
Project Manager: Sally Hyer
Printed by Thompson-Shore, Inc.

Front cover photos:
Facade of 518 Alto Street before street was paved in 1972. (Courtesy New Mexico State
  Records Center and Archives, Historic Santa Fe Foundation Collection, Neg. No. 20807)
Charlotte with Charlie beside a flowering apple tree. (Courtesy Charlotte White)
Hand-plastering by women from Cañones, June 1961. (Courtesy Charlotte White)
Sculptor Boris Gilbertson with his torch. (Courtesy Charlotte White)

Back cover photo:
Corinne P. Sze and Charlotte White, 2000. (Photo by Hope A. Curtis, Courtesy HSFF)

Frontispiece:
Boris's *zaguán* gate, c. 1968. (Photo by Alan K. Stoker, Courtesy HSFF)

Publisher's Cataloging-in-Publication
(Provided by Quality Books, Inc.)

White, Charlotte, 1914-
   Within adobe walls : a Santa Fe journal : selections
from the Charlotte White journals / edited by Corinne P.
Sze : foreword by Marc Simmons. -- 1st ed.
   p. cm.
   Includes bibliographical references.
   LCCN: 2001088151
   ISBN: 0-9708609-0-0

   1. White, Charlotte, 1914- 2. Women--New Mexico--
Santa Fe--Biography. 3. Architecture, Domestic--New
Mexio--Santa Fe. 4. Santa Fe (N.M.)--Social life and
customs. 5. Santa Fe (N.M.)--History--Miscellanea.
6. Gilbertson, Boris, 1907-1982. 7. Artists--New Mexico--
Santa Fe--Biography. 8. Adobe houses--New Mexico--Santa
Fe--Maintenance and repair. I. Sze, Corinne P.
II. Title.

F804.S253W475 2001   978.9'56053/092
                  QBI01-200306

To the late Bill Lumpkins, who saved this house from extinction in 1946. Without him it might not have been here in 1959 (again in danger of falling down) for Boris and me to save once more. Also to Archie West, without whom maintaining it would have been impossible for me here alone for so many years. Finally, to the Historic Santa Fe Foundation, which, I trust, will continue to care for it for generations to come.

CHARLOTTE WHITE
SANTA FE, 2000

Contents

Foreword   ix

Editor's Preface and Acknowledgments   xi

Introduction   xv

Prologue *January 20, 2000*   1

July 28–August 29, 1959 *"I wouldn't even mind living just this way"*   9

May 1–June 8, 1960 *"Waiting for Boris"*   20

June 10–August 5, 1960 *"Nothing like fixing up an old house"*   29

August 11–October 17, 1960 *"I'm in the front building, all clean and warm"*   41

October 31–December 14, 1960 *"The patio is transformed"*   50

December 21, 1960–April 5, 1961 *"Such a long, lonely winter"*   57

April 18–July 29, 1961 *"A man of no compromise"*   66

August 3, 1961–March 3, 1962 *"Piles of wood, vigas waiting to be used"*   74

April 17–August 13, 1962 *"Boris pulling loose ends together"*   77

August 14, 1962–December 10, 1964 *"No time for the house"*   81

July 12, 1965–October 3, 1967 *"Boris's work finally recognized"*   93

October 14, 1967–October 19, 1968 *"Working on the portal in back"* 115

November 14, 1968–January 10, 1970 *"Adobes are going up fast* 126
for the new room"

February 14, 1970–January 21, 1971 *"I haven't had a minute"* 137

February 6–December 25, 1971 *"We may finally finish the house!"* 146

January 4, 1972–January 19, 1977 *"One thing actually finished"* 157

June 5–December 19, 1978 *"Wish we had never started the back"* 176

January 4–November 9, 1979 *"Poor Archie, poor Boris, poor me"* 189

November 10, 1979–August 20, 1980 *"The kitchen is a joy"* 200

September 15–October 29, 1980 *"You can't help admiring his spirit* 210
and guts"

Epilogue *January 20, 2000* 213

Glossary 216

Flora and Fauna 218

People and Places 220

For Further Reading 235

Foreword

The house at 518 Alto Street in Santa Fe has a long and enduring claim on my affections. It is a historic structure, linked to the prominent nineteenth-century political figure and land grant expert Donaciano Vigil. I was a member of the State Cultural Properties Review Committee in 1972 when another member, Dr. Myra Ellen Jenkins, nominated the Vigil House for inclusion on the National Register of Historic Places. It was accepted unanimously.

In the early 1960s, I had become friends with the house's saviors, Boris Gilbertson and Charlotte White, and on a couple of occasions I even occupied it when they were away on winter jaunts to their beloved Mexico. By the 1970s, I also was acquainted with the property's previous owner, noted architect William T. Lumpkins. Over the years, I was drawn to others who had an association with the house on Alto Street and with its remarkable pair of occupants who so lovingly had brought the original ruin back to life.

At the time, I remained unaware that Char was keeping a journal, recording not only the joy and frustration of architectural rehabilitation but including sidelights on her life and Boris's as they intersected at many points with artists, writers, and the numerous interesting and quirky folk making up the Santa Fe community in the second half of the twentieth century.

Char's writings, it is clear to me, serve as a valuable contribution to the social and cultural history of Santa Fe. But more importantly, perhaps, they convey to readers the authentic flavor and atmosphere of the town during a relaxed, freewheeling period that no longer exists. Charlotte White herself admits that under the changed circumstances of today, she and Boris would have been unable to pull off the same hardscrabble adventure that resulted in their reclamation of the Donaciano Vigil House.

From the foregoing, it can be understood why I eagerly accepted the Historic Santa Fe Foundation's invitation to contribute to its newest publication, *Within Adobe Walls: A Santa Fe Journal.* The edited selections included herein were ably prepared by Corinne P. Sze, who worked closely with the author. The finished book, well-illustrated, offers a simple but charming narrative that should appeal to all those seeking to learn more about the magical place called Santa Fe. Charlotte White's account lets us see how the town worked its spell upon two talented people and how they returned the favor by preserving a significant fragment of its architectural heritage.

I am delighted to pay tribute to my two friends, Charlotte White and Boris Gilbertson, by extending their book my strongest and most heartfelt endorsement.

Marc Simmons

Editor's Preface and Acknowledgments

Charlotte White began keeping a journal on July 28, 1959, the day she and sculptor Boris Gilbertson arrived in Santa Fe, New Mexico, from Illinois to take possession of their newly purchased property at 518 Alto Street. After years of neglect, the two small buildings they now owned were barely habitable, but in them Charlotte and Boris saw the potential to create a work of art. For Charlotte, the keeping of a journal was a new and uncharacteristic undertaking that marked a radical break with the past and the beginning of a challenging new life in Santa Fe.

She faithfully recorded the daily details of a project that eventually spanned more than two decades to create the showplace home and gardens that are among Santa Fe's most beloved. Beyond this story, which will resonate with anyone who has experienced the romance and the frustration of renovating an old adobe, Charlotte provides a window into the life of an artist in Santa Fe in the mid to late decades of the twentieth century, a period yet to be discovered.

Most histories of Santa Fe's celebrated art colony, which began to take form after the turn of the twentieth century, conclude in the 1940s with World War II. However, Santa Fe remained and continues to be a mecca for artists. Despite growth and change since the war, when Charlotte and Boris arrived in 1959, Santa Fe was still a very small town and a relatively remote haven where artists could live their chosen lives away from the mainstream of American culture. There were few galleries but plenty of creative people whose ranks Charlotte and Boris soon joined. In her journals, this world forms the background for her main subjects: Boris and the house.

In 1996 Charlotte White donated her home, which had come to be known as the Donaciano Vigil House, to the Historic Santa Fe Foundation (HSFF). The HSFF is a private, nonprofit, charitable organization chartered in 1961 and dedicated to historic preservation by owning and preserving historic properties and by providing education based on the sound knowledge gained from its research efforts.

When it became known that Charlotte wished to share her journals and their invaluable documentation of the house, the HSFF Board of Directors realized that this was a rare opportunity, as it were, to be present at the creation. Because the journals contain much that is highly personal, they could not simply be handed over to an editor to pick and choose at will from their contents. The board decided that Charlotte should read through them first and select passages about the house and other items of interest, including enough detail to follow the thread of her life during these years. Then Charlotte and I met for many pleasurable sessions at 518 Alto, with tape recorder and notebook.

Working in the greenhouse on the south side of the back building—sunny and warm even on the windiest January day—we sat at a long table by the door that looks through the kitchen to the patio door, recording Charlotte reading the passages she had chosen, editing and commenting as she went along. The tapes were transcribed and edited for Charlotte's review, and then corrections and additions were made as she saw fit.

The journal excerpts as read by Charlotte have been only minimally edited for clarity, beyond the necessary decisions concerning punctuation and paragraphing. When in doubt, the spelling of names follows that of the journals. In some cases, surnames have been intentionally omitted. Explanatory information, much of which is in the "People and Places" section at the back of this book, was gleaned from obituaries and other news articles, biographical dictionaries, other standard references, as well as Internet searches, with the possibility for error inherent in each of these sources. Charlotte's spoken comments have been placed in bracketed italics.

Acknowledgments must first and foremost recognize Charlotte White and Boris Gilbertson for seeing the potential of the property and for making their vision real. The late architect William T. Lumpkins, who stabilized the property, keeping it standing in the 1940s and 1950s, patiently answered my questions during several interviews.

Charlotte has additionally given us a rare day-to-day record spanning more than twenty years. Having devoted nearly half her life to the creation and care of the house and its gardens, she has selflessly donated them all to the HSFF so that they can be preserved as a historic property for the benefit of future generations.

This project was undertaken over several years with support from the HSFF. Julie Dougherty was the president of the board of directors who accepted the gift of the property from Charlotte. As the board's property chair, Dale Zinn recognized the significance of Charlotte's journals and provided the leadership that launched the project of their transcription and editing. Ruth Holmes, as chair of the Foundation's publications committee, has guided this effort with a wise and steady hand. Historian Sally Hyer has assisted with many details and has ably shepherded the manuscript through the publication process. Copy editor Denice A. Anderson gave many helpful recommendations.

Donna Quasthoff, American Institute of Architects, provided meticulous, measured drawings of these old and irregular buildings, and Hope Curtis furnished invaluable photographic documentation. Eugene Sanchez, the director of Gallery A in Taos, willingly researched questions about the gallery and its early artists. The staffs of New Mexico's research collections were indispensable: the State Records Center and Archives, the State Library, the Fray Angélico Chávez History Library, the Palace of the Governors Photo Archives, and the library of the Laboratory of Anthropology. Finally, the present HSFF Board of Directors, led by Peter Wirth, has made the completion of this publication possible.

Introduction

Charlotte White was forty-five years old when she began a new life in Santa Fe, New Mexico, with Boris Gilbertson. She had been independent for a number of years, supporting herself as a floral designer in her native Illinois, but she had never before owned a home, much less a crumbling adobe on a dirt road in Santa Fe's ancient Barrio de Guadalupe. The two structures on the property, which she had purchased from the artist and architect William T. Lumpkins, were barely livable. Across the front were one large room and a small bathroom (added by Lumpkins) but no real kitchen. Further back another building was just one long, undefined room, roofed but lacking a ceiling. The space between the front and back buildings was enclosed by the walls of neighboring dwellings lying on the east and west property lines. The patio thus created was filled with dirt and debris; nothing at all of any note was growing anywhere on the property.

In 1946 Bill Lumpkins had purchased the property at 518 Alto Street for $700 as an investment. Abandoned for years, it was then in ruins. The front building had no roof, and its thick adobe walls were eroded down a foot or two. A fire had destroyed the roof of the back building, which was in such poor condition that it was impossible to tell how or when it had last been used.

Lumpkins built up the walls of the front room and installed a beamed ceiling. He filled in the opening across the front between this building and its neighbor on the east with a cement block wall in which he placed an entrance door. He framed in a bathroom against the neighbor's wall on the east property line and enclosed the space between it and the original room with a frame partition that in effect extended the south wall of the main room and created an enclosed entry hall. The back building was roofed but otherwise left unfinished. In both front and back buildings, cement floors were poured. Most notably, Lumpkins installed some of the beautiful nineteenth-century windows and doors he had salvaged from the old St. Michael's College building, which he had renovated for the Christian Brothers after World War II. Others he had left lying about the property.

During Lumpkins's ownership between 1946 and 1959 the property was little used. For about a year, his brother Louis, a contractor, had his shop in the front room and stored lumber in the back. Then it was leased for about a year and a half to Warren ("Bud") Gilbertson, a noted ceramist and Boris's brother.

In 1958, Charlotte and Boris found the property virtually abandoned again, with roofs leaking and windows broken and boarded up. Nevertheless, of all the possibilities they saw, this was what excited them. Finally, in the spring of 1959, after protracted, long-distance negotiations between Illinois, Santa Fe, and California (where Lumpkins was living), it was theirs for the sum of $4,150 plus $72.32 in expenses.

Initially, Charlotte and Boris were taken with the potential beauty of a dramatic property with its large, thick-walled front room and interior courtyard enclosed by neighboring buildings, and they sensed that the neighborhood was old. Only later did they learn of its associations with Donaciano Vigil, a towering figure in the nineteenth-century history of New Mexico.

In reality, the Barrio de Guadalupe is one of Santa Fe's oldest neighborhoods. One of the earliest known maps of Santa Fe, drawn in about 1766 by the Spanish military officer José Urrutia, shows this as an area of furrowed fields with a few widely spaced and modest-sized, rectangular or L-shaped buildings lying along what is now Agua Fria Street (then a *camino real,* or royal road, and the trade route south to Mexico) and on the high ground (*los altos*) south of the river. After the construction of the Guadalupe Chapel (licensed about 1795), the neighborhood was known as the Barrio de Guadalupe. In 1823, as indicated on a Mexican census, fifty-seven families were living in the barrio. The most common occupations were farmer and laborer, with a scattering of masons, cobblers, tailors, shepherds, and silversmiths.

The properties now located on the south side of Alto Street were once part of large tracts that extended south from the Santa Fe River. Here Donaciano's father, Juan Cristóbal Vigil, had established a family home. His will, written in 1832, describes a four-room dwelling, a garden with five fruit trees, and a detached building used as a barn for animals and hay.

As he declared in his own will of 1842, Donaciano inherited a share of this property, including two rooms of his father's house. He also had purchased other rooms and adjacent lands from various relatives and had control of a room and land owned by a nephew. In 1856, he sold an unspecified amount of this property, including a house with a mill, to Vicente García, who proceeded to buy up other adjacent lands. In 1915, as administrator of his father's estate, Marcelino García deeded fifty-seven feet of this property to his younger brother, Vicente García, who eventually lost it to a finance company that, in turn, sold it to the wife of Bill Lumpkins in 1946.

It is difficult to know the precise location or configuration of the Vigil or García buildings because of the vagueness of early property descriptions and because of the time that has elapsed. Adobe was used as a highly flexible medium. Rooms were added with relative ease, and, if neglected and their timbers salvaged, they could quickly dissolve into the mud and straw from whence they came. Boris and Charlotte have created not so much a reproduction of the Vigil home as an interpretation of a Spanish-era dwelling that stands on its own merits as a sublime work of Boris Gilbertson's artistic imagination. With its magnificent entrance gate crafted by Gilbertson, elegant windows brought from the old St. Michael's College dormitory, and exterior walls mud-plastered in the traditional manner, the Donaciano Vigil House has become one of Santa Fe's most distinguished and cherished properties.

Charlotte's handwritten journals faithfully document the day-to-day vicissitudes of the project that lasted, off and on, into the 1980s. They also touch on the many facets of daily life: pets, friends, family, the ever-present neighborhood children, and jobs at flower shops—a not always welcome duty but necessary to finance the seemingly endless house project. There are sharply drawn vignettes of life on Alto Street, so different from the upper-middle-class world of the Midwest that Charlotte had gladly left behind. Always, too, there is the garden, with its seasons, and the weather, which in New Mexico is rarely without its own drama. A horticulturist by profession and avocation, Charlotte has a special interest in weather, which she rarely fails to mention.

However, her main subjects are always the house and Boris, who seems to have had a limitless ability to make real with his hands his vision of the property—but who also placed inordinate demands upon himself in his quest for excellence. Professionally already a well-regarded sculptor, Boris embodied the paradox of the true artist: a "free spirit" expressed through highly disciplined work.

Gilbertson was born in Evanston, Illinois, in 1907 to a Russian mother and a Norwegian father. When he was a child, the family moved constantly; in his teens, he struck out on his own, beginning a lifelong propensity to just "take off." In his youth, as he put it, he would "hit a rattler and go for a ride." Eventually, he knew most of the railroads in the country. A keenness for spontaneous adventure persisted through the whole of his life.*

He was just short of fifteen when he first headed off. Jumping a train in Chicago, he was amazed to find himself in Denver the next morning. There he found a summer job on a railroad construction crew helping the powder man with explosives. In the fall he returned to school with "money in my shoe." After high school he entered the University of Chicago to study physics but soon found that wasn't for him. A job at the university's Oriental Institute restoring finds from the dig at Persepolis in Iran inspired him to enter the Chicago Art Institute to study sculpture. He trained for about six years at the institute and at the University of Chicago but typically never got around to "collecting the degree." By his own account, "I just didn't pay much attention to that sort of thing."

Beginning in the late 1930s, following a propensity to go his own way, Gilbertson lived for about fifteen years in a log cabin in the woods on the remote northern Wisconsin shore of Lake Superior, near the small Finnish–Russian settlement of Cornucopia. There he built a studio and won a number of depression-era, federal commissions for art in public

---

*Boris Gilbertson was interviewed by Sylvia G. Loomis in 1964 for the Smithsonian Institution's Archives of American Art. Most of the quotations here are drawn from that interview.

buildings. His most ambitious project was two marble bas-relief panels for the new U.S. Department of the Interior building constructed in the 1930s under Secretary Harold Ickes. Each was thirteen feet long and five and a half feet high. One depicted American moose and the other American bison. The panels were produced in Wisconsin in three sections, which each weighed more than two tons, and then were shipped to Washington, D.C.

As an artist Gilbertson refused to be pigeonholed. He had no respect for "schools" or "labels," which he felt were the work of "little busy-body critics." To him, art was either good or it was not; it was either an expression of genuine feeling or it was a "superficial spellbinder." He had no use for the company of artists simply because they were artists, unless he had something really in common with them, which wasn't necessarily always the case. His inspiration, he said, came from life.

In an era when abstraction was the vogue, Gilbertson worked from reality. Most of his work depicted animals, often with a great deal of humor, because with animals he could more safely express emotions. As he told an interviewer, "with animals you can say almost anything and no one can criticize you . . . you can make them say all sorts of very corny things and it doesn't seem corny at all . . . any feeling can be evoked, just as in the Russian fables which . . . always involve animals instead of people." One function of the artist, he felt, was to reveal "greatness in the commonplace." Hence the name Charlotte White chose for her book on Boris's art, which was published six years after his death: *Greatness in the Commonplace: The Art of Boris Gilbertson* (1988).

Gilbertson sculpted in wood, metal, stone, and slate. Each piece was handcrafted. His metal sculptures were created with a torch because he felt he remained closer to the materials that way. He never cast his work, and each piece was unique. This required prodigious technical skill and very systematic effort, about "eighty percent just plain dirty work," as he put it. The problem was always to maintain the creative spark over the mountain of technical work.

A student of Oriental thought, Gilbertson returned to the Oriental Institute to study classic Chinese calligraphy after World War II. There he learned the technique of Sumi brush drawing. His delicate creations on handmade Japanese paper, using ink he ground himself in the traditional manner, express his own sensibilities but with an Asian feeling.

Gilbertson's drawings and sculpture are represented throughout the United States in museums and private collections. His work can be seen in public buildings and outdoor spaces across the country, from the marble panels of the U.S. Department of the Interior building in Washington, D.C., to the thirty-five-foot-long limestone relief of a chess game with a large, freestanding king and queen at the Chess Pavilion in Chicago's Lincoln Park, to the fifteen-foot-high steel-and-bronze figure of the Prophet Elijah on the grounds of the State Land Office near downtown Santa Fe.

In the journals published here we are witness to the arc of Boris's life in Santa Fe: his early years of struggle working on the house while beginning a new career in the Southwest; followed by his ever-growing success as an artist represented by galleries in several southwestern states; and, finally, his progressively debilitating, chronic illness, in spite of which he valiantly persisted with his work as well as with the seemingly endless task of finishing the house. Through it all he never let go of his spirit of adventure.

Charlotte White has had a long and enduring relationship with the Historic Santa Fe Foundation to which she has entrusted the Donaciano Vigil House for preservation. She was a hardworking member of the HSFF Board of Directors for several terms (1967–72 and 1978–80). Another board member, Dr. Myra Ellen Jenkins, first noted Donaciano Vigil's nineteenth-century ownership of the property. Through her influence in 1962 the property was one of the first buildings listed by the Foundation as "worthy of preservation" and thereby eligible to display its shield-shaped plaque.*

CORINNE P. SZE

---

*The HSFF Registry of Buildings Worthy of Preservation to date contains nearly eighty historic resources in Santa Fe and environs. Through the efforts of Dr. Myra Ellen Jenkins, the Donaciano Vigil House was designated by the HSFF as worthy of preservation in 1962, and it was listed in the New Mexico State Register of Cultural Properties in 1969 and in the National Register of Historic Places in 1972.

Prologue

January 20, 2000

I was born in 1914 in Paxton, Illinois, a small town about a hundred miles south of Chicago. My father was born there, too, and my mother lived in a little neighboring town. It was named Ludlow after her father, a gentleman farmer, who arrived there in a covered wagon. His grandfather was Israel Ludlow, who did the surveying of Cincinnati, Ohio, under George Washington. Israel married Charlotte Chambers of Chambersville, Pennsylvania, and that's who I am named after, my great-great-grandmother.

I don't really know much about my father's family except that they had a farm in Paxton. My grandfather on that side was English and was a wonderful man. My grandmother was Scotch-Irish and came over to this country when she was quite young. I don't know how they ever met. My father was born on the farm, and he educated himself. Like so many influential and wealthy men at that time, he was self-made. He began as a clerk in the little bank in Paxton and worked his way up to a high position in the Federal Reserve Bank.

When I was four years old, we moved to Evanston, Illinois, when my father took a job at the Federal Reserve Bank in Chicago as head of the department that examines the bank finances. I was the baby in a family of five children, a mistake, I'm sure. My oldest sister Dorothy (we called her Dot) was sixteen years older than I; Treet (Theresa) was fourteen years older; and Kay (Katherine) was twelve years older. I had one brother, who was eight years older. He was named Ludlow, my mother's family name. Within the family we all called him Brud; to his friends he was Lud.

We moved into a large, three-story house in Evanston. Until my father died, our lives were secure and very conventional. My mother was a wonderful woman who lived for her children, as very few women do these days. My father was so preoccupied with his job that I didn't see much of him, except when we were together in the big garden out back. He loved to garden, and so I worked with him there. My mother was no gardener,

1

but she loved the wild outdoors. She was very close to the earth. I have something from each of them.

I had a wonderful childhood. We had beautiful red oaks in the yard, and I loved to climb in those trees. In the fall there were piles of leaves, and we would make leaf houses all over the front lawn. We raked them into low walls with doorways. You never jumped over the walls but used the doors. An old Italian lady came around with a huge hurdy-gurdy on wheels, and Dad would pay her to stay in our yard. All the neighborhood kids would come over and we would dance.

Times were so different then. You trusted everybody; there was no reason not to. In the 1920s there were hobos who would go from city to city jumping on the trains. They had regular camps around the country, and I am sure our house was marked in some way. We had quite a line of them coming to the backdoor asking for food. Mother never turned them down. She kept dishes and utensils to one side, just for these hobos, and let them sit on the back stoop to eat. Sometimes they would do odd jobs for her, but always she fed them. These days you would no more think of feeding a guy who came to the backdoor; you would call the police.

Probably the most beautiful thing I ever experienced was what my mother and father did for Christmas. The other children were so much older than I that it was really for me. Before Christmas there was only suspense. On Christmas Eve my folks must have stayed up all night because I saw nothing ahead of time. On the big morning we all had to come downstairs at the same time; I was naturally up early going around to wake the rest. Together the five of us went into the living room and there was the Christmas tree, all decorated—the lights gleaming, a fire in the fireplace, the music box playing, and all those presents. It was like magic, a fairyland.

After being up all night decorating the tree and getting everything done, Mother would make a very special breakfast and then Christmas dinner for the seven of us. I don't know how she did all that; it was her life. The tree with all its decorations was up for just a week. We had a tradition in the family that it was bad luck to have the same Christmas tree up in two different years. So the day before New Year's we would madly take down everything and put it all away. How they ever did it all, I don't know. I never even saw where they hid the Christmas tree beforehand.

My father died in 1930 when I was sixteen. He had been next in line for president of the Federal Reserve Bank in Chicago, but someone from Washington, D.C., was brought in instead. It was a purely political decision. I think that position had been his goal all his life. When he found out that he wasn't to have it, I think it killed him—I really do. Soon after he had a cerebral hemorrhage while coming home on the commuter train. Unfortunately, he was very ambitious. Boris always said ambition was an evil thing, and I can see why.

When he died everything changed. He didn't leave anything because investments were against his religion, even though he was a banker. Being a Scotch Presbyterian, he didn't believe in using money to make money. He wasn't a churchgoer and neither was Mother, but they both had great faith. In his work he didn't have anything to do with investments. We had been living just on what he earned, and we were really broke after he died.

My father didn't believe in credit, either. He had always said never to buy anything unless you could pay for it. However, he did buy the Evanston house on credit, and after his death we couldn't pay the mortgage anymore. This was during the Great Depression, and under President Franklin Delano Roosevelt's New Deal there was a program that helped us. The government would take over your mortgage and you could live in the house until your equity was used up. We lived there that way for quite a few years.

By the time Mother had to leave the house, I was married and my brother was in New York. She moved into an apartment and took what furniture she needed. It was the first time in her life that she had been free of the house and all those five kids. She became a different woman and enjoyed herself thoroughly. That's probably one reason I never wanted children. People who have children should make it a career in order to bring them up right. I never wanted to do that. I loved my freedom too much to be tied down raising a family—but I've always had wonderful dogs.

My brother and I were the only ones still home when my father died. My sisters were all married and gone by the time I was twelve. They all led very conventional lives, marrying successful men, having children, and doing all the things you were supposed to do. Dot, the oldest, married a boy from Paxton. They went together when she was in her teens

3

and were married secretly for a couple of years before anybody knew about it. She was still living at home while he was going to law school. He became a leading attorney in Chicago. Dot's daughter Karin lived in Santa Fe from the late 1960s to the early 1980s. Her husband, David Jackson, was headmaster of the Santa Fe Preparatory School.

Treet also married someone locally. Her husband was a prominent businessman, and they had a beautiful home in Evanston. They had a fancy summer home on Lake Vermilion up in Minnesota. She fell in love with the north woods and moved up there after her husband died. Treet was the one I felt closest to; we had a great time together. She loved the outdoors, walking though the woods, sailing in the boat. After she was widowed, we took trips together, and I went up to visit her when I could.

Kay, the youngest of the three, loved gardening. She was very close to the earth, and she loved animals. Shortly after her first husband died, she lost her only son to appendicitis. He was only seven or eight years old. She remarried a widower who was on the stock exchange in Chicago. He had a son just the age of the little boy she had lost, so she raised him. She and her husband moved out to Santa Fe even before I did.

My brother and I were different from the others. He was very unconventional. We weren't close until I started growing up at about fifteen. After that he was a big influence on me, and I thank him for it. He was a concert singer with the most gorgeous bass-baritone voice. He moved to New York City because he thought he would have a better chance for a singing career there, but he lacked the confidence to have a good stage presence. He got nervous and upset every time he had to perform. Toward the end of his time in New York, he made his living doing weddings and funerals; as he said, marrying and burying people. He was a dear, dear guy; we were very close.

After I graduated from high school I was faced with having to make some money, but I wasn't raised to do anything. If my father had lived, he would have insisted that I go to college. He was a great believer in education, although he himself never went to college. He couldn't afford it; he had to work. But I hated school. I was so glad to get out of there that I never, never wanted to go back. Even now I can't face it. I started taking something at the community college but I just couldn't do it—the homework and all those awful things that I associated with school. I got my education from reading books and from people. My brother got me on that path when I was fifteen; I became an avid reader because of him.

So after high school I needed a job. I had a friend whose sister worked in Mandel Brothers, a big department store in Chicago. She got me a job there. At one point, I was in charge of setting up a show of linens and tableware in the rug department where Harold Marks was the buyer. (I don't know why they gave me that job; I never did much of that at home.) He asked me out to lunch, and we went together for about a year. He was eight years older than I, my brother's age. I was four days short of twenty when we got married during Hal's lunch hour.

Soon we took off for Long Beach, California, where his uncle was in the oil business. He had an apartment for us and gave us a Model A Ford coupe with yellow wheels and a rumble seat. After a year I was sick of all those things growing and blooming all year long, so we came back to Evanston. After Hal was drafted into World War II, I got a job with Alcoa. They made sheets of aluminum for airplanes, and my job was to mark allotments for shipping. I quickly decided that wasn't for me, but I had to get another job. I couldn't stand the thought of being in an office all day and I had always liked flowers, so I decided to become a floral designer. I hadn't had any experience, but I finally found a florist who would take a chance on me. I just learned by doing. So began a thirty-five-year career.

I first met Boris Gilbertson when I was fifteen years old. Like Hal, he was the same age as my brother. (Boris's brother, Bud, was my brother's friend.) Boris did a marble head of me that I have still. It was very flattering to have a mature man interested in me. However, my father was alive then and would have nothing to do with my being mixed up with a twenty-three-year-old man. So we went our separate ways and each married other people. Later we met again through mutual friends in Evanston.

Boris was half Russian and half Norwegian. He was born in Evanston, but I don't know much about his early life except that he was a rebel just like I always was. I can't remember what his father did, but the family traveled all over. Both he and his brother became artists. Boris worked his way though the Chicago Art Institute driving a cab at night.

During World War II he lived in northern Wisconsin by Lake Superior. Boris never drank because there was alcoholism in his family. I thought that took a lot of character. But he had smoked three packs of cigarettes a day since he was twelve. The first year or two we were here in Santa Fe, he stopped cold and never had another. That takes character, too.

Boris and I depended on each other but for entirely different reasons. He was a very strong man, and he had such mastery in his art. He could do anything he put his mind to, and he created such beautiful things. He was an artist with all his being. His art was a very important part of my feeling for him, and of my life, really. Of course, for him art *was* life. Practically everything he did was somehow or other wrapped up in it. It was a compulsion. He just had to do his work. He lost all track of everything else when he was working. I felt responsible for him, even before he became so ill—like a mother, almost. He just didn't seem to be able to take care of himself in practical matters. He counted on me in so many different ways. I had such faith in his work and wanted to make it possible for him to devote himself to it.

Everybody liked Boris, people of all ages. He had such exuberance and a wonderful sense of humor. I never knew anybody who loved life the way Boris did, and his enthusiasms were infectious. The way he could tell a tale, elaborating anything to make a story out of it; he would have been a marvelous writer.

He wasn't always an easy person to be around, though. Time never entered into his plans. He was fascinated with clocks (the mechanisms, that is), but they didn't have to tell the right time. He had absolutely no sense of time. He never liked to meet a schedule and was always late. I get things done ahead of time so I don't have to worry; he put everything off until the last minute, when he would then be desperate. He never would make plans that required a certain day or time. I never knew when he was coming back from a trip, and he didn't either.

I first came out to Santa Fe in 1952 on a vacation with my sister Kay. We drove from Illinois together in my Jeep station wagon. I remember when we arrived in Taos Plaza, we saw an old wagon with Indians wrapped up in blankets. We couldn't believe we hadn't wandered onto a movie set. We were so enchanted that the next day we decided to take the back road from Taos to Santa Fe through all the little villages—what is now known as the High Road to Taos. It was a dirt road then and took quite a while. We just couldn't believe the whole thing was real— coming down from Truchas into Española, it was all so beautiful.

In Santa Fe we looked up Boris's brother, Bud Gilbertson, a very well known potter by then. He was renting this house from Bill Lumpkins and making his pottery in the unfinished back room. His kiln was in the *placita,* and he was living in the large front room. Little did I guess that one day I would be living there.

Anyway, my sister and I both fell in love with Santa Fe. I had wanted to get out of Illinois, so while we were here I got a job with a local florist as well as a place to live at El Zaguán. The rent was $35 a month for apartment number four, furnished and including utilities. I went back to Illinois and sold or gave away everything I owned except my clothes, books, and some records. Within a month I was back in Santa Fe. I lived and worked here a year and then went back to my old job in Illinois, which paid a lot more. Within a few years my sister and her husband built a house in Santa Fe and settled here permanently. That's how Santa Fe grabs you.

In 1958, when Boris and I decided that Santa Fe was where we would like to live, we came out for a month's vacation to see what we could find to buy. Boris suggested that we look at Bud's old place over on Alto Street. It was a complete shambles, just falling apart and all boarded up—hadn't been lived in for years—but it was for sale. Mr. Maes, the neighbor who had been watching over the house, came over and asked if we would like to go in and see it. We did; Boris, naturally, fell in love with it immediately and knew exactly what he was going to do. It took a year to make arrangements to buy it. We spent a month's vacation starting to fix it up, and the next year we moved to Santa Fe for good.

It was all so different then. Alto Street was a dirt road. The stone wall in front of the house wasn't there, and there were cement steps up to the front door. The large entrance had been partially enclosed with cement blocks. The *portal* in the patio wasn't there, and the patio was full of debris. Bud had built a cement slab there for his electric kiln. We didn't realize that there was a well and only found it after we brought the patio down to its original level by hauling away tons of dirt and debris.

Except for a couple of trees in the patio—a small, tough elm and a cottonwood (both of which I later removed), plus a small tamarisk—nothing much was growing anywhere. There were boarded-up doors and windows in the west wall of the patio, and there was junk piled all over.

Boris loved it. It was a challenge for him. I would never have even thought of attempting such a thing; it was a complete mess. This place never would have become what it is without Boris. I know of people who looked at the property when it was vacant and for sale and thought it was beyond hope. My sister wondered why we would want such a dump, but Boris and I had both been to Mexico and loved it—to Alamos and Taxco, which are national monuments and are preserved with character, which should have happened to Santa Fe many years ago. Those trips were an inspiration because this place looked so much like Mexico. I think that's what guided us in what we did to the house.

It is remarkable to realize now that in fixing up the property we were able to do just as we wanted. It's a good thing we didn't have to get permits because we would never have been able to do the things we did—especially the way things are now. There were no inspections or building permits then; it was wonderful. I can't believe all that we did to this old house. Of course, we knew nothing of its history when we began; it is lucky we didn't spoil it.

Boris and I have put so much of our lives into this house over so many years—so much thought and time and even money, which was never easy. That's one of the main reasons I've stayed in the house so long. It becomes part of you, and you feel responsible for it. As long as I can, I'll keep it going. I wanted it to be preserved, and that is why I have given it to the Historic Santa Fe Foundation. I feel sure they will take care of it, and it won't be sold. Nothing is ever sure or certain when you are gone, but I hope the Foundation will keep and protect this old place.

The whole story is in my journals. The minute we got in this house, I started writing about it. I never in my life kept track of anything or had any system at all. I've never understood how I managed to do something so unlike me, but I am glad I did.

July 28–August 29, 1959

"I wouldn't even mind living just this way"

July 28

Arrived yesterday from Illinois at 518 Alto with the little Jeep's arse dragging a thousand-pound load, among which was Boris's grandfather's workbench that he had made many years ago and is prized above all of Boris's possessions. It's eight feet long, so naturally hung out, making it necessary to leave the tailgate open. *[I think Boris spent a lot of time with his grandparents when he was a child. His grandfather was a woodworker and must have been an influence on him. Boris's son has the bench now.]*

We also had an eight-foot piece of plate glass we eventually hope to use for a skylight in the bedroom. *[We didn't use the plate glass as a skylight; we used it in the old doors back here in this building—they were the front doors when we came. The glass had been all broken and the doors boarded up when we came. We made room for them in the back building facing the patio.]* And tools and clothes, charcoal stove, cooking basket *[full of cooking stuff]*, cots, sleeping bags, an air mattress, and so forth. We were very lucky, for which I am most thankful. The Jeep has won the name of El Burro, which is an honor and a compliment.

Now for the house. With the sun coming up over the Sangre de Cristos, my beloved mountains, I sit in our patio surrounded by the very old adobe walls. It is weed-filled, with paper, cans, old stovepipes, tar paper, and assorted rocks; but there are a few tough trees that have survived neglect, one of which stays—the others are to be transplanted. It will be truly beautiful someday. The house is even more wonderful and full of promise than I had remembered. Of course, we didn't dare look at it too hopefully before, for fear it wouldn't be ours. The footing needs attention and above the windows where years of rain have washed away the adobe. How I hate to see that precious adobe return to the ground.

The house was full of children wandering in and out from the minute we unboarded the front door—from sixteen to two years old. All

9

from across the road. One of the older boys, named Mike, helped us unload and hose out the front room. Nice Mr. Maes, who has kept an eye on the place, fixed the toilet; outside of that, the plumbing was intact and they had men up here to turn the water on inside of two hours. *[Bill Lumpkins had put in the bathroom across from the front room.]*

Spent our first night here. Such luxurious camping out. Running water. The candlelight and shadows on the thick adobe walls. Smell of piñon. Cozy beds. Slow dripping of a slightly leaky roof that will soon be fixed. The front room is fine. We will be working on that first so we'll live in the back. So much to do. What first?

July 30

Missed yesterday. So many things to do. Never have I been so happy. I wouldn't even mind living just this way. I have a table with a fruit bowl, candles, and lovely piñon branches with beautiful green cones as a centerpiece. Bought two most comfortable and nice-looking, canvas-backed, basket-type chairs. Cook right at the table on the hibachi. Boris hung a piece of wood to hang our clothes on backed by the tarp, which gives us privacy where our cots are. And the elegance of a bathroom and "kitchen" with running water—all cold. It is the fanciest camping out you can imagine. *[When we came Lumpkins's added bathroom was really two rooms. A tiny room with a hot water heater and a sink was attached to the bathroom itself, which had a shower stall, a toilet, and a sink. I guess the previous tenants had used the smaller room as a kitchen somehow or other. We took out the door between the two rooms to put in a gas heater. There were two doors into the hallway, one from each of the small rooms. We closed off the original doorway into the bathroom and use the one that went into the "kitchen." Boris made the door.]*

We have decided to plaster with real adobe, no fake. The idea of covering up those old, old, lovely adobe bricks with nasty plaster has bothered us every time we talked about it. It never has the feeling or the warmth of the real thing. We are on the lookout for a man who can do a nice job and not ask $3 an hour. The footing has to be dug and two windows put in on the south wall because we are using some handsome old doors that will not let any light in on the patio side. *[I don't understand this; it doesn't sound right.]* Anyway, someday the patio will be so elegant we'll want a good look at it from the front room. Boris took the broken glass out of the front doors and put plywood in *[which we left for a while, of course].* Also drew a picture of flowers and Mau-Mau *[my beloved African gray parrot]* with La Casa Blanca *[the "White House," a pun on my last name]* drawn on it. It is such ideas and little touches that he will be inspired to do that will make this place really great.

He found a huge, hungry black widow spider under a rock in the patio yesterday—hope there aren't too many of them or any more, I should say. He has it in a jar. I'd feel better if it were smashed. Saw a baby horned toad in back this morning. If they aren't moving, you can't even see them for they are exactly the color of the earth.

Ginger Gray and Charles Hagerman called on us last night. They are such nice people—such good friends. Right at the start they love the place and its spaciousness. *[A potter herself, Ginger had worked for Bud Gilbertson, helping him with his pots.]*

July 31

Neighbor boys and Boris got the footing dug in front yesterday. *[This footing is baffling to me because the front room didn't need a footing. It has those great river rocks as a footing. I've forgotten so many things in all these years, but I think for some reason we thought we should put a footing on that west wall of the patio. We had never worked with adobes, and we didn't know what we were doing really. I don't think this footing was ever necessary.]*

Still trying to track down an old-timer to do the adobe work. Got stuff for the back roof, which will be on in a day or so. It seems to take so long to get going and money disappearing like mad; but it's for things we'll need for years to come, and guess it's all part of owning a place and getting started. *[You see, I'd never owned a house before.]*

Want to pick up my Santa Fe car license today. It will make us feel even more that we belong. Glorious sky last night from the roof where we later want to have a deck. *[We never did.]* You can see all around the city—the Jémez and the Sangre de Cristo mountains. Each day is so beautiful—hot sun, cool shadows, magnificent country.

It is most discouraging and depressing, the price of everything. So much to be done. Thought we could do more ourselves. We'll just have to—it's the only way we can swing it.

August 1

Truck of adobe bricks arrived. First load: eight men and two boys; two men very "tight." Second load: six men and three boys; "tight" ones still with us. Third load: three men and one boy, one "tight." Lovely bricks. Seventy dollars per one hundred, plus $20 delivery, which is well worth it. With a stack of them in front and the footing dug, it is beginning to look as though something is going on.

I worked on the back roof yesterday and this morning, scraping it and getting ready for the tar and tar paper. It is too hot now. We can't even touch the stuff. Hope to get it done later today or tomorrow morning. Had a beautiful downpour last night. The way the rain beats down on the flat roof is wonderful. To watch the sky all around gathering for the storm is magnificent.

An old Spanish guy was here yesterday about plastering. All he could think about was what gold might be in the walls—willing to split it with us, of course.

August 2

Boris is on the roof putting a new one on *[back roof]*. It is hot now, and I hope he comes down soon. Besides, it is Sunday and we are taking the afternoon off, eating out, and going to a mariachi concert in the Plaza tonight.

Still trying to track down a man to put the front adobe on. It is a job to find them. We'll have to find someone soon. I knocked down the silly little fireplace in the front room this morning. Saved about two dozen adobe bricks from it. *[There was a little stuck-on fireplace on the north wall of the front room, right in the middle. Just a few adobes piled up with a chimney. Bud had it built by an Indian woman. After I got it down, I discovered there were electric wires going right through the wall with chimney and fireplace on top of them, but being adobe, it didn't ever ignite.]*

Spent last evening sitting on the front stoop with three of the neighborhood children. Duchess and Juanita are handsome little girls. Such energy and devilment. Those children sleep when they are tired day or night. Makes no difference. Otherwise they are just having fun.

August 3

It is unnecessary to say it is a glorious morning. They all are. The intense light, hot sun, beautiful air, the soft breeze that ruffles the leaves on the little cottonwood in the *placita*. The sound that the leaves make and the way the cottonwood looks against the intense blue sky. The shade also will be welcome. *[The cottonwood didn't stay because it wasn't in the right place. There was also a small Chinese elm that I took out later.]*

Think we have found a man to do the work the way we want it—an old-timer, sober and intelligent who does beautiful work, Señor Delfino Montoya. He can't start for another couple of weeks.

We went to Truchas to look at the adobe plastering. Lots of straw in it, which makes it look like some of the fancy Japanese papers *[that Boris used in his work]*. Few cracks, sturdy. Hope we can have ours done that way.

The sky at sunset was wild, sun spotlighting parts with rain shafts and lightning behind it all. The sky in the evening is never the same. Each day a new dramatic effect. Amazing. The clouds are always more beautiful than any we've seen. Went to the Plaza last night. Looked like Mexico. The children drove home with us, stopping for a jumbo sundae—more than anyone could eat, except me, of course.

August 6

Finished tarring and papering the roof yesterday *[of the back room]*. I did it just because it's my house—for no one else would I do it. *[I don't remember how I tarred the roof. I must have used tar paper. There was no ceiling. It was leaking everywhere so we wanted to do that first for protection. When we finished the back room in 1979, we put the ceiling in and a lot of insulation. There were only two by sixes holding up the roof. We did the vigas from underneath the roof, which isn't easy. The front room supposedly has eight inches of dirt on the roof—I don't know.]*

We've both been working like bulls. Slowly things are getting done. Boris does such a perfect job, being a perfectionist, that it takes longer; but it's done right. Like the windows having to be evened *[leveled]* out.

Each evening my little friends Juanita and Duchess come over and we talk Spanish. They are darling and call me their God-given mother. So begins another busy day. They go so fast. Too fast. *[We were just out here on my vacation for a month to work on the house.]*

August 7

Most discouraged. It goes too slowly. I guess we'll have to find someone to work or we'll never get even the front done before we have to go. Wish I could do that work. I've been cleaning bricks, old ones from the prison. It's a hell of a job and I'll never make two thousand. *[The bricks were from the penitentiary way out in the country. They were tearing it down. Every brick is from there. So you can imagine—thousands of them, I guess.*]*

It rained from late yesterday afternoon until seven this morning. It's clearing now and maybe we'll get some things done.

August 8

Stopped raining long enough to get cement poured. *[That's that dumb footing that we thought we had to put in the patio over on the west wall between the two houses.]* Found a laborer at a dollar an hour to help with the bull work and clean bricks. He's a good Spanish guy with about twelve children. No job. How do they survive? He speaks no English, but with fingers and gestures he and Boris get along.

Last night we had a little shooting on Alto Street. Were awakened at eleven by Mike knocking on the door saying someone was trying to break in. He was home alone with six little ones and was frightened. Boris cut quite a figure running around in his pajamas, flashlight in one hand and .38 in the other. Cops came, shot into the shrubbery. No sign of anyone. Watched from empty-paned front window, hugging the wall, gun in

---

*New Mexico Territorial Penitentiary: Established 1885 near present St. Francis Drive and Cordova Road. Red brick manufacture began as a prison industry, 1886. Supplied bricks for many public and private projects, including additional prison buildings, walls, watchtowers. Replaced by new facility, 1956. Highly prized, old bricks salvaged. The names, Pen Road and the Pen Road Shopping Center, are the last area reminders of this once imposing facility.

hand, just like a horse opera. It is really a shame how they leave little children alone. If they survive, guess they're tough. Maybe that's better. This journal was going to be about the progress of the house, but since there is no progress I will fill in with life on Alto Street, of which there is plenty.

August 9

The sheepherder we have working for us showed up drunk today wanting an advance $3. I would have told him to go to hell, but not Boris.

August 10

We've decided to have the roof finished by an expert. Hot tar and gravel, ten-year guarantee. Hope to have it done today. It will cost $100 but will be worth it to have one thing finished. *[That's this roof in the back. Can you imagine? A hundred dollars!]*

The sheepherder is here again toting, leveling. He is a steady worker, which is something. Boris spent yesterday filling in a big hole in the wall caused by erosion before the roof was fixed.

Certainly hope *Señor* Montoya can come next week to get started on the front. *[He never did show up.]* Nothing seems to be getting done. I keep telling myself that if Boris wasn't that way he wouldn't be what he is to be an artist. One goes with the other.

This is truly a wonderful spot, and Boris thinks from the shards and flints and the old adobe that it must have been a very old campsite for Indians long before the Spanish invasion—being right on the river would be a likely place.* *[I saved those things that we found as we were digging around in the patio and took a big box of shards over to Marjorie Lambert, who was an archaeologist with the state. She dated some of them back to the 1300s, showing that the Indians did camp and live along the river. The shards are still in the shed out back.]*

Ginger and Charles dropped by yesterday with a delicious water-

---

*Spanish invasion: Juan de Oñate established the first Spanish colony in New Mexico in 1598 near San Juan Pueblo north of modern Española. The Pueblo Indians rose in revolt in 1680 and drove the Spanish out of New Mexico. Beginning in 1693 Diego de Vargas reconquered the province with considerable bloodshed.

melon. Met "our children" on the Plaza last night. They run to greet us and cling as though we were magnetized, especially to Boris.

August 11

This glorious country! Every morning is a joy to get up. The light is blinding; it takes several minutes to really see when you come in, even if you haven't been in the sun.

The roof is beautiful. The color of the gravel is wonderful with adobe. I'm going to have the front done next spring. Slowly this room is taking shape. Boris is doing a perfect job, naturally, and that takes longer but also lasts longer, too.

August 12

The front is more of a problem than we had suspected. Evidently before the roof was fixed the water had run down into the wall at one end and eroded the adobe. Big holes are under the surface. They have to be cleaned out and filled in like a cavity in a tooth so that we won't have trouble later on. *Mucho tiempo.* Oh well, things are always more involved than we expect, and I must learn to be patient. Boris got ahold of some sand with lots of mica in it. We think it will look great in the final coating of adobe and will sparkle in the morning sun, which should delight the neighbors. *[We didn't do that.]*

August 13

The sheepherder is with us again. When he is here, he really works but certainly is not pleasant to have around. Got another lead on a man for adobe work. Now to start trying to find him through brother, cousins, and so forth.

August 16 (Sunday)

Today we have a jackhammer. Mr. Roybal next door works for the city and he got ahold of a city one and is helping Boris crack the stuff up. Why they put such thick steps in I can't imagine. It's a terrific job and hope Boris doesn't overdo. He's really remarkable to be able to throw that big thing around and know where and how to throw it, and also to do the beautifully delicate drawings he does. Amazing. *[When we came, there were narrow cement steps that Bill Lumpkins had put in up to the front door. We couldn't have that, so Boris took them out.]*

Last night we took the three children to the circus. I don't know who had the most fun—the children watching the circus or us watching the children watching the circus. We had cotton candy and balloons. There were lots of animals, for which I'm glad. The most wonderful to me were the trained chimps, which I howled over. Duchess liked the elephants best.

The adobes are almost where we want them. The windows are sealed with mortar and new lintels. Boris has really been working like an ox. It's remarkable how he takes it.

August 18

We have a good floor; *that* we know. The jackhammer wouldn't even break it up. Just made little holes in it. It's poured concrete over wire mesh. We had to tunnel under it and then break it to get our *zaguán*. *[That's the cement floor between the bathroom and the east wall of the front room. Lumpkins had created an inside hallway with a plasterboard partition that continued the south wall of the front room across to the bathroom, which he had added. We took the partition and the floor out. Later we took dirt out. The whole thing was unbelievable.]* The front is going to look quite different with the big drive *[up to the door]*, which the sheepherder and Boris are digging out. What a job and what a mess.

Boris made a little piñon "stove" in the patio to cook on—cheaper than charcoal, and I think I'll like it better. It is easier to regulate the heat. *[This was just a rock-enclosed area for a fire.]* We only have about ten more days here. How quickly a month has gone and not nearly as much done as hoped. Hate leaving it. Hope it won't be long before we get back.

August 19

Signed my will today leaving everything to Boris. He is to distribute some of my personal belongings as I desire. It's simpler and cheaper that way.

Today I can't use the bathroom for our sheepherder is tunneling and breaking up the floor in front *[hallway]*. It will be a feat to even use it when it's available. Need a ladder. Love my piñon stove, and it's so nice

17

to have the campfire going at night. Got some marshmallows; the children have never roasted them.

Never have we seen so many men looking for work, and yet it is so hard to find anyone to work. They love the idea of earning some money but are not willing to do anything for it. Ambrosio is really a good worker, poor guy. It's heavy work, too. Was offered $35,000 yesterday for the place when it's finished—not interested.

August 22

Siempre mañana. Still seem to be always waiting for something to get done. Now it's to have a mountain of sand, stones, and cement hauled away by the Rios Wood Yard, where I buy two laundry tubs of wood for sixty cents. It would be wonderful fill, but unfortunately now no one wants it.

The front is really beginning to look elegant. It looks so tall and grand. The idea of "friend" *Señor* Montoya wanting $5 per hour has spurred us on. That was with Montoya's brother-in-law as helper, which we certainly don't need. We told him no, and Boris will do it himself. There! Since I have no pen and the candle is insufficient light I'll wait until *mañana.*

August 24

How quickly the days go by. Unbelievable. Such a busy place this is. Rios never did show up so told him not to bother. Got the Senas. A thirteen-year-old boy drives the truck and helps his very handsome grandfather—I'm sure he isn't fifty, if that. Our helper is bringing adobes inside for safekeeping through the winter. Boris is busy laying up adobes, and I'm still scraping paint from old doors.

Took my little girls shopping this A.M. Yesterday was Duchy's birthday so told her I'd get her a fancy hat to wear to church. All the little girls have them, and they look like birthday cakes. Also one for Juanita—I won't be here for her birthday. When we get to town, we discover without a doubt that a petticoat would be much more exciting, so they chose red tulle with red ribbons and bells around the bottom—very pleased.

Ginger and Charles—our first dinner guests. Grilled hamburgers, salad and fruit, roasted marshmallows. Saved enough for hungry mouths.

Four of the children were here for their first marshmallow roast. What fun!

Got some DDT this A.M. Think there must be bedbugs in the walls.* *[They loved me; they didn't even touch Boris.]* When we first came I slept on the low cot and every night I'd get bites, so I changed to the high cot. No bites, nor did Boris on the low one. Last night they found me on the high one. I poured DDT around the floor and on my cot legs. They can live evidently without nourishment. Wonder if that's it. There was no one here for years. Anyway, it was awful.

August 25

Another dark day and rain this morning. Boris has taken off to the hills for a few hours; we'll see. He couldn't stand it anymore here, and I can't blame him. He certainly deserves some pleasure and relaxation. Ambrosio bringing adobe in between showers, cleaning bricks when it rains. Had tons, five loads, of stuff hauled away front and back. Looks much better. Now if the rain will stay away for a few days.

August 28

Getting ready to leave our house. Hate the thought. Got all the adobes inside, the windows boarded up, the front cleaned up, gravel in the drive. How different and grand it looks. We'll work and live for the day when we return with bag, baggage, and Mau-Mau.

August 29

6 A.M. leaving. Our children came to say good-bye last night and as they left in unison said, "God be with you on your journey." I detected tears in their voices, and surely there were some in my eyes. *Hasta la vista.*

---

*Bedbugs: Tiny, nocturnal, bloodsucking insects that spend their days in wall crevices of old adobes and are known to live for a year without food. They were the scourge of nineteenth- and early-twentieth-century travelers to New Mexico as "hereditary lords of the soil" with whom accommodation was routinely shared. The insecticide DDT, introduced in the 1940s, proved highly effective against insects that threaten crops and carry diseases such as malaria. Peak usage coincided with the publication of Rachel Carson's book, *The Silent Spring,* in 1962. Finally banned in the United States in 1972, it is still widely used internationally.

May 1–June 8, 1960

"Waiting for Boris"

May 1

Back to stay. Children pouring in as soon as the door opened. Boris will stay here, Mau-Mau and I are at Kay's because of the cold. *[My sister Kay had moved here.]* A rugged trip with rain and terrific winds.

May 2 (Monday)

Boris's birthday. Bought a chocolate cake with pink flowers and writing, candles. All the children came in after school. It was fun. Twelve of us. Boys next door starting digging out the old well in the patio. Believe what keeps them going is the hope of finding a treasure. Maybe when we get down deeper we will. *[Of course, we never did finish digging it out.]* It's a square well, boulder-lined. We are only about four and a half feet down. So far beer cans, bottles, and broken pottery of Bud's. *[Bud Gilbertson was Boris's brother, the potter. We had visited him here when he rented the house from Bill Lumpkins before we ever got it.]* Cooked steak on a campfire in the patio. Ginger and Charles stopped in.

May 3

Have planned with two boys next door to make adobes from patio dirt for five cents each—very nice boys around twenty. They have no jobs and seem happy over the prospect of the work. If we bought adobes, they would cost seven cents, nine cents delivered. So we furnished our own water and the patio gets leveled, too. Also, it's fun to think of our house being built of the dirt in the place. We inquired around for a good adobe man to start on the front and walls. Someone who is reliable and a good worker since you pay by the hour. So anxious to get going on it.

May 5

Even the sky is crying; Boris is gone. It's empty, lonely, and sad here without him and incomplete. He is as much a part of this place as the sun on adobe walls. No sun today; no warmth. I just hope I don't disappoint him in what I do in his absence. No adobe making today.

May 6

A beautiful sunny morning. The boys should be able to work on the adobes today. I'm going to work at the flower shop this weekend and every weekend for a while. The extra cash will come in handy. Can't understand this town—prices are so very high and salaries so low. How empty and sad it is here without Boris. He is such a necessary part of the place, and how hard it is to get going without him. May he soon return.

May 10

The neighbor boys have made four hundred adobes. The dirt in the patio wasn't good enough, they said, so they have started digging in the back. I have my garden in; it's really just an experiment. I have a lot to learn out here—it's so dry. Mau-Mau is here with me in the patio. She'll be chirping like a sparrow soon. There are so many things to do; must start on something.

May 11

Ambrosio is back. Walked in this A.M. looking for work. He needed it badly, I'm sure, so have him cleaning up the back and he will start on the patio wall. Boris would like to have him here. He has a soft spot in his heart for him. I'm sure I can keep him busy. Have another man coming this afternoon to see about starting on the front. Hope it all gets going and fast. *[When we came, on the common west patio wall there were boarded-up doorways and windows. To cover them I decided just to build another adobe wall over the whole thing. So the west wall is now about four feet thick.]*

May 16

Today things are really popping. Adolfo Romero and helper started on the front today with Ambrosio. A lot of the adobe has to be broken out, and then when you put new adobe over old you have to anchor them into

21

the old with spikes. *[Oh dear, that's not true.]* Adolfo gets $2 an hour but seems to know what he's doing. Told him I wouldn't pay a helper more than a dollar. The poor front wall has to be hacked away where the water leaked down. It hurts to watch them do it, but it must be done.

May 17

The building up of the adobe on the front is almost done. *[That's the front outside wall.]* Tomorrow Adolfo puts the brick coping on.* Then the plastering with mud. Had three loads of junk hauled off today for $30. That's the end of that. *Muy caro [very expensive].* I'll do it myself. That's what I get for feeling sorry for the workman. He wanted work so badly.

I've almost decided not to have a Heatilator fireplace.** One large enough for that room would look hideous, all out of proportion. May just have a nice corner fireplace built and have a panel-ray gas burner, which we'd probably need anyway, and I know it would look better.*** *[Well, as you see some of this turned out differently. Boris designed the corner fireplace and we did put in a Heatilator. We also had a gas furnace put in the corner—all walled in—to heat the front room.]*

Got a small wood-burning stove for the back room. As soon as the adobes are out I'm going to fix it up in here so I can move in on a moment's notice. Wish Mau-Mau were a German shepherd—I wouldn't

---

*Brick coping: Several courses of fired bricks placed at top of adobe parapet walls to prevent erosion. Often arranged to simulate classical dentils. Resulted from American influence and the availability of fired bricks after 1846. A defining element of the styles known as Territorial and Territorial Revival.

**Heatilator: Registered trademark of Heatilator/Hon Industries, which sells fireplaces, stoves, and related products. Company began 1927 with invention of a "heat-circulating fireplace." Also refers to device built into fireplace to direct output of heat into the room rather than up the chimney.

***Panel ray: Rectangular, vertical, thin-panel, gas wall heater. Frequently found in older homes lacking central heating or in added rooms. Corner fireplace: Traditional Hispanic adobe fireplaces were shallow with arched openings and usually placed in a corner.

hesitate a moment. Talked to Boris this A.M. How wonderful to hear him and know he is there.

They have started on the brick coping. It's going to look lovely. Ordered five hundred adobe at ten and a half cents delivered.

My neighbor Olympia tells me that this house used to be, years ago, a gambling place, and she is sure that there are treasures buried here. As I told her, I could dig up the whole patio, tear down all the walls, find nothing, and not even have a house left. It is something to think about, though.

I must have a new roof on the front. Will get ahold of a man to give an estimate. The trees that we transplanted look a little sad but I'll water and hope. My corn is showing and the nasturtiums. *[Being a compulsive gardener, I had to have a garden. When we moved here there was nothing growing in the patio except a Chinese elm, a small cottonwood tree, a very small tamarisk tree, and some woodbine on the north wall of the back building facing the patio. The back was absolutely barren—no plants, no fences, no gates or anything. One other thing had survived all the years of neglect. There were some true Solomon's seal—just a few plants growing on the north side of the patio. The reason, I'm sure, was that moisture dripped down off the back roof. I don't know where it came from; you don't often see the true, although there is a lot of false Solomon's seal up in the mountains. It spreads and it blooms beautifully, and I've transplanted it elsewhere on the property. I tore out the woodbine and replaced it with ivy that I started from two little cuttings a friend gave me. Now it covers a lot of the wall. I replaced the elm in the patio with an apricot tree. The tamarisk is still there and has gotten huge. Everything else I planted over the years.*

[Within the first few years we began to put in plants. This first spring I ordered fruit trees from the East, and the boys next door dug holes to put them in. Boris got loads and loads of topsoil for the garden in the mountains with his pickup truck. I got starters for lots of things from Olive Rush: the hen and chicks over by the west wall of the patio, the lily of the valley planted under the tamarisk, and the little fragrant violets out in back under some of the fruit trees. The crab apple tree in the patio was just a tiny shoot that had come up from the root of hers.

[In the back Boris built all the fences and made the gates and built that

23

little shed. He also dug the hole for the little pond. I started the big Russian olive in the back from a little twig I put in the earth in 1961. It's partly dead now but I'm just leaving it—I like it and the birds love it. The pussy willow bush I started from a twig in the ground, too, but the other smaller Russian olives I started from seed. I always had a vegetable garden in back and froze the produce to use all winter. After Boris died (in April 1982) there wasn't much use in having it anymore so I have turned that spot into a perennial garden. Sometimes I wonder why I did; it's a lot of work and water to keep it going all summer. So you see everything that is growing here I planted as we went along.]

May 19

Ambrosio's son is like a little wild animal and my shadow. Didn't come today. Bitter cold, rain, windy, and overcast. Don't think I'll have to water except maybe the trees. The coping will be done today. Tomorrow should be the start of mud. I'm trying to get the back room cleaned out of adobes so I can straighten it up. Those darn things are heavy—twenty-five pounds each—especially when I have to move about two hundred. I think it will be quite cozy, though, with the little stove. Warm enough even for Mau-Mau, I hope.

[It's a long story about how I got Mau-Mau. When I first lived in Santa Fe, in 1953, I took a trip to Juárez with some friends and fell in love with an Amazon parrot in the market. I had Pancho smuggled across the border in a shoe box and brought him back to El Zaguán, where I was renting a place, and then back to Illinois. He was a wonderful parrot—he screamed and never talked—but he adored me. One morning I got up and there was an egg in the bottom of Pancho's cage, so I knew I had a Pancha.

[I don't really understand why but this upset me greatly. I was so nervous about it that I called Brookfield Zoo in Chicago and talked to the curator of birds. I mentioned that sometime I wanted an African gray because I'd heard they are the most wonderful of all parrots. By coincidence he happened to have one for sale that had been born at the zoo. They couldn't keep her because she was crippled. Her mother had sat on her wrong and had broken a wing and a leg that didn't heal properly. I then made the horrible decision to take Pancha to the Brookfield Zoo and buy Mau-Mau.

[So that's how I got Mau-Mau, a fantastic parrot. Because she was crippled, I handled her a lot and we became inseparable. She said everything—it was unbelievable how she answered questions and asked questions and had comments on everything that happened. If a dog came in and you asked, "What's that, Mau-Mau?" she would say, "That's a bowwow." I could go on for hours about Mau-Mau, who, I'm sure, was actually a he, not a she.]

May 24

A letter yesterday and today from Boris, and as always they read like poetry. I wish sometimes he would bother with what he calls "trivia." How he is. When he will be here. But such beautiful writing expressing magnificent thoughts.

The house is developing. The front is done all but the final mud *[that's the outside]*, and, of course, *el zaguán*, which awaits Boris. I'm having a new roof put on the front like the back one. Mr. Spiess is going to put pumice under it to change the pitch so that the water will drain out of one large *canal* on the patio side. *[Which we did not do.]* We'll leave *canales* in front for looks. Then I'll have two layers of coping on the top. Have painted the bathroom white and will paint the floors adobe color. Have ordered a glass block that has vents in it as a window for the front wall *[in the bathroom]*.

It's cold and dark and windy. Soaked my garden for I'm working at Flor-Al tomorrow. *[That's the flower shop.]* I hate it, but each hour is an hour for Adolfo.

May 27

The front looks lovely, such a perfect job of mud plastering. *[I don't understand that. I thought we first had it plastered later by women.]* Roofers came yesterday and spent one and one half hours shoveling pumice up to the roof to change pitch, but when they *[the roofers]* saw how much and what weight, they decided it was very foolish. So they shoveled it all down, making jokes about it. Decided not to change the pitch. Too expensive. Could pay several years of water bills for what it would cost; so today they're all busy putting a roof on as was, *canales* in front. *[One was stupidly placed right above the door.]*

Adolfo is working on the patio wall. Probably won't finish until Tuesday. Then to the front room patio wall *[south wall]*, door, window, and so forth. Then the fireplace and finishings. He put pieces of wood in the adobe bathroom wall for towel racks, also a medicine chest. Still trying to find an electrician; they charge fantastic prices.

May 31

Patio wall on west almost up. *[That's where Adolfo laid the whole new wall against the common wall.]* Didn't realize it was such a big one. Then I start on door and windows of front.

It's turned cold just now and looks very stormy. How it can change so suddenly! I'm frozen! No further news from Boris. He should be here this week, I hope. Our nice double mattress arrived. Horrible color, but guess you won't see that. Can't find legs, so I guess we'll have to make some.

The bathroom floor looks so nice. Ran out of paint when I had about two square feet in the shower stall left. Hope it won't be noticeable for I can't find the same paint anywhere. The Berrys were in this morning trying to play the guitar, or wishing they could play it. *[I don't remember them.]* We'll have to find someone who can. Adolfo's son-in-law, who is helping him, is very nice and a good worker.

June 1

Feels more like October. Cloudy and cool. Boris arrives Sunday. How happy I'll be. How wonderful it will be to move in here and live. Must get the bed up and things organized. The bathroom is all done, window and all, and looks like a different place. That is a surprise for Boris. *[I hadn't told him a thing about it. I painted the walls and the floor and put those glass bricks in for ventilation. One of them opens and also gives light to a certain extent.]*

Had an electrician here last eve. He wanted to really do a job—new wiring, my fuse box was obsolete, and so forth. Three hundred bucks. This morning another one came, Johnny Montoya. He seemed most friendly and cooperative. What I want done would be $30. New meter, new switch box, because of course it's just where the fireplace goes, block out outlets in driveway, fix outside wires, light, and bathroom light. I was so happy I could have wept at the difference. Have the doorway knocked out, ready for cement and door. Boris will have to fix the door and make a frame. *[That doorway is from the front room into Lumpkins's hallway, facing the bathroom. There was an opening there without a door. So Boris took one of several old doors that was just sitting around and adjusted the opening to fit the door. He made a frame for it out of another door and also the panels on each side.]*

Oh, how happy I am; Boris is coming to fix all those things! Think I'll keep Adolfo for a week after Boris arrives and see if we can get to the point where we can do it pretty much by ourselves.

June 3

Boris, naturally, has postponed his departure. Got the heat-form fireplace this A.M., $80 plus grilles at $16. Hope the size is right. Will try to wait for Boris before actually designing it. His ideas are better than mine.

June 5

Mau-Mau and I have moved in *[the back room]* while waiting for Boris. I've corralled all my belongings. They are all here and, I must say, it's full. This will be my first night alone here. Hope I won't hear too many noises as it gets dark. It's an experience anyway. Should have watered the trees and gardened, but I am hoping for rain, which it looks as though it will come but probably won't. I suppose that every rattle will sound like someone trying to get in. Hope the wind dies down.

June 6

Had a wonderful night; wasn't at all frightened. *Bueno!* The little stove warmed it up from sixty-five to seventy-five degrees in an hour this A.M. My shadow, little Ambrosio, appeared at 7:30 this A.M. and spent most of the morning with me. He is a pathetic and appealing child. He tried to disguise his lack of cleanliness by a dose of hair dressing, but I could still smell him through it. How I wish to get him soaked and washed and clean. Bought a secondhand Kelvinator refrigerator for $80. It's a nice-sized one with a freezer on top. Hope the electricity works in the back now so I can use it back here and also hope that soon they get the power on. Well, I love living here in spite of all the inconvenience and roughing it.

"My men" came late today. Called to tell me. Will finish the corner in front where the wires were moved and then make the platform for the fireplace. Can hardly wait for Boris—tomorrow night or maybe Wednesday.

June 8

Boris really should be here today. Monday night it was so cold I put Mau-Mau in her basket and took her to bed with me. Last night I took her to Kay's so I wouldn't have to worry about her being cold. Did I sleep! Lovely sleep.

Adolfo put a brick sill for plants in the patio window *[of the front room]*. He leveled the floor there and will do the same in the window they are now cutting through—all three feet. *[We put a window in between the big doors and the west window in the south wall of the front room facing the patio.]* Then the door goes up for which Boris will have to make a frame.

Adolfo placed the fireplace yesterday. Made a raised brick hearth, which I like for practical purposes. Put the firebrick on the bottom of the fireplace and sank the heat form six inches into the wall. *[The Heatilator brings the heat into the room, but you would never know it's there to look at it. The grille where the heat comes out is on top of the mantel. I designed it so that it wouldn't show. The intakes are at each end of the hearth.]*

I'm going to build the fireplace out eight to ten inches. *[I made the fireplace deeper by bringing the opening out.]* It's too shallow and I sank it *[the floor of the fireplace]* two inches below the hearth to make it look taller. Am leaving the designing to Boris. Sure hope he arrives in the daylight. Want him to see it all.

Adolfo tells me that a long time ago our house was headquarters for a notorious gang, the Silva gang, bandits. So the stories go. Have found bones, hair, and corncobs in the old adobes we're taking out for the window.

June 10–August 5, 1960

"Nothing like fixing up an old house"

June 10

Boris did arrive Wednesday evening at eight o'clock. Had a quick, good trip, and I was so delighted to see him. Seems impossible that we are here together in our adobe hacienda. Have gotten the "kitchen" organized with everything together except water. So much handier, really fun. *[That was the kitchen I fashioned in the corner of the front room.]*

Still raining; it's the fifth day. Adolfo is working on the fireplace. Do hope it turns out to be magnificent. Boris is drinking coffee. Between the heating pad and the stove, we keep Mau-Mau warm. Wish it would stop raining and get warm.

June 12

At last a glorious, warm, sunny day. Boris is busy fixing up the front for a shop. He has to fix doors, windows, and make door frames. Don't know when I've been so happy. Feel wonderful and think Boris would say the same thing. Today we are going to take off for a while; maybe pick up some coal in Madrid. The little stove eats it up. We're going to have Adolfo start the patio wall of the front building. Leave fireplace for a rainy day.

June 14

Another glorious, warm day. Adolfo has started on the patio wall of the front building. That will be wonderful to see and a relief to have done because of the way the rain comes down the wall. Boris has taken out the old lintels and put new ones higher to make room for the beautiful, old door. It's getting there. Ginger and Charles were here for dinner.

June 15

Another glorious, hot, sunny day—cool shadows, fresh, sparkling morning—such a place. I could never get homesick for Illinois. I love it so here and feel that I belong. Outside wall is going up fast. Adolfo leaving holes so baby sparrows can get out. Boris is cleaning bricks with his air compressor. Goes fast. Doorway ready for frame. *[That's the big door into the patio on the south wall of the front room. There had been a French door there, but we wanted to use another of the old doors from St. Michael's College that Bill Lumpkins, the previous owner, had left lying around outside. Since the opening wasn't big enough for these doors, Boris had to enlarge it. I always thought Lumpkins got those old doors and windows from the Loretto Academy building, but if he said St. Michael's that must be it.]*

June 16

Patio wall of front building done except for plastering *[with mud, of course]*. Brick coping on; looks wonderful. I hope Spiess comes to finish the roof tomorrow. Then let her rain. Had wiring around the door fixed, ready for plastering. Now "kitchen" light doesn't work. Oh well, someday everything will be attached and working.

June 19

So starts another week. Hope this one shows a lot of progress. Never as much as I hope. Unfortunately, Boris and Adolfo both love to talk and find lots to talk about. I'm taking the windows and doors apart to fix. We discovered they were put together with square nails and pegs, all handmade, of course. When it gets done, we'll be elegant. Adolfo only has two days left. Then he will be back for a few days in a couple of weeks to plaster inside. Must start doing it all ourselves.

June 20

Another hot day—must be around a hundred degrees. Even Mau-Mau says, "It's kind of hot in here." Boris got some old lumber two by twelves for the gate at six cents a board foot instead of eighteen cents. It is wonderful old wood; the building was eighty years old. *[I'm not sure where he got that wood. I know for his shop out back, Boris went out to an almost deserted little town on the way to Juárez someplace. Was it Sidney? He got a whole barn of weathered wood to build that shop. This may have come from there also.]*

Hope to get a plasterer on the inside wall tomorrow and put Adolfo on the fireplace. Then the front will be mostly done. The rest we do ourselves except final inside plaster, which Adolfo will come back in a couple of days to do.

June 21

Fireplace almost finished—bricks and more bricks. Boris has designed it, and it is going to be elegant when painted white. *[They plastered it and we painted the plaster white.]* Wonderful for display or arrangements. Not another one like it. *[That wasn't true forever. A friend of ours, Zig Kosicki, asked Boris if he could copy it. He was a doctor here who was building a house on Garcia Street, near Camino Corrales. Zigmund and his wife were good friends. He was an orthopedic surgeon, and they had moved here from El Paso. I met them when I looked out the window one day and saw them looking at the house. I asked them in, and that is how our friendship began.]*

Tomorrow is Adolfo's last day except when he comes for a couple of days to put on final white plaster inside. Wish we could afford to keep him all summer. We'll miss him. Boris is busy fixing door and windows. *[Front room patio door, that is. He didn't do the windows finally.]* Next week I hope we'll get to the drive, the wall across knocked through, and the front finished. *[The stuff we had to tear out of here before we could start anything! There were the concrete block wall across the front, that big plasterboard wall inside across the zaguán, the cement floor in that hallway, and the cement steps up in front.]* Wish it weren't all such heavy work; then I could do more. Mau-Mau is really a patio parrot and loves it out there. Talking, whistling all day.

June 27

Boris has started knocking out the front. What a job! *[That's the very front where Boris constructed the big gate that's there now. The space between our front room and the building next door on the east had been partly filled in with concrete blocks. Lumpkins had installed one of the old St. Michael's doors as a front entrance. We replaced the cement block wall with Boris's gate and eventually put the old door on the north wall of the back room. That's the larger door facing the patio.]*

31

We have an obstacle course to get to the bathroom, with shoring propping up the ceiling. Yesterday I sifted dirt, mixed mud and straw, and filled in holes on the south wall. Adolfo is coming back for a few days to catch up on a few things. Must get more bricks for coping on the wall. We've used hundreds. *[That's more of those bricks from the penitentiary they tore down].*

Went out to see Mrs. Ernest Thompson on Saturday. She is quite a person. The stuff she has is fantastic—drawings, paintings, books, collections of things—and such a wild house *[Seton Castle].*

June 28

Adolfo is working on the south wall front. We're so anxious to get it done that Boris has been his helper. I hate to see someone with all his talents and art and feelings mixing mud for a plasterer, but it saves us $8 a day. All the dust, sifting dirt, sifting sand, knocking out walls—it's really almost a lost cause trying to keep things halfway clean, to say nothing of yourself.

June 29

Adolfo is putting a brick coping on the west patio wall. Decided to keep him another week to finish walls around the patio. *[We kept him and kept him.]* Boris just has too much to do, and it is too discouraging to see so much undone. I'll have to get the wiring done before we finish the inside wall. *[Finally, I think, one of our neighbors who knew something about electricity came and did it.]* I'm going to see about a furnace; we'll need it up front this winter. It would also heat the bathroom. *[We tried to run the heat across the roof but it didn't work so we put a little heater in the front bathroom.]*

June 30

Coping on wall finished. Now to start north *[patio]* wall of the back room. Tons and tons of mud go into such a project! *[The wall was so eroded from being neglected so long—for years and years water had run down that wall from the roof. It had to be built up again with adobe.]* Another hot day for the men in the sun. Wish it would rain to water the ground and cool the air. I don't mind, of course, but working in it is something else. There was a prairie dog out back this morning. Where it came from? Where it went? Poor confused thing.

Adolfo is working on plastering the west wall. Should finish and start on finishing coat of front room outside. Don't think Boris feels well—the heat or work or both. He won't admit it, but I notice he takes every chance to rest in the shade. Hope he is all right. My poor peas are about to give up in this heat. Never saw such gorgeous pumpkin plants; they love it, as does the corn and squash. May have some marigolds and zinnias and nasturtiums. This intense, dry heat is hard on everything. My little willow is all right; has new growth. So glad.

July 2

Got *vigas* for the drive *[zaguán]*. When that's done the worst is over. Fred Montoya stopped in. His great-grandfather lived here, and he remembers the house well and is full of information about it. He says it's older than the Guadalupe Church and is the oldest house around here. The well was sixty feet deep. He said there should be gold coins, as they aired them in the patio. *[Whatever that means.]* He has pictures and things, which he says he'll give me. *[I never got them.]* Everyone knows of this place. It really has history. If these walls could only talk!

July 5

It's been raining since two this afternoon; it's now eight. Still at it. It does nothing halfway here. It's hot and dry, then rain. Yesterday I had what is known as the Santa Fe trots, and do you trot. Trotting across mud-strewn patio, dodging puddles and wheelbarrows, and so forth; the obstacle course of timbers holding up *el zaguán's* roof. Missed a trip to Charles's folks' ranch and some wonderful mariachis from Mexico because of it. Felt fine today, but Boris had a slight attack.

Got the door frame in and plastered up for the door from the front room to *el zaguán*. *[That's our front door from the* sala *to the* zaguán—*not the one to the street but the one into the house where Lumpkins had just an opening.]* Have been removing paint from doors and so forth so Boris can fill them in, repair, and sand them. Think I'll start painting window frames tomorrow. Am anxious to get the front at least finished.

Then we can move up there where the fireplace is and have a clean place to live. There is a fire in the fireplace tonight and fun to see smoke come out of the chimney.

July 7

Heard yesterday that the man who built this house helped finance and build Guadalupe Church. *[I'm not so sure about that.]* So must see if I can find out when that was first built. *[You see, we still didn't know it was a historic house, how old it was, or anything about it really.]*

Spent today in Taos. Took some of Boris's work to show them at a new and lovely gallery called Allied. *[Later this was Gallery A.*]* They were properly impressed. I hope it leads to something. It's the nicest and most elegant gallery I've seen in these parts, run by my friend Frances Good. *[Her sister was a friend of my sister Dot. I looked her up and that's how we got involved with Gallery A.]* Beautiful trip, such magnificent country. Came back by a back road along the Rio Grande and picked up some handsome lava rocks for the patio. Shopped in Española, where prices seem to be a little cheaper. Am constantly amazed by the high food prices here.

Boris is gone for another load of brick, getting them for a cent a piece from a young boy who worked at the pen. Why didn't he come around sooner? He has two thousand!

July 10 (Sunday)

The front is out. *El zaguán* is open *[where we put the big front gate]*. Boris is busy putting up the roof and *vigas* today. *[He's building the* portal, *I guess.]* We're going into the bathroom right on Alto Street, in view of all. Nice to have such a lovely view of the mountains. *[He has knocked out the cement-*

---

*Gallery A: Opened May 15, 1960, at 133 Kit Carson Road. Founded by artists Eric Gibberd and Mario Larrinaga as "a gallery of dignity where worthwhile paintings could be shown without an accent on prestige value or commercial financial gain." Moved to 105-107 Kit Carson Road, 1990. Allied Artists of New Mexico remains the corporate name of the business.

block enclosure of the doorway and it was wide open.] Boris was up until 10 P.M. making temporary plywood doors for the front. It is wonderful to watch him move those heavy things around. It must impress the neighborhood. Our backyard looks like Rios's wood yard—piles of lumber, *vigas,* rock, all kind of brick, adobes, sand, and so forth. It is a glorious day.

July 11

Poor Boris. He's having a hell of a time building the "hall" roof backward, trying to get the *vigas* in to fit under the roof instead of building the roof on the *vigas.* *[This is the area between the* sala *and the bathroom up front where Lumpkins had created a hall. It was already roofed. For the long* portal, *he could put the* vigas *up before the roof.]*

July 13

The *vigas* are up. Looks so nice. Start on the gatepost tomorrow. Hope the bulldozer comes to level off the patio and cut the bank in front. Then I can plant a garden in the patio, and Boris can get to the stone wall in front. *[Boris built the stone wall from river rock.]* Adolfo comes back to finish the front and patio walls *[of the front building].*

Last night a neighbor's cousin was here—red hair and freckles. Has been in the pen for rape. Wife left him. Has another. He is tough but wiry and has been run over by a tractor. He and his brother played guitars and sang. Most of the neighborhood children wandered in. We had a fire in the fireplace and we furnished beer. It was wonderful. Not the beer— neither of us drinks the stuff. Mau-Mau loved it—cha-cha-ing and olé-ing, dancing and yelling.

July 15

The tractor with the shovel and dump truck did arrive—at eleven o'clock instead of six. Worked to 12:30. Won't be back until this evening or tomorrow. *Siempre mañana.* Wish I could relax and be that way too. Maybe if I live long enough. *[Over eighty years old and I still haven't changed.]* Boris is busy on the gateposts. Hopes to have shovel *[on tractor]* push them in place. Hope it works; they must weigh a half a ton. *[Those are the huge posts on either side of the gate.]*

Can hardly wait to start fixing and planting the patio. As soon as it is leveled off am going to get manure and peat moss to work into the beds. Filemon gave me a beautiful turtle. Was going to keep it for the patio; but since I discovered it is herbivorous, I'm not so sure. *[Filemon was the stepson of a neighbor and was probably in his teens at that time. He was a good friend of Boris's and over here a lot helping him.]*

July 16

Gateposts and beam across in place. How big they look. *[Boris must have bought the posts at the lumberyard.]* Front almost cleaned off. *[That means all the dirt and cement from breaking out those steps and making the parking space that was there before the sidewalk was put in by the city.]* How high the house looks. Tractor won't be back for a week to finish. Didn't get to do the drive or the patio.

July 18

Front being finished by Adolfo. How wonderful it will be. Tractor coming in nights with lights to finish getting things level. *[There had been those concrete steps up to the front door.]*

July 19

Front final plaster coat on top washed off already. The mixture wasn't right; too much sand maybe. Adolfo's idea because it's easier to work. We're going to experiment.

One of the original *vigas* Boris took out of *el zaguán* must really be old. It has a big hole in one end where they put a rope through it to be pulled by a burro—no chains. *[I don't remember where that* viga *was situated when it was taken out, but it had a hole in it that they used to drag it down from the mountains. I saved it, but somehow or other it got sawed up. I was just sick.]* Wish we could really find out when this place was built. Everything is a mess. Things started everywhere. All of a sudden my helper will be gone.

July 21

Didn't think the mess could be worse but it is. Patio is practically impassable. Am putting one of the old doors in the patio wall of the back building where we are living. *[That had been the front door facing the street that was all boarded up when we came.]* Has necessitated knocking a considerable amount of adobe wall out to make room. Result: layers of dust and adobe, everything a complete mess.

Next comes the moving of a window on the same wall. At night we have to hang a tarp over the opening of the door to keep out the cold. It is like waking up in a cave. Maybe someday it will be straightened around and pulled together—I hope. I say there is nothing like fixing up an old house, especially when you're living in it. *[Lumpkins had put one of the old windows in the very back corner of the patio wall where my bedroom is now; that is, on the west end of the back building. We filled that in and used the old frame and window when we cut another opening on the south wall of the front room facing the patio. It's the one between the door and the existing window on the west corner. There had been a window in the back room on the north wall, where the smaller door is now. We left the old frame and put in the door.]*

July 22

Door in and mess cleaned up. What an improvement! Trying to save the lovely vine, poor thing; hope some of it survives. *[Later I found out that woodbine is not really a lovely vine. I got rid of that in a hurry and put in ivy.]* The last day of men helping. Will be nice to be alone. We'll have a lot of mud-throwing to do; and if Tony with the tractor ever shows up to get the patio cleaned up, it will begin looking like something.

Thrill of the day: saw Igor Stravinsky and his wife on the street. He's here to conduct his opera, *Oedipus Rex.**

July 25

It's 10 P.M. and we have lights strung in the patio for the tractor and shovel to work. He's been here since six and how different it looks already.

---

* *Oedipus Rex:* Opera–oratorio. Text by Jean Cocteau after Sophocles. First performed, 1927. Paired in double bill with Giacomo Puccini's *Gianni Schicchi* by Santa Fe Opera, 1960. Igor Stravinsky's *The Rake's Progress* also was performed that season.

It is going to look enormous. *[The patio, that is.]* We're almost down to the original level, finding the old flagstone around the well and other spots. *[We took all that dirt out of the patio. It had risen way above the base of the wall. You didn't see the stone footings anyplace. There was a step up to the patio from the French door that was there. We made the patio level with the bottom of the door. Later we put a brick step from the patio into the front room to keep out water. When we found flagstones, we realized that that was probably the original level. It wasn't a complete thing—just pieces here and there, and we didn't leave them. We didn't have any idea of actually restoring the place because we didn't know it was anything historic. We were just fixing it up to live in.]*

I've been slinging mud all afternoon. Boris is experimenting with a final coat using lots of straw. Think it will look wonderful. Have also discovered that mud sticks beautifully on plaster in the *zaguán* so we can cover that up, cheating, of course. *[We had it all redone later—correctly that time around.]*

We are tired, so is Mau-Mau, but the show must go on while we've got the guy to work and he wants to. He tells us he's sure there is gold in the well. It used to shine at night under the water. It's so much nicer when it's just the two of us working here together with no workman. We have lots of mud to throw.

July 27

We're on again, off again. Tractor started in at 1:30. Thought here we are, we'll finish. Something broke. A trip to Española and already they, including Boris, have been gone two hours seeing about it. Oh well. Everything seems to be at a standstill until this is done, but I'm still happy and loving the life. It certainly beats working, which I hate—the going to a job every day. Hope something works out so I don't have to do that.

July 28

Yesterday afternoon they got going with the tractor again until four and worked most of today. Still at it at nine tonight. Working on front with the "help" of all the neighborhood children from three to sixteen hanging on the tractor, throwing rocks, dodging cars. Pancho, a neighbor dog, adding to the confusion. Wild! Maybe tonight we'll see the end of this business. Found a lot of flagstone under the foot of dirt.

Spent hours watering. Everything is so dry. This is supposed to be the rainy season, but no rain for more than a week. Planted tuberous-rooted begonias in our first flower bed by the back building door. Hope the vine survives. Can hardly wait to get started on the flower beds. *[Eventually, I decided not to have any flower beds in the patio but just to use pots of flowers and have the beds in the back.]*

Going to Taos tomorrow to see Frances Good. Hoping she will have some ideas about what to do about selling Boris's work. In the evening I'm going over to Olympia's for a hen party for her daughter, who is being married next month.

July 29

Whoops, a flat tire *[on the tractor]*. This A.M. a trip to Española to have it fixed and a wait of five days to have it vulcanized. So the tractor queens it in the patio sans tire with only an hour or so of work left to be done.

August 1

Boris is busy on the front stone wall. We got a load of handsome copper deposit rocks out at the old copper mine near Cerrillos—beautiful turquoise green. They should look wonderful in the ferny bed I hope to have on the shady side of the patio. *[I had that as a garden, but I took it away when I planted the ivy. The rocks are strung around in the patio now.]*

August 2

Another hot day and no rain. Tractor still in the patio and will be for several days. Couldn't fix the tire; have to buy a new one. Won't get it until Friday and this is Tuesday. Boris is doing beautiful job, of course, on the front stone wall. His touch will really make it something. Going to Taos tomorrow.

August 4

A real storm halted work on the wall. It's almost finished. I went to Taos yesterday to see about getting Boris's work in another gallery. Réalités is interested but wants to see more and also to see Boris, so we have to go back tomorrow. Another day away from the house and Boris has to leave next week for Illinois for a month. He's hoping to get the big doors hung today, or to start anyway. *[Having lived in Illinois and Wisconsin a great part of his life, there were things that had to be taken care of.]*

Guess I didn't mention how amused we were Monday, August 1. We couldn't imagine what was going on. Streams of people all dressed up, walking down the road toward town—looking so happy and festive. Then when the mailman came into sight, a little boy across the street came calling to his mother, "Here comes your check." That was the answer. Half of Alto Street must be on welfare. Then the bill collectors start streaming down the street, knocking on closed, quiet houses that had been shaking with noise and activity a few moments earlier.

The rain on the walls has made them a beautiful dark color with the shining gold straw.

August 5

The gallery took several of Boris's things. Mrs. Barbara Kennedy is very nice, and I think it's a good place. We came back on the Truchas road; it was beautiful. Had another look at the wonderful mud work they do so well.

Tractor still here; think we'll put a little fence around it. Poor Tony. They got the tires on wrong so back again to Española. Will this ever end? We are both so tired, we're shaky. So to bed.

August 11–October 17, 1960

"I'm in the front building,
all clean and warm"

August 11

Boris left for Illinois early this morning. He told Tony to get his damned tractor out. We had waited three days for him to come back to finish. We got two men in the neighborhood to dig with Boris to finish cleaning up the drive and front.

Ray Gonzales fixed the light in the bathroom. How elegant it is to actually see in there. *[We had been using a kerosene lantern.]* We spread gravel all over the *placita,* and how elegant it is. It looks enormous and so wonderful. We really feel it's on its way now.

This afternoon I'm going over to my sister Kay's to get a lot of perennials to put in the beds I've been fixing with manure and peat moss. Next year we'll have pretty flowers blooming. It's going to be a truly lovely place. Last night Boris hung some of his slate carvings on the *placita* walls. It's going to make a magnificent gallery, such light and surroundings.

August 13

I have been throwing mud this A.M. Hope to get all the walls covered with the first coat before Boris returns. It's the mixing that's the work. *[I soon gave that up.]* I have a phone! Can't get used to the idea. Thought it might be a good idea while I'm here alone. *[Boris was in Illinois for a long time. While he was gone, I got the front room all done—the inside work, that is.]*

Have been trying to catch a mouse for four days. Four times he's taken the food without setting off the trap. He must be smart. Boris should arrive in Evanston today. Should get his airmail card Monday. Do hope it wasn't a miserable trip. It seems strange here alone.

August 14

It's lovely, empty, and quiet. Storms have been all around but no rain here, which we need badly. Threw mud all morning but, being Sunday, decided to clean up and be lazy. I read all afternoon, lying under the tree. *[That was the Chinese elm in the patio. We replaced it with the apricot that is there now.]*

August 16 (8 A.M.)

Already the smell of piñon fires, green chile, and tortillas cooking is everywhere. Don't feel too chipper, so will use that as an excuse not to throw mud. Will work at the windows and take it easy.

August 17

The furnace arrived today; finish installing it tomorrow. The problem, it seems, is getting the gas hooked up and passed by the building commissioner. It all gets so complicated. The hole we made in the wall isn't large enough, so will have to put the furnace in the front room in a corner and build a partition. Hope it doesn't look too bad. *[We had thought we'd put the furnace outside in the wall south of the door into the* sala, *and that's why we dug a big indentation. We left it because we thought it would look nice to have something there. Years ago in Mexico we got the ceramic stove that's there now.]*

The older brother to the neighborhood kids is home. He has been dishonorably discharged from the U.S. Marines. It isn't the happy laughing group it usually is. They all wish he'd leave. I don't dare get involved, especially with Boris gone. An older sister, who disappeared a month ago, writes from Long Beach (California) that she's married to a sailor; she's sixteen. "He's so nice, he bought me a TV," she said.

August 18

A week ago today Boris left. Seems ages. Heater put in. Pipe insulated on the roof. Looks big enough for a factory even though pipe itself is only six inches. Looked for the satellite *Echo* until my neck was stiff.*

Echo: The first communications satellite project of the National Aeronautics and Space Administration (NASA). *Echo I* was a one-hundred-foot-diameter balloon made of aluminized polyester, launched August 13, 1960, as a passive reflector of radio waves back to the ground.

Unfortunately, I didn't see it but did see a beautiful shooting star leaving a path behind it like a skyrocket, which I'm sure was more of a thrill than the *Echo*.

August 23

Had gas connected, which involved having location of meter changed because it was in the neighbor's yard on the east. Cost $78. Now have to have an electrician to hook up fans and thermostat. So it goes. Put quite a bit of mud on. Two or three more days' work and it should all be done. Ready for a final coat, which I hope Boris can do for he does such a beautiful job. Two weeks tomorrow he left, and in another week the time will be getting shorter until he comes back. It's after the halfway mark.

Yesterday was Duchy's birthday so I took her to the Plaza to pick out a present, a baby doll and miniature bath kit. Also a cake, which I decorated with bright pink letters and animals and candles. Hope she was pleased. She seldom shows emotions; guess she is so used to keeping everything inside.

August 29

Fans and thermostat hooked up. So now all I have to do is get windows in and a door hung to keep warm. It's so very dry, I soak things all day in the garden. The sun seems hotter than ever. Mike's puppy, Snowball, lives here now. They can't take care of him. He's not the kind of a dog I want; mostly collie, smart and good and devoted. What am I to do?

No letter from Boris. How long it seems. I hope at least the one-half mark is over. The neighbor children and I went to the Plaza last night for mariachis. The people are fascinating to watch, mostly the Spanish, even though I'm sure it's put on for the tourists, which I never seem to see. *[How it's changed!]*

August 30

I planted a butterfly bush and a mahonia today. We had a nice shower this afternoon; how good it sounded and smelled. Spent the afternoon with sweet old Olive Rush. I went over to see her and her charming old adobe and beautiful gardens on Canyon Road. *[Now that is the Friends Meetinghouse.]* She has lived there for forty years and planted all the big trees herself. I love her paintings. They have a fairy story quality, like elves, fairies, and pixies—charming and lovely. I came home with flowers, apples, and plants. *[Many of my plants are starters from her. All my Castilian roses and my hen and chicks, my lily of the valley. This crab apple tree in the patio was just a little tiny twig when I planted it. That was from her garden, too.]*

September 1

Somehow three weeks have gone by since Boris left. I don't know how; it's so lonely and empty and pointless. Locked in my adobe walls, I feel like the princess locked in her tower waiting for the knight on a white horse to rescue her.

Watched the first of the month parade up and down Alto Street. Even the taxis were busy tearing up and down. Women loaded down with bags and boxes, smoking tailor-mades. A day for celebration and a night, too, I'm sure. Tomorrow night I'm taking Olive to see the burning of Zozobra and the melodrama. It's Fiesta, and I suppose I should see some of it, although I don't look forward to it without Boris.* No word from him for more than a week. How much longer will it be?

September 2

Just saw Dr. Myra Ellen Jenkins, who is in charge of the New Mexico State Archives. She had found some old documents about this house. The name on the abstract of title was Donaciano Vigil, but his father, Don Juan Cristóbal Vigil, left it to him. In the will are mentioned orchards,

---

*Santa Fe Fiesta: Yearly September weekend celebration commemorating the return of Diego de Vargas to Santa Fe in 1692, which began the reconquest of New Mexico after the Pueblo Revolt drove the Spanish out in 1680. Begun as a religious observance in 1712; expanded for tourism in the 1920s by Santa Fe's business and creative communities to include a reenactment, secular parades, a melodrama, and a candlelight procession to the (first) Cross of the Martyrs, which was dedicated in 1920 and is now owned by the HSFF. Zozobra, a giant effigy of "Old Man Gloom," is torched on the first night of Fiesta to begin the festivities. Conceived by artist Will Shuster in 1926.

five or seven trees each, pastures, and corrals. Donaciano sold it in 1856 to Vicente García and moved to Pecos.

September 3

Wouldn't have missed it: La Fiesta. What color! What carnival atmosphere! What getups! Every kind of person. The native population really eats it up. The Plaza was surrounded by stalls selling everything—tacos, hot tamales, cotton candy, popcorn, and so forth. Every inch littered with people, children, food, dogs, and debris. So sorry Boris isn't here. He'd get a kick out of the mood, too, I'm sure.

September 5

A letter!

September 7

Spent the morning experimenting with final coat of mud. Used sifted dirt and lots of straw. Throw it on *[the wet wall]*, smooth with trowel. Then go over it with lots of water and trowel with a rubber sponge. Looks pretty good. *[I did a lot of the exterior, but, of course, it was all covered up when we had it done right.]* Brought sweet Olive Rush over to see the house. She loved it since the time Boris's brother Bud lived here.

September 12

Finished the mud work on one wall of *el zaguán*—doesn't look bad. Not as nice as Boris's, though. It is too hard work for me; I was sore all over. Really I shouldn't do it but hate to admit it. Can't be much longer before he comes home. Today is Mike's birthday and so must go and get a cake.

September 17

Just got back from four days at Kay's. Had a touch of pneumonia, so she took care of me—very good care. It was most pleasant lying there gazing at the mountains, with Mau-Mau for company and food brought to me on the hour. But it's good to be back even though no letter was waiting for me. *[Every day it's "Haven't heard from Boris" and "Certainly he'll be home soon."]*

September 20

I'm having the two patio windows fixed to save time. Would have front ones done if I could get them out. *[The windows were all broken and even some of the mullions. They needed a lot of work. I had Mr. Roybal next door come and take those windows out; we took them over to a man named LaCerte. He was such a nice man. He repaired all the windows. Then I had Mr. Roybal come and put them back in. So I got the glass done and the furnace in; and, as you know, the fireplace had already been put in so I had heat. I could move my bed and what furniture I had up to the front room and live there. There was the bathroom up there across the* zaguán. *I fixed a little kitchen in the corner of the big room. I had the refrigerator moved to the front and put a partition so it didn't look bad from the rest of the room. I cooked on a two-burner electric plate. There was no water; the water was across the* zaguán *in the bathroom. After I got that all done, I lived up there.]*

September 22

A cold, rainy day. Have to keep the little stove really hot so Mau-Mau and I don't freeze. Put in a pyracantha today. The orange berries are so lovely against the adobe wall. No word from Boris.

September 24

A letter yesterday from Boris and no mention of when, so I'll just wait some more. Surely it will end someday, this waiting.

I went to Georgia Gonzales's wedding this A.M. at the nine o'clock Mass at Guadalupe Church. Then took Duchy and Juanita to the reception in the public hall. Children of all ages rushing around. Much parading, marching, and dancing. Everyone having a wonderful time. Paper plates and cups, sensible, really. It was fun to see everyone weeping when the bride and the groom left. So I guess the whole thing was a big success.

September 25

A dreamy, special letter from Boris. Still no definite word about his coming. Had five little girls "helping" me water this afternoon. Playing games and tearing around in the patio. What a mess they left, but it was nice to hear their little voices. They were having a lovely time with a "balloon" that they had found. Blowing it, biting it, and chewing it. It made me cringe. It finally broke, and that was the end of that, thank goodness.

September 26

It seems I'm preoccupied these days with keeping warm, especially evenings and mornings. Hauling ashes, coal, and wood; or following the sun, which is hot and lovely. Put a heating pad on Mau-Mau at night. Mr. Roybal is going to put in the windows and hang the door tomorrow *[from the front room into the* zaguán*]*. It's a start anyway.

September 27

How elegant and beautiful the windows look with all the whole pieces of glass. Never knew windows could be so exciting. I didn't even mind washing them—a job I usually loathe. The door is up but doesn't quite fit. Has to be planed. How can I wait to get it all fixed? I want it where it will be.

September 28

How many things we just take for granted. How beautiful the reflections are in my windows. Like framed colored pictures—bits of the garden, a green tree branch dipping down. We should all be without things occasionally to appreciate them. *[I was living back here and looking up front to my new windows.]*

September 29

Yesterday Kay and I went up the Aspen Ranch road among glorious, brilliant gold aspen to dig some more meadow rue. They call it maidenhair fern out here, which it definitely isn't, but it's pretty stuff for my shady garden. Still no Boris. Surely any day now. Took two more windows to be done. Got them out myself.

September 30

The patio is covered with what looks like mothballs and such a racket on the roof and windows. A hail thunderstorm. It's really coming down. Of course, this means I will have to get a fire going and the wood is running out. Oh where, oh where is Boris?

Taking the last window over to LaCerte tomorrow with measurements for the front screens. So by Wednesday that should be done.

October 1

No Boris. He said he'd be back in September but naturally didn't make it. He has no conception of time, never can gauge it. He's always twice as long at something than he thinks he will be. He isn't aware of it, but I am. I should learn after all these years of waiting, but I always hope. Took over last window measurements for screens. Get them next week.

October 5

Vigas stained; windows and door in. Scrubbing floor, waiting for plaster, then paint the floor, then move in! Heat's on, and it heats up in no time. Simply wonderful. It is going to look so beautiful and hope it will be all done this week. Won't Boris be surprised! Mr. Roybal is making a partition around the furnace.

The mountains are golden now with aspen. I do hope they hang on for another week so Boris and sister Treet, who arrives Friday, don't miss them.

Sister Kay has been so wonderful to me; don't know what I would do without her. Mau-Mau and I are over there again. I simply couldn't stay warm here. It was ghastly—I couldn't leave the stove for it would go out. Hope I never take things for granted again, like heat, hot water, and so forth.

October 6

Today was my day, if I had only heard from Boris. I got a part-time job at Dressman's Flower Nook three days a week, starting next week. *[I got a different job. I was still working in flower shops, you see, when all this was going on.]* The Noskin Gallery in Albuquerque sold a small horse and wants lots more. *[Jack Noskin was a dentist in Albuquerque. His wife had a gallery in Albuquerque's Old Town.]*

How could so many nice things happen in one day? I stained the *vigas*. Hope they are not too dark. *[I went up the ladder and stained all those* vigas *on the ceiling of the front room. It was new wood and I didn't like the looks of them. I think I stained them a little too dark.]* I say this week I can do no wrong. If anything is wrong, it's Boris's fault for not being here.

October 11 (Tuesday)

This is a day to celebrate! I'm in the front building, all clean and warm. It looks beautiful and cozy. The fireplace is so elegant. The Indian rugs and baskets are lovely. *Vigas* don't look too dark. Painted the floor adobe color. Walls aren't white enough. Will paint them later. How wonderful voices, music, sound behind the wonderful thick walls, high ceiling! Mau-Mau likes the way she sounds, too. Won't Boris be amazed and delighted!

I start working Thursday for three days a week at Dressman's. I'm not looking forward to it, but it will at least keep us in food until things get started. I think the new connection in Albuquerque might work into something. Sounds promising anyway. *[That must be Noskin's.]*

October 15

We had snow today. Cold and dark. How thankful I am not to be in the back building.

October 17

How wonderful it is to have a home—a warm home. Sunday morning I woke to see the patio covered with snow after a terrific hailstorm during the night. Roses still blooming. Nothing nipped except the begonias. Still dark and cold. Brought the geraniums in. How can I wait?

"The patio is transformed"

October 31

Boris got home ten days ago. The days aren't long enough and the evenings are the same—poof! And when he is gone, how slowly they go. We have spent three days going out into the hills to chop piñon for the fireplace. How wonderful to have the pitch-filled, fragrant wood to burn and a man who knows how to handle an ax and saw!

Boris is busy fixing and straightening the back building for a shop. What a mess it was. *[That's this building where we sit.]* He bought a big, old potbellied stove and has put up shelves and has pushed back all the numerous boxes and so forth, so it should work out fine. Hope in a few days he can start fixing the drafty doors in the cold bathroom. We have to do a little knocking out of walls for doors and closing in doors for our outside–inside john.

Went over to Olive's this A.M. for an ornamental crab tree, a little one. I put it in the patio; hope it lives. *[That's the big tree there now.]* Wet down all my plants today so they will freeze wet. Want to put some bulbs in next week.

We have had a flow of trick-or-treaters tonight. Have run out of stuff. Boris carved a wonderful pumpkin from the garden, which we have a light in out in front. The children are very impressed and can't believe it's real. Boris spent all day carving this pumpkin. *[He didn't make holes in it. He just took off the outer surface, so the light shows through. It was a piece of sculpture. Gorgeous.]*

Tomorrow we go to Albuquerque to case the Noskin Gallery, which has some of Boris's things. Hope it works out as well as they lead us to believe it will. They have a beautiful metal bowl and a humorously elegant metal giraffe to take.

It's cold but oh, so warm and cozy in here. How thankful I am to be warm in such a charming and impressive room.

Mrs. Lambert of the anthropology museum has dated the shards we found on the property.* Some of them go back to the 1300s.

November 9

At last the boards are off of the front windows. What a delight to look out of clean, whole pieces of glass to the glorious mountains, constantly changing with the light. Always touchingly beautiful—now with snow. Have painted the frames white and hung salt-sacking curtains until we get the inside shutters made. Have the curtains in two parts, as the shutters will be, so we can keep the bottom closed.

Boris has gotten some lovely used planks, *vigas,* and plumbing— for the future bathroom in the back—at the Santa Fe Indian School very cheaply. He is busy closing in the bathroom in front, making doors, and so forth. It's going to look wonderful. Planted bulbs in the patio so it should be beautiful come spring.

The Noskin Gallery has sold another piece, a small metal bull, and wants more. Dr. Jack Noskin, who is a dentist, is coming by Saturday to pick up the giraffe. Hope Boris can have something else by then. It is most encouraging, and the *dinero [money]* is always welcome. Still working three days a week. It seems at times I'm in the ribbon-and-tulle business instead of flowers; will be glad when I can leave it. Hope I can get going somehow on my own next year. *[I was thinking of having my own shop. I'm glad I didn't! I never could have made it because I'd have to do everything to get it the way I wanted it. I'd be awful to work for.]* Oh, how happy we are—a dream of so many years come true!

November 12

Bathroom all finished with nice weathered planks. How nice to have all of the pipes out of sight. It is warmer in there, too. *[The planks on the outside,* zaguán, *wall of the front bathroom. There was another door from the hallway into the bathroom. We had to take it out because when we*

---

*Anthropology museum: At this time Marjorie Lambert was in charge of the Palace of the Governors (1955–64) and was its curator of anthropology and exhibits (1959–63).

removed all that dirt, where the zaguán *is, the door was left way up high. We covered that all up with the wooden planks. That's the frame wall that Lumpkins put up to create the bathroom. It is not thick.]*

Boris has his shop all fixed up in the back building, and it looks wonderful. Lots of nice light and room. Kept cozy and warm by the big, old potbelly. He seems so delighted with it. It's been many years since he has had a decent place to work, and I know it will make a big difference, as well it should.

Never get over being delighted with the glorious view of the Sangre de Cristos changing constantly or with the fireplace or this elegant old house or our finally being together. As much as I hate housework, which is never ending, I even find pleasure in that. It looks so nice when it is kept up. We love it.

Little Benny is Boris's shadow. A ten-year-old neighbor boy whose father was killed two years ago. He's a big help and a darling little boy. The other children drift in and out. The other kids don't come over much anymore, though still very friendly.

November 13

What a joy, sweet pleasure it is to stand here looking out of the window across the patio into the back building, watching Boris working with his tools and metal as he creates another beautiful object.

Fire in the fireplace as usual. Cooked our dinner in it. Baked potatoes wrapped in foil and broiled steak. Mau-Mau dozes. She loves it here now and is going all day. I'm ready for bed, too. No telling when Boris will be in. He gets started on his work and nothing else exists.

November 17

Boris is still busy hauling lumber and *vigas* from the Indian School, mostly for the *portal,* which he laid out today. *[That's the* portal *in the patio.]* Snow on the mountains; roses in the patio. Nights around twenty-seven degrees, days fifty-seven.

Benny is here every evening. He and Boris work in the shop pounding out things in metal. Two nights ago I had a birthday cake and ice cream for him. He was twelve. He's a sweet child and fun to have around.

We're going to Taos for Thanksgiving dinner at Barbara Kennedy's of Réalités Gallery. *[I think it's still there.]* She is having several local artists and a charming French couple, Marcel Mayer and his wife. He is a sculptor and a very good one. It should be fun, I hope, and very arty. *[Taos was the place to be for galleries. We didn't feel that there were any good ones in Santa Fe at that time. Later Boris did have an opening here and eventually had a couple of little galleries. Noskin's was in Old Town in Albuquerque. Once he got started in Gallery A in Taos it went fast. He sold every single piece. Then he got other galleries in Fort Worth and California. He worked so hard. Looking back I don't know how he produced all that work, especially considering his health—this thing periodically creeping up on him. Of course, we didn't know then that it was emphysema caused by all the dust and fumes he was inhaling in his work. He just didn't feel well. He went to the hospital more than once. As the doctor said, he had the heart of a bull, a very strong heart to put him through all his hard work. It's a good thing we didn't know.]*

November 20

Today went with Benny to Golden to get a load of wood. A lot of dry trees that have been bulldozed. Came home in the dark, precious new moon, the light of Santa Fe, silhouettes of the mountains, tired and hungry, our pot roast hot and done and delicious. *[Boris got a Dutch oven for the fireplace, and before we left we banked it with hot coals.]* Tomorrow I am going to bake bread in the fireplace.

November 25

A month from today is Christmas—our first one in our own home. How wonderful it will be. Will be working full-time the last week or two, which I don't look forward to. The party yesterday, Thanksgiving in Taos, was quite a turnout. The Mayers were out of town, a big disappointment.

Have been making bread all afternoon. Should have started in the morning; didn't realize it was a day's job. Kneading, rising, mixing, rising, forming, rising, baking. It will probably be awful but I'll learn, I hope. Boris said he'd get ready the right fire for baking in the fireplace. I'm now busy burning wood like mad to get coals.

Boris has started the *portal*. Put large stones in as foundations for the posts with pipe to go up into them. He's so anxious to get going on it, to get it done before snow, and so delighted to do something from scratch instead of correcting other people's mistakes. My bread smells good. *[Those stones were from the penitentiary quarry up on Cerro Gordo and Gonzales roads.]*

November 28

It *was* good. Tomorrow I'm going to have another pot roast. Ginger and Charles are coming for dinner. Yesterday we took Filemon to Cañones. What a spot; beyond description. Magnificently, spectacularly, awesomely beautiful. Lots of water, lots of Indian ruins. The day was snowing, cold, so couldn't explore. Can hardly wait to get back. Would love to have a retreat there.

Today Olive Rush was here. Sweet, wonderful lady. She wants Boris to have a show with her at the Art Museum next spring.* Sounds like a wonderful idea and hope it works out. She refuses to grow old spiritually, constantly trying new things and interested in everything. Full of enthusiasm. Says Boris's work surpasses anything around, and I know it does.

Posts up for *portal*. Now we get the *vigas* up. He has rigged up a winch so it won't be quite such a backbreaking job. *[He did all this himself.]* Wish we could have it done so he could spend all his time on his work. Seems such a shame to take the energy and time away from it. Roses still blooming despite cold weather and snow. Mountains are covered with fresh snow.

December 3

A beautiful blizzard is raging off the Jémez. How magical it is, so exciting. How cozy it is inside and fun to look out. The patio is transformed.

---

*Art Museum: Santa Fe's Museum of Fine Arts, located northwest corner of Palace and Lincoln avenues. Established 1917 as a unit of the Museum of New Mexico. Unless otherwise identified, this is the art museum to which Charlotte refers throughout.

The little tamarisk bush is lovely. Each twig wrapped in white. We are together in our house and it's December.

The posts and *vigas* are up on the *portal*. It looks enormous and elegant. What a difference it makes. It all looks so huge. How exciting it will be to wake up with all white. Too exciting to go to bed.

December 4

The mountains have been so magnificent today that it was hard to tear myself away from the windows. Constantly changing with the clouds, sun, and light. Covered with snow. A wonderful day, and how extremely happy we are in this cozy, elegant house. Baked bread tonight. Even better than last time. Maybe I'm getting the touch. Boris wants hot rolls every night.

As always, little Benny is here working with Boris in the shop. He's here every minute that he's not at school or eating or sleeping—even eats with us at times. Darling little boy and loves carving and working at something while Boris works. *[I think he is the only one of all the kids we knew here who finished high school. He says we were responsible for him doing that. He now has a job at Los Alamos. Every time I see him, he thanks me. He did this for his younger brothers and sisters as they finished high school. His sons have graduated from college. It does go on—just from one little boy.]*

December 8

We have lots of snow. Haven't seen the tops of the mountains in days. Clouds always hanging over them. How deep the snow must be up there. When they do show, how lovely they will be.

Went to Albuquerque last Tuesday night to take some things to the gallery. They were delighted with them. If they would only sell before Christmas, how happy Boris would be. Went to a local hangout for coffee. It was quite a gathering of artists. Really nice people. I'm working now every day except Sunday until Christmas. Will be glad when it's over. Hope next year it will be different. *[Every year I say this.]* It isn't that I mind working, it's just the routine and being away from 518 so much—a place I love to be. The evenings are so short, and I have to go to bed early to get up at six. It's all worth it, though; and surely next year I should be able to do something on my own.

December 14

Tomorrow is my first birthday in our house. May we have many more here together. It's cold and lots of snow on the ground. I'm working tomorrow, of course, but Kay is coming over in the evening. I know it will be fun to come home. Such a wonderful home to come home to. Boris has been able to do some work. Just finished a magnificent metal *toro*. Very handsome.

December 21, 1960–April 5, 1961

"Such a long, lonely winter"

December 21

Boris is gone again—first Christmas in our new home. I just didn't think it would ever happen again. I just didn't think I could face it again. I knew we were too happy. Eric, his son, needed him; he's not well physically or emotionally. Boris couldn't live with himself if he didn't go. How I hate his making that trip again, as did he. *[Boris and Eric were always very, very close.]*

If it weren't for the children, I'd forget Christmas. It was to be our first in our home. Next year, I always say. But it will mean a lot to the children—the tree, presents, and all—so I'll go ahead and hang wreaths and so forth. Children file in from the time I get home from work. I won't have time to be too lonely. It is lonely, though, for Boris loves being here. How wonderful the children all are; so thankful they like coming here.

December 25

It was a lovely Christmas, though Boris isn't here. I know how he would have enjoyed the children. This house was made for children and a Christmas tree. Seeing them all sitting on the floor by the tree, singing Christmas carols, laughing over the windup toys and playing games was wonderful. All last evening and all today. I had little presents for them under the tree. Mau-Mau loving it, too. I burned *luminarias* out front last night, hung wreaths out on the windows. Among my visitors was little Ambrosio and his sister, Lupe. They were so dirty and ragged, actually smelled. It made your heart ache. And so quiet, but I'm sure not missing a thing. Mike played very nicely with Ambrosio, and Juanita obviously let Lupe win at checkers. Last night from 10:30 to midnight the bells were ringing furiously in the clear night air. I could here the screams and shouts of quarreling, too—drunken, loud, and disenchanted. It was sad. Such futility, it's no wonder people just give up.

Mau-Mau and I had dinner in the hot sun by the window. Steak and baked yams cooked in the fireplace. Then I went over to see Kay, whose house as always was the picture of Christmas. So back home, really home. Thinking of my Boris. Wondering where and how he is and how he found things—and missing him. So very sad that he missed today, for it would have helped to take the distaste of Christmas from him. So happy not to have to go to work for three days. What a luxury to sleep after six and not to be dog-tired at night. And my freedom! I certainly don't have a chance to get very lonesome; but it is, even so.

1961

January 2

This seems to have become a second boys' club, girls, too. Haven't even had a chance to read the intriguing books my brother, Brud, sent me. Every evening the children are here playing games—dominoes, pickup sticks, and I've taught the boys chess, which I am delighted to see they like. No word from Boris in more than a week.

There are so many gangs of boys, always stabbing, fighting, and even shooting. Two shot in Ranchos de Taos yesterday over some girl. Why are they so violent? They just don't have anything to do. If I could just get enough of them interested in things like chess and carving with Boris, perhaps when they get older they will escape all that. It's worth trying at least.

January 8

A letter and a wonderful one. Boris is in fine spirits, very optimistic. However, he won't be back for two weeks. Eric is better.

The boy across the street has skipped town. Family hopes he won't come back. No doubt got into a jam. What a future he has!

Boris would have laughed at me if he could have seen me last night. Thought I heard something in the patio. So I took my flashlight and my Colt .38. Searched every corner of the house. I even looked down in the well. No one, not even a cat. As I came back a bird flew out, so I guess that's what it was.

January 9

No, no, not again! Had a suspicion a couple of weeks ago, but now I'm sure. Bedbugs! One must have come in on someone. Hope it isn't pregnant. Have doused bed with DDT. *[Imagine using DDT like that!]*

January 15

It's going to be another sunny day and warmer. No snow on the mountains, and the skiers are most unhappy. Even though it stays cold, there is a promise of spring in the sun and air. Suddenly I am reminded of where I actually am, and I give thanks to the powers that be. How many years have I dreamt this. Of course, Boris not being here is not part of that dream, but he will return, and I hope to stay. I wonder, though, if he ever will.

Benny still comes over every night. Last night I gave him a book, *Learning Spanish Through Pictures*. He can't read or spell Spanish at all, and this is wonderful for him.

Between DDT and insect repellent, no more bites yet.

January 25

Boris is still gone. It seems when he is gone I reach a point when my nerves take over. Monday night I heard a mouse under Mau-Mau's cage. Got up, went to the back building for a trap; with shaking hands set it. Didn't catch anything.

After no signs of any mice when Juanita and Benny were here last night, we heard one trying to get in at the door where one had gotten in before. I had plugged it up. We set a trap and in minutes had one. Then we came into the house and one was lying dead under the chair from the poison behind the shelf. By that time I was a wreck. Juanita and Benny having a ball; loving my screams of fright, which gave them great courage for more hunting. So I had Juanita stay all night. Put up a cot, air mattress, and sleeping bag, which she loved. Benny wants to have a turn at it, too. So think I'll have one or the other stay here until Boris comes back. It's a comfort to have them here. What will tonight bring? Benny and Juanita, I know, are for more excitement. They are dear children, and I'm thankful for them.

Mau-Mau loved the excitement last night, yelling and laughing and bobbing her head. She also said, "Hello, Benny," which made him burst with pleasure.

January 29

Juanita and Benny have been taking turns staying the night with me. They both seem to love it. Having breakfast here, sometimes dinner, when Juanita's mother is drunk or there is nothing for Benny to eat. Last night thought I'd stay alone, but Juanita came running over to get away from her sister's worthless boyfriend, who went after her. So she stayed all night. Poor, sweet, frightened little girl. Wish I could get her out of that horrible environment. She is really different from the others. Do hope she can escape. Wrote Boris that we have to hurry and get more room for our family.

It was a glorious, bright day after several cloudy, snowy ones. The mountains are again visible with a new white coat. Boris still doesn't know when he'll be back.

February 7

Had a birthday party for Juanita—ice cream, fancy cake with "Happy Birthday" on it. Had Valentine cutouts for them to make, which kept them happy and busy for hours. So now, since they asked me to, I made a box where they could put their Valentines for each other; we will open it on the fourteenth.

Still no word from Boris as to when he will be back. Benny and Juanita love staying here and I love having them. Juanita is here most because I feel she needs it most. They are both wonderful to have around. It stays so cold; only one warm day in a month. The sun is hot, though, and a couple of daffodils are poking shoots up in the bed by the south wall.

I was so in hopes Boris would be here for Valentine's Day. It doesn't seem like it. He's been gone since before Christmas. Each day I long for a letter telling me that he is on his way.

February 14

Boris has been very ill. First time I've ever known him to admit it, so it must be bad. Metal poisoning from working on his metal with the compressed gas. He's still in Illinois and can't travel until he's stronger. We will open the Valentine box tonight. I'm so concerned about him, and he is so far away. Do hope it has no permanent effects, his vision and balance and so forth. Maybe he'll get off next week.

The daffodils are coming up like mad, and the rosebushes in the sun are getting new little sprouts. The buds on the elm tree are swelling. I worked today and we were very busy. I've asked for a raise. Will I get it? Also, I'm going to start working four days a week. My salary for three days just doesn't make it; a depression is on its way and unemployment rises rapidly. President Kennedy really got into a mess.* No matter what happens he'll be blamed when, of course, it all started before he got in.

Have again been attacked by *chinches*. The one night after a month that I didn't use repellent, they struck. Don't think I'll ever go to bed without dousing myself with it. *[Oh God! It's a wonder I lived through it.]* Never have I seen anything so illusive or hard to get rid of. We never see the damned things, but man do you know they are there! It is horribly depressing to me; and it ruins everything—peaceful sleep—just imagining you feel them or hoping you won't wake up with huge sore welts on your face, especially. Where do they come from? The children? Who knows?

February 20

Boris is sick with pneumonia. *[This could have been the beginning of his illness, emphysema.]* Ordered five fruit trees for the back—a pear, an apple, a dwarf apple, and two dwarf peach. I'm going to get a wisteria for the *portal*. It's all very exciting. The sun is really hot, though the air stays cool and nights are cold. Had the exterminator in Saturday. Couldn't live with those *chinches* any longer. Hope that's the end of them. He said he may have to come back in thirty days in case eggs hatch.

---

*When U.S. President John F. Kennedy (1917–1963) was inaugurated in January 1961, the country was in an economic slump. In his first days in office, Kennedy proposed a program to "restore momentum" to the U.S. economy. In early February the U.S. Department of Labor officials stated that unemployment was the "worst since early World War II" and that the country was in a "full-fledged recession."

The children still spend their evenings here and, once in a while, a night. They do their homework here, where at least there is quiet and interest. You can't blame the children for not doing well in school. Their parents give them no help or interest. A lot of the parents don't know English. Surrounded by fighting, yelling children, with the ever-present television on full blast.

March 9

Still very cold but for the first time in the evening the air had the feel of spring. It's been such a long, lonely winter; Boris has been gone almost three months. Hoping he'll blow in this spring on the twenty-first. He's getting better every day. Got the flower beds all fertilized, and I'll plant peas Sunday out back. A robin has been singing every morning and how exciting it is. I stand in a trance, listening.

Benny, Juanita, and Duchy still come over every evening to do their homework. Then we roast marshmallows or have ice cream. Must get a corn popper; they would enjoy that. Got some cheap cotton to have the girls make themselves skirts. Will wait till Boris gets back, so Benny will be in the shop with him.

Have a light outside the big doors in the patio. How elegant and lovely it looks with it on. Hope to get two Indian women from Santo Domingo Pueblo to do the mud work next month. *[They never came.]*

March 12

How beautiful it was to see the children rush in with their arms full of pussy willows today, breathless and excited. We bunched them in bunches of twenty-five, and tomorrow after school I'm taking them to the Plaza to sell them to the florists for two cents each.

Spring is really on it's way, even though it stays cool. The sun is hot; the robins and house finches sing each morning; and I put two rows of peas in. The patio is exciting, with the bulbs shooting up and the rose-bushes and plants getting green. Think I'll order some more gravel to put on the drive in back. It will look so much nicer. The trees haven't come yet; all ready for them.

A letter from Boris says it will be two more weeks. He is much better but dizzy from not smoking. His system was so full of nicotine and so used to it that the effects are like dope. It seems impossible that he will come, it's been so long.

March 14

What a day! Almost too glorious to stand. Worked outside all day again. Planted peas Sunday. Put gravel on the drive in back and the trees arrived. They look so little. I was having a miserable time trying to hold them and shovel in the hole. Had to push wheelbarrows of good dirt from way in back and haul water by the bucket since I can't for the life of me turn the hose faucet on. It wasn't but a few minutes after the first tree was in that children were everywhere, delighted to find something going on and eager to help. Then I got three more trees as bonuses—apples and a grapevine—for which I had to dig holes. Fortunately, Johnny, Benny's fourteen-year-old brother, and his friend Robert were around, so we got it done. It looks like a young orchard.

March 19 (Sunday)

Hope this is winter's last fling. True to form, March is raising hell. Four inches of snow this morning and more is falling, but it's more like rain now. We need the moisture badly, though. I'm sure it's good for all my trees and so forth, even though I soaked everything well Wednesday. Been raining and snowing ever since.

Boris's letter—"It won't be long." This has been going on for weeks and weeks, so I pay little attention. "Wolf! Wolf!" you know. I won't believe it until I see him. We've lost out on his show at the gallery with Olive Rush; it's to be on April 17. I'm so embarrassed about it that I haven't mentioned it to Olive. It really seems that he could have been back by now. *[The show was at the Art Museum. I have an article on it.]* I wonder what is really the answer. Maybe he really isn't strong enough yet, but I talked to him more than a month ago and he was getting better then. Could he take that long? Do hope he is all right.

The mass of little birds in the patio is lovely to see, eagerly devouring the food I put out. Have some new friends. Think they will be most enjoyable.

Boris said he might call this evening. Guess he decided against it. Juanita, Duchy, and I popped corn on the fireplace last night. Benny went to the show. Boris did call. Sure he'll be home for Easter.

March 22

Glorious warm day. My daffodils, scilla, and shoots of myrtle coming up through the leaves under the trees look like a bit out of the flower show. Planted a row of yellow wild roses out back by the fence. Got them from Olive.

The most depressed letter from Boris. He is most discouraged about selling his work, almost ready to give up. No wonder he's not here. Oh well, something will turn up somehow. We'll hope for the best.

March 23

A day that makes just being alive wonderful: the air, the sun, the birds singing, flowers blooming, dirt to dig in.

March 26

This morning I woke to find one inch of snow on the ground and cold. My poor, sweet daffodils were bending at the waist, frozen solid, but they thawed and later on were none the worse. It's amazing. Benny and I dug holes for some little Russian olive trees I hope to go dig with Kay *mañana*. Also think I'll try to get another piñon for the front. He stayed last night and the two girls. He and I had a wonderful evening with popcorn, and then I sat and just watched them play and act silly like three little cubs. Their laughter and expressions were most entertaining. I love them. He was here for a big breakfast and lunch. He has grown four inches in three months but is too thin. Think he'll be fascinating to the girls when he grows up. Duchy and Juanita, I believe, think he is already. It amazes me how very modest the children are coming from such big families with no privacy.

A wonderful letter from Boris yesterday with drawings. He really thinks he'll be home this week. Can't believe it until I see him. I'm going to dye eggs and have an egg hunt in back Easter morning. There will no doubt be fifteen children; hope it's a nice day.

March 31

Last day of this month, thank God. Boris called Tuesday. He'll drive but hopes to be here tomorrow. We had a lot of snow yesterday A.M., and it's been lousy cold, but today promises to be lovely. I'm so thankful for Boris.

As for me I'll not know what it's doing for the next two days and nights. I'll be in the salt mines fixing things for Easter. For the pittance I get paid it's hardly worth the effort. Heard yesterday that living costs here are second highest in the country; Washington, D.C., is first. I believe it. Everything except housing is higher than even Chicago—utilities, gasoline, food, everything you need. I don't know how all these poor, which there are more of, too, make it when salaries are half as much. Doesn't make sense. *[Some things never change.]* Must be off to work.

April 2 (Easter)

The sun came out for our egg hunt. Had four dozen dyed eggs and about the same of candy eggs. Didn't take fifteen children long to find them all. Much excitement. The apricot blossoms are blooming on the huge branches I brought in Wednesday. How thrilling it is. Still cold outside but promises to be warmer tomorrow. A letter from Boris. He'll be here Tuesday or Wednesday.

April 4

Children just left. Waiting for Boris. Got a cake with "Welcome Home" on it and steak. Surely he'll be here tomorrow if not tonight. Glorious summer day. You wanted to cry and call and dance when you stepped out in it. It was so warm. Trees are bursting; apricots in bloom. Is there anything like spring?

April 5

No word, no sight of Boris. He must have left or he would have let me know. Horrible day. Cold and snow all day. Of course, we need the moisture, but how exciting a warm rain would have been. Last night the flashes of lightning over snowy mountaintops were really dramatic. Nothing, black, and then suddenly a flash, spotlighting the white mountains.

April 18–July 29, 1961

"A man of no compromise"

April 18

Yes, Boris is here. Arrived the sixth. Of course, have been very busy. *[I didn't do anything on the house when he was gone. It was all outside work that was left. I'd finished the front room while he was gone before, so I was living up there.]* We got *vigas* from a mill in Pecos for almost half of what they would be at the lumberyard. Also, slabs with bark to make a fence eight feet tall in back. What a wonderful difference. *[Those are the* vigas *that about twenty years later got put up in this room. They had beautifully aged, naturally weathered, stacked out in back here, and then I found that wonderful stain at Valdez and I stained all the wood for the ceiling and it perfectly matched the naturally weathered wood.]*

Got a load of lava rock in for rock work in the patio. *[It's on the west wall there.]* How beautiful it looks instead of cobblestones. Blends in better instead of slapping you in the face; and Boris does such a beautiful job of laying it. The Indians haven't shown up for mud work. We will have to look for someone else. Too bad.

Duchy and Juanita are here busy on their skirts. Bought Benny some high tops for his helping us; he's so pleased. It's good not to be alone. Sleep the whole night through and how quickly the evenings go.

April 25

The *portal* is finished and now for laying brick in *el zaguán* and *portal*. How huge it looks and what a wonderful place it will be to sit in the summer shade with a breeze gently blowing through the doors. Now begins the watering—trees, garden, and flower garden in the patio. Yesterday we went and dug out big yuccas for the front. They just suit it with rocks and piñons. There is so much to do; I hate going to work each day, but that too is a necessity.

It's still cold. Will it ever warm up? The fruit trees are out all over town. Lovely, and the lilacs push on in spite of the cold. Juanita brought us some yummy hot *sopaipillas* for dinner.

Little boys are busy helping Boris haul gravel—after ice cream, of course. Can't believe what a terrific difference there is in the place in less than a year. Unbelievable.

May 5

Sleet and cold today. Lilacs in bloom. Fruit blossoms almost gone. The little flowering crab apple surprised us by blooming. Corn, squash, and pumpkins in. *[When Boris was gone that first year I was here, I ordered all those fruit trees. I planted them first so they would grow and I could enjoy them before I dropped dead or something.]*

Boris has started laying brick in *el zaguán*. It's going to look elegant. On May 1 Marva and Jack Noskin and Peter Hunt were here for dinner. *[Hunt was a friend of Jack's. I didn't know him.]* Steaks cooked in the fireplace and garlic bread. Had a gay, talkative evening.

Tuesday, May 2, was Boris's birthday so we took off for the Indian ruins in Cañones on top of a high mesa. Sheer drops. What a view; scrambling up and down the mountainside, a real workout. Trying to find our way down was an adventure as it was getting dark. Sliding down sandy slopes to find a sheer drop, scrambling up to try again. Finally found a sand slide. *[It really wasn't sand, it was pumice.]* That took us almost all the way down as the stars began to appear. We made quite a picture laughing as we went, Boris with a knapsack full of dwarf piñons, picks, and shovels. *[One little piñon tree is still by the big rock on the east side of the front room patio door. I keep it trimmed back so it stays small.]*

The ruins were unbelievably wonderful. Houses line the edge for a mile—all built of lava rock cut in shapes of adobe brick. Found four arrowheads. Virgin territory; no digging. Boris dreams about going back to dig and screen. Little Benny can hardly wait to go, too. Next time it will be easier since we know the ropes. There were moments when I really thought my time had come, crashing off the drop. Felt like finding a safe place and curling up till morning but knew I couldn't. No choice but to go on. Sometimes you feel like that about living, too. My job, for instance, but know I can't quit. Anyway, I hope someday.

May 7 (Sunday)

Boris had half of the bricks laid in *el zaguán* when he discovered some lovely blackish ones that were much to his liking. So out came the red ones and he's busy doing it over. A man of no compromise.

May 8

Boris finished laying the beautiful, dark bricks in *el zaguán*. They look as though they had been there forever. Only to find out they all have to come up again to lay a sewer and water pipe to the back building. It's all so discouraging and so much horrible bull work for him. Sometimes I wonder why we ever started this. Money going fast. Not sure we can finish.

May 14

A rugged two days at the flower shop—Mother's Day. Glad that's over. Boris decided not to lay the sewer under the drive but to run it along the wall so bricks don't have to come up. He's not laying the bricks, he's creating them. *[Instead of going along the* zaguán *we cut through the patio. The only bricks we had to take up for the sewer were the ones between the front building and the bathroom. The gas pipe to the back is under the* banco.*]*

The little boys are kept busy loading the wheelbarrow and piling bricks. They love it. They take time off to ride each other around on the dolly and play horseshoes in the back.

May 17

Three beautiful days. Lots of sun, except for today, which was at least warm. We packed a lunch and went up into the Sangres to see what was happening. The aspen are just beginning to leaf out and fresh tender green things appearing. Had lunch by a rushing stream. Thought of horrible Illinois. Came back with a truck full of little trees. *[Of course, I'm sure we weren't supposed to do that.]*

Boris has almost finished the wall along the driveway in front and then back to his bricks. *[I guess he is making the wall out in front.]* Do hope he'll get to his own work soon. Have decided not to have a show at the Barn Gallery until August. *[The Barn was located on the north side of Canyon Road where you go down off the road.]* House is beginning to have recognition. People are curious and impressed. Hate the thought of going to work tomorrow.

May 19

Stone wall by drive finished *[that's out in front]*. It's a work of art. Boris built a flower bed in it, and when we get it planted and the little trees it will be beautiful to see. *[I decided not to have any flowers, anything I had to care for, out in front. I had too much back here. So we put only plants that grow naturally there.]*

After I came home from work, we went back up to the mountains—Benny and his friend Ronnie rode in the back of the truck—for a load of yummy black dirt. It was so lovely up there. The aspen dressed in fresh chartreuse and the streams gurgling over the rocks. Got home about dark for delicious stew. The children joined us. People are beginning to wander by the house and ask to come in and look.

May 25

Took off for Cañones yesterday. Snooped back roads and brought back a truck full of lava rocks and cacti. Crickets chirping in the patio, lovely sounds.

May 29

The two ladies from Cañones arrived. They start on the mud *mañana*. Are sleeping on cots in the back; cooking on the hibachi. It will be interesting to see them work and wonderful to have the walls done in the old way. They speak no English, so Benny will be interpreter and perhaps I'll be forced to use what Spanish I know—which will be good. Of course, tomorrow being Memorial Day, I go to work at dawn. Tomorrow night we take Benny to his first circus. If I could only write, what a book all this on Alto Street would be.

May 31

What a day—chopping straw for mud, mixing same to fill in holes, and so forth—getting ready for the ladies to put on the final coat. They've finished the front except for going over it with a wet sheepskin and paste (flour and water) and screened dirt to fill in cracks. *[We built a fire in the patio for the finishing coat. They got a big kettle and made a paste out of tortilla flour and water, which they mixed with the mud for the final coat. It dried like cement and it lasted for years.]*

It's causing a lot of comment out front, seeing them work. These days most people, if they do use adobe instead of cement blocks—horrid things—cover them with wire and plaster. Think it is going to look lovely. The *señoras* are cooking with piñon on the little stove I used last summer. It will be fun to look back on, but right now we are looking forward to our peace and solitude again.

Streams of children are in and out—mostly in—all day. At times I get very tired of being patient with the little ones. Fern and Rose helped me all day. *[Those were Benny's sisters, nice little girls.]* Then they had a ball taking a shower for they have no hot water at home. The circus was a flop, a fraud. Nothing but a corny vaudeville show. A horrible disappointment.

Boris has a time keeping up with the *señoras*—straw to chop, dirt to sift, and mud to mix. Benny is a big help, and so ends another exhausting day. Will the day ever come when we can just sit leisurely and enjoy our efforts?

June 6

What wonderful ladies. How hard they work and what beautiful work. They have finished the front and have done all the other walls except for the final going-over with sifted dirt mixed with paste made by boiling tortilla flour and water. It fills in all the cracks and looks gorgeous.

The weekend was something. People and children swarming in and out. Much talking and laughing, yelling, running children. Mau-Mau joining in—loving it. *[All their friends from Cañones came down for the weekend.]* Really feel if more people could know about this art there would be more adobe used. None of this sand stuff that washes away, like the local men use. It will no doubt be a lost art when their generation is gone. Think I'll tell the paper about it tomorrow. Perhaps someone is interested in preserving the old ways. Bet no one in Santa Fe has such beautiful walls.

June 14

Paper didn't come, of course. Too bad. They missed a good bet. Ladies gone—miss their Spanish chatter, laughter, smell of piñon and tortillas. Was almost sad to see them go. They want us to come and see them. One of them has a little house in an orchard that we can stay in.

Boris is still throwing around three-, four-, and five-hundred-pound stones, much to the amazement of everyone. Little girls coyly lower their eyes and little boys beam with pleasure at the strength. The ladies from Cañones called him *"superhombre" [superman]*. It's impressive, I must say. Hope he doesn't overdo. He used the rocks for the drive in front and is now making a low wall between patio and *portal*. They are from the original old penitentiary, quarried dark limestone from about 1880. He plans to carve some of it, too. He must get at his own work next week.

No rain. How dry it is! There are more and more people in to look at the place each day, it seems. I should charge admission to keep it going. Dr. Jenkins and her friend, Miss Hull, were over to see the house and loved it.

June 19

Olive Rush, Ginger, and Charles were here for supper last night. They are really our best friends. Went with Olive to an open house at an old house that the Old Santa Fe Association* bought on Canyon Road, the Rafael Borrego House. They have fixed it up and it is charming but not elegant, like this one.

We went snooping around the country today. Went to see Los Alamos for the first time and last. Most impressing to see how and why billions of our taxes are spent. Could live beautifully on the money it takes just to keep all of those darn lawns watered. Every house has

---

*Old Santa Fe Association (OSFA): Founded in 1926 in opposition to the establishment of a "culture colony" on city-owned land. Stated goals were in part "to preserve the . . . historical structures and traditions of Old Santa Fe, to guide its growth . . . [so] as to sacrifice as little as possible of [Santa Fe's] unique charm. . . ." The HSFF was founded by OSFA as an educational and charitable foundation eligible to receive tax-deductible gifts.

one. Ridiculous!* Looked for Indian ruins we found several years ago but couldn't find any. Looked for fossils Charles told us of over by Santa Cruz Reservoir but didn't find any. Boris was most disappointed. Had a lovely rain this P.M.; need more, though.

June 25

Had dinner out in the patio. Boris made a pine table and benches, wonderful in the corner under the tree. He must start on his own work, though, and let the house go for a couple of months. He's going to work under the *portal.*

Wild storms all around but not a drop here. Just terrific wind. Dr. Jenkins and friend Miss Hull were over this evening. Children in and out all day, as always. It's a refuge for them, I guess. Mau-Mau on the patio loving all the activity, laughing and squealing like they do.

July 5

So dry. Water, water all the time. Still, the flowers look lovely, and the patio is a joy. We eat out there a lot. Boris has gone to Albuquerque alone. Juanita and Duchy spent the evening sewing on their skirts until the machine broke. Poor thing, it's been longer than I can remember since anything was done to it. Glad I finished my skirt before it went out.

July 8

The rainy season is upon us. It's at it for the third day. Last night walls, roads, and God knows what were washed away. Never heard or saw a better storm from 1 to 3 A.M. It came down like a waterfall. Our lovely new wall is blistering in spots, and the outer coat is peeling. Makes me sick. There must be an answer. Hope we'll find it.

Edgar Britton, his wife, and friends came by the other day. He's having a show here at the Barn on Canyon Road. Old friend of Boris's— hasn't seen him in thirty years, a sculptor. They live in Colorado Springs.

---

*Los Alamos lawns: Los Alamos, with its rows of government houses on numbered streets with front lawns that need watering in this desert state, presents a strong contrast with other northern New Mexico communities.

July 11

Our beautiful walls are not holding after all the rain. The outside coat blisters in spots, loose from the undercoat. Why? We aren't sure whether it's the mud, whether it's because they didn't wet the wall underneath, or whether it's the sand underneath. Anyway, we're experimenting with water repellents, emulsion of asphalt *[which we didn't use],* and water sealers to see if we can find an answer to this darn thing. We are determined to have mud walls. *[Well, we didn't use any of this. We just weren't used to adobe, you know. Eventually we accepted it all and took what came. Recently, I did make a terrible mistake with a new product called "adobe," which was recommended. The theory is that it breathes so when it gets wet it dries out and doesn't seal like most coatings do. Unfortunately, it doesn't weather beautifully the way adobe does and is peeling off like paint—awful, very ugly. It just makes me ill. We have to take it all off because it's water repellent and you can't throw wet mud on a dry wall.]*

Had our first *calabacita [baby squash]* last night from the garden. Boiled it with onion, very little water, and butter. Delicious! Boris is working on bone sculpture. Mad! Paints designs and faces on vertebrae and so forth, bones he picked up. Mounts them on dowel rods or wires. They are really wonderful. It will be interesting to see if they sell.

July 14

Had a very nice evening at Peter and Marion Krebs's place. Lovely people. *[That's Marion Love of the* Santa Fean *magazine.]* John and Bernique Wallace were there. *[Bernique was a painter. I didn't know her well.]* Boris has gone to Albuquerque with drawings, which are selling. If we could get enough outlets, we could make it. We'll try Gallery 5 here in Santa Fe. *[I can't remember at all where that was. It's come and gone like so many.]*

July 29

Very warm for Santa Fe. Terribly dry. Boris going to Illinois again next week for a garden job in Lake Forest; we need the money badly so he feels he must go. Don't look forward to two months alone again. Had hoped this wouldn't be necessary. *[I don't remember this job.]*

August 3, 1961–March 3, 1962

"Piles of wood, vigas waiting to be used"

August 3

Boris has gone. Left early this morning. Even the sky is crying. Can't believe he's gone again. That's why he went, a job, a prospect. We need the cash. *[Nothing got done while he was gone. The inside was all done and I was living up in front. The only thing left, of course, was this back. I couldn't do it. My journal now is all about the weather, my job, and how weary I am of being here all alone. The neighbor kids practically lived here. Some one of them was always here at night. I made Christmas for them and then I did Valentine's Day for them. For Easter we had an Easter egg hunt. They kept me occupied.]*

August 15

Guess I'll not put anything more down until Boris comes back. Things go on as usual except we've had days of rain. All is green and lush. Nice not to have to water. My sweet little girls, Juanita and Duchy, spend almost every evening with me and the nights. Don't know what I'd do without them. I think they would move in if their mother would let them. A week from tomorrow is Duchy's birthday. Plan to take them and their mother to Olympia and Carla's house, with a cake, for the afternoon. *[Carla was Olympia's daughter.]*

    I was hoping to go back to Illinois next month but they don't need me to work, so I don't know whether I'll go hog wild and go anyway. Think I might and drive back with Boris. Haven't heard from him in ten days. I'm very concerned. Wondering how he is and how things are going. Can't understand why he doesn't write.

September 3

Believe it or not, this morning after raining most of the night, we had a snowstorm. Picked corn in it. Almost froze my hands. Still raining at noon. Poor Fiesta, which is in progress. The freakiest weather I ever saw. Yesterday it was sunny and tonight it is supposed to be thirty-eight degrees. Hear from Boris occasionally. Hope things work out for him.

September 27

Back slab fence up. The Taos Indian, who is a friend of the Lappins, came with braids encased in blue wool. *[I'd never seen anything like that before. Joe and Gladys Lappin were retired neighbor friends. She was an excellent seamstress and made some wonderful things for me.]* His helper was like something out of Dostoyevski or Steinbeck but really most willing and appreciative. Spent the last two days on it. Now I can hardly wait to get it cleaned up back there. Don't think the neighbors like the fence. They can't see each other or yell across. In a way I am sorry, but it is wonderful to have the privacy. Boris's work goes well in Evanston. Sold something and has others to do. No word about when he'll be back. *Que serà, serà.*

October 12

Winter on its way; snow on the mountains. My giant pumpkin vine frozen. Aspens gone. Glorious days, frosty nights. No promise of when Boris will return.

November 16

Everything goes along about the same. The four girls, Juanita, Duchy, Fern, and Rosy, come over almost every night to do homework. Juanita usually stays the night. It has gotten colder. Have had snow, which is melting down the walls, taking mud with it.

I'm very weary of being here alone with so much remaining undone or half done on the house. Piles of wood, *vigas,* and so forth waiting to be used.

New Year's Eve

Mau-Mau and I are again alone to begin another year. A week ago tonight the children and I decorated the tree. Hung wreaths with bright red ribbons in the front windows. *Luminarias* on the wall outside. It was gay and happy; they made it so. Christmas morning they all came in for their presents. Popcorn balls and candy. Tonight we will take it all down and so begins a new year. I know it will be a happy one. Boris I'm sure will be home soon. He hasn't been well and I'm very anxious about him. Surely it won't be much longer, and then we can live together forever and find peace, wisdom, love, and happiness.

1962

January 16

The weeks pass. One very much like the other. Working four days a week. Three lovely days to myself. It's been miserably cold. Last week the pipes all froze, including the john. It went to five below zero or more for two nights. Had it thawed out with an electric gadget for $15. Thank heaven no broken pipes.

Still no word from Boris. One of his drawings that I sent into the Dallas show was accepted. Took his giraffe and drawing over to the Art Museum here. Know that too will be good news. His work is finally being recognized here, as it should be. If he'd only get back so we could really get going on it, but he has done several jobs in Illinois.

March 3

Seven months ago Boris left. Contemporaries Gallery opens April 7. *[This was near where the Bull Ring restaurant used to be on the Old Santa Fe Trail.]* Have signed up Boris for it. He must get back to get things organized. He hasn't been well at all. Naturally, I'm concerned, especially when I don't hear from him.

April 17–August 13, 1962

"Boris pulling loose ends together"

April 17

Boris got back on the tenth of March. *[I wrote and told him I might get married to an elderly friend of my sister's.]* I left for Chicago the eighteenth and went up to Tower, Minnesota, with my sister Treet to spend ten days with her and Dot.

Boris finished the brickwork under the *portal* while I was gone. It looks elegant and tremendous. Patio looks lovely. Crocus now gone, also daffodils, leaving bleeding heart and columbine. My two little peach trees, only a year old, are covered with brilliant pink blossoms. Put radishes and lettuce in; will plant corn next week. Boris got a lot of cholla and yucca today to put in front and started fence in back.

Looks as though I would finally get the plaque for the house *[from the Historic Santa Fe Foundation]*. One of the oldest around and authenticated. Hope it goes through.

This is Easter week; I'll be busy at the flower shop. Will be glad when it is over. The weather is beautiful. Will dye three dozen pullet eggs for the children for Sunday. They are still over here every evening and any other time they aren't in school. What does the future hold for them?

May 8

The old house was voted last week to receive a bronze plaque not only because of its antiquity but its historical value. So maybe that will bring something interesting.

Boris is busy pulling some of the loose ends together, such as fixing moldings on windows. He made a paneled frame for the door into this front room building, squared it off, and it looks beautiful, thick. No end of things to do. Patio looks beautiful. Crickets merrily chirp every night. I feel constantly beat, though, from working and don't even make enough to keep things going. *[All along we are talking about money, money, money.]*

77

May 23

What a joy this place is. Have been planting the patio, hanging begonias under the *portal,* bright pots and boxes of geraniums. On the north wall the spots of bright begonias. Boris made a little pool by the *portal,* and I got a reedy water plant—cattail—for it and goldfish. It is so lovely, all of it.

He fixed the big door to the patio—with latches and such—so it works. Also the screen door works and finally I can just walk out through it to the patio. *[That's the big door into the patio from the south wall of the sala.]* He's starting on the front gate and the wellhouse. *[Boris built the wellhouse, but we never had the well completely dug out.]*

I've quit my job; I love it! Something will turn up, I know it. *[Well, I went back later, I'll tell you I did. Pretty soon, though, Boris was making it on his work, which was wonderful.]* This job and career stuff is not for me. I hate routine and adore my freedom. I love being home and just keeping things going here inside and out. Keeps me busy all day.

Poor Boris has little time for his own work, but we feel we must have the place looking elegant by the time the plaque is up, which should be next month. Finished getting my corn, squash, and pumpkins in. The back is even beginning to be beautiful. All that will be left is the back building, which is a project in itself—but that too will come.

May 28

The gate is almost finished with the door cut into it *[which they call a "needle door"].* It's put together with carriage bolts, the last big black ones in town. The new ones are all horrible chrome-plated things and cost eleven cents each. More than one hundred of them. Think maybe I'd like to sell this place and go to Mexico or maybe rent it. I'm sick of this darn cold weather.

May 30 (Memorial Day)

The gate and the little door within it are finished and, of course, are wonderful. Boris, as always, has done a beautiful job, and his touch has made them truly lovely and elegant. Damn cold again tonight. Will it ever stop? Four chameleons survived. *[I brought the chameleons back from the circus because I felt so sorry for them. When I was little, my brother and I always had to buy chameleons when we went to the circus.]* Horny toads hatched out; they're all over the place. Buying a new car. *[Since Boris was selling his work, we were getting rich.]*

June 30

Eric, Boris's son, was here for a week a couple of weeks ago. He loved it all, and how happy Boris was to be with his son. Brud will be here the fifth of August, and I can hardly wait. Boris is having a show at the Barn Gallery and is busy getting things together.

We have a new pet, Edgar Nevermore, a raven. Mike brought him over, a poor, weak, half-starved nestling. In ten days his feathers have gotten soft and lustrous with his diet of meat, cod-liver oil, egg, pabulum, and bone meal. He can't stand up but is getting stronger, always hungry. We can't get near his box without his beak flying open and his calling, "Caw, caw." Mau-Mau hears him; "Edgar the crow," she says. "Caw, caw." Otherwise, she is indifferent to it. She, of course, doesn't know that she herself is a bird. I have a patio full of chirping crickets, wonderful night sound.

August 1

Today the plaque was put up. It looks quite impressive and will be interesting to see how many wend their way over here. We had hoped to have an "open" sign out and perhaps someone would buy something, a drawing and so forth, but I've since had to go back to work to eat. *[I don't like this; I'm always complaining.]* But I hate to work, as Mau-Mau says. I won't be home much to see; maybe something else will turn up, I hope. My dear brother arrives Sunday with his friend Bill.

Edgar died. Just as well for he had no use of his legs and don't think he ever would have. Mau-Mau still says, "Poor Edgar the crow." The big horned toad laid eggs and the patio is full of baby toadies. We really have to look before we step. *[They were about the size of my thumbnail.]* Also another lizard is added to the collection, and inside we have four more birds. Two fire finches—my favorite color, shocking pink—and a pair of gouldians, who are fantastic birds. *[Gouldians are also finches.*

The males are beautiful, with brilliant colors. I bought them to get them out of Woolworth's.]

Boris is to have a show at the Barn Gallery opening the twelfth, a week from Sunday. He's been turning out a lot of wonderful things, and it should be a great show. A small metal horse was stolen in Taos a few weeks ago. He was very flattered. We hope to be reimbursed.

The Alfred Kings of the King Ranch in Texas were over the other night. They bought a piece of Boris's years ago and wanted to meet him. Wonderful people and even threatened to buy another piece.

August 13

Opening over. Beautiful show. Everyone really impressed. The Kings bought a lovely metal bird and Dr. Kieva a few drawings. *[Dr. Rudolph Kieva was a psychiatrist in Santa Fe; he bought several of Boris's things later on.]* People will come back, and I know this is the beginning.

August 14, 1962–December 10, 1964

"No time for the house"

August 14

The little old burro, the Jeep, was hard to part with but traded it in on a 1958 Volvo station wagon. Boris has a new toy and has done nothing but work on it since he got it at 3 P.M. yesterday.

September 27

Got back from Denver and Colorado Springs last night. Took back Ed Marecak's paintings and Edgar Britton's sculpture. *[They were also in the show at the Barn Gallery.]* Spent most of our time with the Brittons, who are very nice. Marecak is a real artist, a vital and interesting man. Loved his work; traded for a piece of Boris's. *[I have that painting in my guest bedroom. I like it very much.]*

A few weeks ago we went to El Paso to take some things to Ferrell's gallery. It should be a good connection. Gallery A in Taos has asked for us to come in; we are very happy for we feel it is the best around here.

I spent all day today planting things in pots to bring in the house. *[I used to put things in pots for the winter.]* The house looks like a conservatory and is very lovely. Every window stuffed with green and blooming things. Have given Ginger a lot, about two dozen geraniums, and still have loads for myself. Patio looks gorgeous; no frost yet. My chrysanthemums are spectacular. Everything bursting with growth except, of course, the roses, which I am about to give up.

The Barn show was quite a success both financially (it is such a relief to have the pressure off) and as far as connections go. Brought back some goodies from Juárez that belong here: lovely pots and jugs and a leather-and-wood settee. Really would enjoy living in Mexico.

October 11

Still no frost. Evenings getting colder, though, and come the full moon in a few nights that will be it. Have a fire going in the fireplace every evening; during the day the patio doors stand open with the sun streaming in.

1963

February 12

We've had a very cold winter. Down to eighteen degrees below zero in January. The house next door, which is part of the original place, has started to collapse after all these years. Roof leaks, water drips down the walls. The only thing that holds it together is chicken wire. When that goes, as in front, the whole thing will go. *[This is the house on the east. It was fixed later.]*

We have a new parrot, another Pancho, an Amazon from South America, a poor, neglected bird Boris found in Albuquerque. Got it for Christmas, which was a flop and anticlimax. *[I think because of my disappointment in not having our first Christmas in the house together, we tried too hard.]* A smart, lovable, gorgeous bright green. So with six finches, two parrots, fish, chameleons, and three windows bulging with plants, I'm tied. *[I who love my freedom.]*

Boris says he is going to start on the house when the weather breaks. We'll see. He's now starting a slate carving for the Goods in Taos for their bathroom wall. Gallery A has done very well. Sold six small things since December 2. Hope the big ones go soon.

May 22

Spring is here. Even though it's cool, my patio has come to life: geraniums, fuchsias, lilies of the valley, violets, and begonias bloom. I, too, have come to life.

Boris's beautiful work is really selling, which is a great stimulant and an inspiration to him. Also what a great relief not to be bogged down by constant lack of money. People love them; and his works get better and better. He can hardly keep up with it, and I am sorry to have to part with them for they are so beautiful. It's been a long, hard struggle for us both, and finally it will reap its fruit. I must really try to hang on to some of them. The Castilian and copper roses are in bloom in back, and the fruit trees look lovely. Boris has started a strawberry bed and I have planted sweet peas, gourds, and nasturtiums. It should all be gorgeous.

The house made the paper last month; most gratifying. Pancho has developed into a character and has gotten his new brilliant feathers. He and Mau-Mau are still distant, jealous of the attention of the other. What a clown he is; Mau-Mau is the egghead.

We have opened a gallery in Cerrillos, behind the Tiffany Saloon, Thursday, Friday, and Saturday evenings. No business but lots of people and interest. It may develop; but it's fun in the meantime. *[There was a little room in the back where the bar was, which we opened into a gallery. I don't remember that it had a name. The whole building burned down in the 1970s, but we had left by that time.]*

Boris has no time for the house now. If things continue to go well, perhaps we can hire some work done. It would be a wonder if we could get to it. It's a wonderful old place.

August 29

Everything is going so well. Gallery A in Taos has sold so much that Boris can't keep up with it. I can't believe it will continue. This is the season. It's wonderful for both of us after wanting and working for so many years. Can't tell what a relief it is not to be under financial pressure constantly. In fact, I'm taking a month off; longer, I hope. We enjoy being associated with such fine artists at Gallery A: Eric Gibberd, Malcolm Alexander, Chuck Stewart, and Mario Larrinaga. We have been to gatherings up there with them and enjoy it tremendously. Frannie Good, the director, is a friend and a marvelous person. We have given up the gallery in Cerrillos. We just didn't have time.

Boris's son, Eric, is here. A wonderful boy, and I love having him around. He and his father have taken off for Chihuahua, Mexico. Should be back *mañana*. Hope they are having a grand time.

Having a party for my brother Monday. Guests will be Jack Schaefer and his wife Louise; he is a Western writer. Chuzo Tamotzu and his Louise. Tom Dryce and wife Ada. *[Tom was a painter who exhibited with us when we had the gallery at Tiffany's out in Cerrillos. He had a gallery on Canyon Road. Tamotzu was a Japanese artist, a painter. He did ink draw-*

ings. He and Boris were great friends. They had a lot in common—the same kind of humor and appreciation for the arts. Louise, who is ninety-six now, says she will never forget me making dinner in the fireplace.] The Ewens, Petersons of the Santa Fe *New Mexican [she was a reporter; I don't remember what he did]*, the Lappins, Rogers, McAuliffs, Ginger and Charles Hagerman, of course. *[The Ewens, Doc and Lillian, were acquaintances. He was a painter who did a drawing of our well for a magazine. The Rogers and the McAuliffs were also acquaintances; I don't remember their names.]* Eric will be gone, unfortunately. We hope he comes soon and often. *[I remained close to Eric after Boris died. We always call each other on Boris's birthday. He works for the Vermont Division for Historic Preservation.]*

We have had an unusually warm, wet summer, and so everything has grown like mad. It's getting quite lush around here. Can hardly wait till the "boys" get back from Mexico with all their goodies, which I know they will have. Fiesta is this weekend, so there is much going on.

Boris purchased two Spanish walking mules from Mexico.* They are beautiful creatures, not like Missouri mules. Smaller than a horse and very appealing. Hope Boris has the time to take them out in the hills, which is why he got them. They are his pride and joy. He built a corral in back for them, so we have quite an establishment.

What a change takes place in a few years. Just in three and a half years, the children have all changed and begun to grow up. All they think about now is boys, or girls, as the case may be, dancing, and silly talk. So they seldom come over anymore except to use the phone for some silly or private reason. They have lost their childish charm and appeal. Too bad. Most of them hate school, and many quit before high school to do nothing but deteriorate.

---

*Boris Gilbertson on his mules: "I like to keep fairly close to the earth . . . to which end I purchased several mules. . . . Spanish walking mules . . . beautiful little animals, very intelligent and they can be very mean and ornery. . . . [I use them] to ride and get out in the country. They'll go twenty or thirty miles in a day over the roughest country . . . barefooted, no shoes . . . you can sit and listen to them eat, crunching grain, just the feeling, the smell of animals is real great. . . . I rather imagine that I could prefer the company of my mules to a great many artists."

September 17

The aspens are starting to turn on the mountainside. Long, fat strings of beautiful red chile are making their appearance on house walls to dry in the sun. The evenings are very cool. Fire in the fireplace is cozy. Days shorter. Chrysanthemums bursting in warm glowing color. Alas, mice are coming in, so out come the traps. Winter is on its way.

Last night we took some pieces to Gallery A in Taos, and Frannie told us of a composer working there at the Wurlitzer Foundation who is terribly enthused over Boris's work, Felix Labunski. So we went over to see him. What a charming and intelligent man. A magic afternoon. He and Boris had a great deal to talk about. He even played some of his compositions for us, which was exciting, lovely. He may come to see us on the weekend.

September 24

Have made reservations on the plane for Chicago Thursday. *[I was going to see friends and be with my sisters, Treet and Dot.]* Boris doesn't like my going for it means he has to cook and so forth. I think it will be good for both of us. Mau-Mau will be at Kay's; Pancho and finches at a friend's. If the plane doesn't make it, it matters little. Boris is on his way, which I have worked for for so long, and actually doesn't need me much anymore; and I would just as soon never be an old lady. *[And here I am, an old lady!]*

November 16

Arrived back the sixteenth after a glorious trip and vacation. Enjoyed my jet rides and loved being with Treet and Dot; not having a damned responsibility or worry. Felt and looked like a new woman, but, alas, the magic is already wearing off. Back to the grind and the push. Was hoping by some miracle things would be different. Boris did get a lot done while I was gone—perhaps I shouldn't have come back—and had my plants in the house in wonderful shape. Mau-Mau isn't too chipper; Pancho the same clown; the mules looking like Mongol ponies with their new winter coat. Patio still hasn't frozen; all the nasturtiums and sweet peas out back are gone. Glorious weather. I feel disenchanted. Maybe it will pass when I get rid of this damned cold.

We want to go to Mexico in January. Boris has so much to get done, though, before we can go. It will surprise me if we actually do go. And then, of course, nothing has been done to the back building. Oh well! *[How many years later is it that we finally get the back done?]*

December 4

Still the beautiful weather holds. Boris is working on two gorgeous big flying birds he hopes to have done by Saturday for Gallery A's Christmas opening. I've had a beautiful fuchsia dress made for the occasion. Last night Jack Schaefer came over to read to us a new short story called "Cowboy's Christmas," which he would like Boris to illustrate. Charming little story. *[Boris didn't illustrate it.]*

Feel good again and things going well. Boris also has made a magnificent bronze bird for Gallery A's artists' Christmas tree. Very Russian looking; the *Firebird*, it's called. Even the gallery business is very slow. They have sold few things recently. Not one month had gone by since he started with them a year ago that they didn't sell something. It's wonderful. *[It's always up and down in the art business.]*

1964

January 2

What a prophetic and glorious way to start the year. Gallery A has sold today a $1,200 piece to Bishop Jones, who already has bought four pieces. *[He was an Episcopalian bishop from San Antonio, Texas. He and his wife had a house on Bishop's Lodge Road and were very well known people.]* It is one of the most beautiful Boris has done: two flying birds, very large, highly polished and magnificent. We plan to leave for Mexico, a grand tour in a few weeks, and that makes it all the more possible.

Boris was the featured artist in the *New Mexico Magazine* this month. The weather is warm and sunny like spring, but how badly we need moisture. Boris did a sterling silver owl for Frannie Good for Christmas; it's her "fetish," and she loves it. Dear Felix Labunski dedicated a prelude to Boris; we were very touched and flattered. Things like that mean a great deal.

January 15

Boris left this noon for Dallas; Ferrell has not paid us for what he has sold. Disregarded all correspondence and phone calls, so Boris has gone to collect all his things, or try to. We've given him every chance and can't be bothered anymore. It's just added expense and time that can't be afforded. It's maddening.

The house finch was singing today. It sounded like spring, but it's very cold and still no snow. Boris has so much to do, but we are hoping to get to Mexico in three weeks.

February 20

In the meantime, Boris had pneumonia and an X ray discovered that his lungs have been damaged by metal dust, so we are still here but taking off *mañana*. Boris seems to feel well again. When we return we'll look into the metal poisoning business but feel the vacation will do him a lot of good. God knows he deserves it. *[That was the real beginning of Boris's illness. Way back then, there were signs of his lung problems. From now on, he would have this. It was emphysema, and it killed him. He smoked most of his life, but he quit when we came out here. It was his work, inhaling all of that stone dust and metal dust, all that polishing and working with his torch. He thought he was indestructible.]*

Marc Simmons is staying in the house. All the birds are at the Bartletts, the mules on Archie West's ranch near Cerrillos. *[Albert and Hillary Bartlett were retired friends. She was a dear; we used to walk our dogs together. We met Archie at Tiffany's Saloon when we had our gallery there. His father was the artist Hal West.]* Boris finished a gorgeous bronze bird for the biannual show at the Art Museum. It should be *the* piece at the show, if the judges have any sense. Unfortunately, it is to be judged by photographs and not the actual sculpture, but still it's beautiful.

It's cold and snowy; I'm so glad to be taking off. We plan to be gone six weeks. We're taking the truck. Boris has made a platform so we can sleep in it, if we wish, storing our stuff underneath. Taking a camp stove, food, and so forth, in case. It all seems impossibly wonderful. Going down by way of Chihuahua, Durango, across the mountains to Mazatlán, and then to Mexico City and Cuernavaca. It should be a marvelous adventure. *[We also went to a place on the west coast above Acapulco before it was discovered. There was no electricity or places to eat; we had red snapper every day. Delicious!]* Boris wants to find a place perhaps to work in the winter and be here in the spring through fall. We'll see. *[Of course, it never turned out that way.]*

June 3

Had a marvelous trip, six thousand miles in Mexico. What a magnificent trip and such sweet, kind people. Kept a diary of the trip so won't go into that here.

Have a dog, a darling pup, six months old, part shepherd and part golden retriever, we think. She is beautiful and sweet; good and intelligent; devoted but not sloppy. Looks like a shepherd, a lovely milk chocolate color with golden eyes. Vixen is what we call her.

Eric is coming again. He is on his way to Mexico City to study Spanish for the summer. He is a darling, and I look forward to his visits. To think Boris was just his age *[twenty-three]* when we first met. *[I was fifteen.]*

Boris's work continues to sell. It's marvelous. I'm working only two days a week, and how I adore my freedom and being home. Boris is feeling much better, and I hope he continues to improve.

June 25

Sylvia Loomis was here today to interview Boris for the Archives of American Art and made a tape recording of the same. The gallery business is much slower this year; I may even have to work extra days. Also, there are added expenses, such as having a fence in the back part of this place for the mules, which are coming back here because there is no pasture or water at Archie's. Of course, the time to put the fences in, which Boris doesn't have, is taken from his work, and he can't seem to catch up.

The patio is so beautiful and the garden has produced wonderful strawberries, succulent Bibb lettuce, and rhubarb. Watering constantly. It's clouding up but still no rain.

August 5

Another large piece, $1,800, sold for cash to Mrs. Tobin of San Antonio—two flying birds. *[She was a friend of Bishop Jones who bought several things. I don't remember her first name.]* The lovely one that was rejected by the show also has sold on time to a man in Colorado. Smaller things sold, too. Boris has a hard time producing enough. Strange and wonderful after all these years. He's been offered shows in Oklahoma City, Fort Worth, and San Antonio, if he can just get enough stuff together. *[He didn't believe in casting things, so everything he did was from scratch with his torch. He couldn't just take something and have five or six or ten made. He just wouldn't do that.]*

Eric has been here for two weeks and will be for another week. He is a dear boy and we will miss him when he is gone. Vixen is a darling dog. I love her. So devoted, good, and sweet. All our pets get along beautifully. Tom, the mule, and she are great friends, licking and nuzzling each other. Vixen and Pancho play, and Mau-Mau adores the dog. *[They used to kiss each other.]* We have had some really good rains, and everything is growing like mad. One of the peach trees is so loaded that even with props I worry about it breaking.

Had hoped to get to working on the back part of the house this fall but the money goes so fast, I doubt that there will be anything left by then. *C'est la vie.* Damn it, I so wish I had enough to really get at it. *[As you'll see, we didn't get started then.]*

August 29

Ingeborg Botlini, a potter from Argentina, and Mrs. Park, an artist and teacher from Korea, have been here; there was much entertaining for them. Wonderful people and real artists. Mrs. Park is a Buddhist, and her lovely soul and wisdom shine through. One evening they were here and she spent all evening with the brushes—calligraphy and watercolor. So wonderful to watch her work and how happy we are to have her things. We gave her a little silver owl that Boris had made me for Christmas. She had admired it; he says he'll make me another. I hope he will.

He has so much to do, I don't know how he'll get it done. The gallery still keeps him busy. He has orders from San Antonio, where he has a real cult. Wants a show in the spring. Hope he can keep up with it. To think of all the years he sold nothing. It is wonderful and most stimulating for him, and I adore not working except weekends.

September 9

We've had nothing but a steady stream of company this summer. We have done a lot of entertaining, which is rather difficult at times without a kitchen, but the patio and *portal* help a lot. *[My God, the company we had! I don't know how I managed up front, with no stove, just two electric burners. It was quite a day, I can tell you, when I got my secondhand Chambers stove.*]* Marty and Bob Brodkey are still here. He's a professor at Ohio State in chemical engineering, a real brain and a darling guy. *[We met the Brodkeys at Boris's show at the Barn Gallery on Canyon Road. They had rented a place in Santa Fe for the summer. Bob was taking pictures at the show, and he and Boris got to talking about their cameras. They became very close friends and he was quite a collector of Boris's work. For quite a few years the Brodkeys came out to Santa Fe in the summer.]*

Mr. Labunski, the composer, is back in Taos. He came to Santa Fe just to see us. Had lunch here; then Boris took him to Taos in a cloudburst and rock slides. He brought us a tape of the prelude he composed for Boris. Must find a machine to play it on.

Boris got knocked down by Jerry yesterday *[one of the mules]*; he was roping and saddling him for company. Hit his head and bottom.

October 6

Just had a two-day visit from a student from Germany. A really intelligent guy and charming. He has worked and saved for this trip and was so impressed with the United States that he would like to come back,

---

*Chambers stove: Gas range pioneered by John Chambers, who in 1909 began producing his "fireless cooker," a cast-iron stove so well insulated that it cooked with the gas off by using retained heat. In the 1930s, the unique "thermowell" was developed for "fireless" stove-top cooking. In the early 1980s, the Chambers brand was purchased by Whirlpool and subsequently retired. Nevertheless, these cherished old stoves remain in demand for their high quality. Thousands remain in use, and there are Chambers specialists to refurbish and maintain them.

especially to the Southwest. We had a delightful trip to Denver last week. Stayed with Muriel and Walter Hutner while Boris repaired the large heron that someone tried to lift. It is anchored in cement in front of their home. *[Walt Hutner is a doctor in Denver.]* We took a piece Boris had just finished. Five soaring swallows, a really great piece. Polished bronze. Everyone was impressed, as they should be.

Went to see Ed Marecak, whom we like very much and think is a fine artist who will be recognized some day. *[He was a very interesting man. He didn't show his work much and wasn't well known. There were stacks of his paintings at his home. I think he just painted because he had to and he also taught in Denver. His paintings were very, very interesting, beautiful. I don't know what ever happened to him. I've tried to track him down when I've been in Denver, but he seems to have disappeared.]*

My brother is moving to Santa Fe, which is exciting. So far no frost, but my flowers look as if they are tired and need a rest.

December 10

Winter is here. It's been cold for weeks with snow on the ground; it's bright and sunny, though. Next week I'll be fifty. It seems absolutely impossible. I well remember saying in my teens that I never wanted to live beyond that old age. But here I am, and, I must say, I'm not ready to go. There is so much to see and do yet. So much to learn and know; as long as you are alive, at least there is a chance of doing and seeing, but there are brief moments when death would be welcome, few and brief. I can't believe either that this short life on this earth is all there is to it. There must be other forms or other places or both. It's too bad we don't remember from one life to another, or is it? Maybe it is best.

Boris's work goes well but not as much sold this year. Gallery business was much slower. Seems there is always a check of some kind coming in each month. Believe one of the most difficult things for me to do is to criticize his work, for I know he's so superior to me, but he wants me to, and for some strange reason, when I do find something wrong or something that bothers me, it's right; and when corrected, he too sees that it's better. I suppose that when you work on something so long and so closely, you fail to see what a fresh eye sees.

Boris was in San Antonio taking a few things to Stewart Reynold's gallery. *[I don't remember this gallery at all.]* Coming back the "short way" through Chihuahua, Mexico, of course. We would so love to go down to Oaxaca and Mitla again this year, but if we do get any money I so want to finish the house. Boris says, after four and a half years, that I am impatient. *[He still said it after twenty-two years.]* Perhaps I am, but how I would love a kitchen. And even a bedroom. Maybe I'm middle class after all.

Christmas is almost upon us again, and I hate the thought of working every day the last week or so.

Street facade of 518 Alto as purchased by Charlotte White, November 1958. (Courtesy Charlotte White)

Rear facade of back building, November 1958. Charlotte and her trusty Jeep on right. (Courtesy Charlotte White)

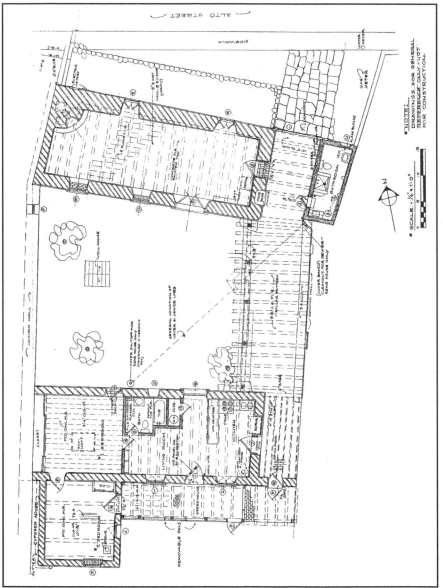

Floor plan, 1995. (Drawn by Donna Quasthoff, American Institute of Architects [AIA])

Alto Street facade before street was paved in 1972. (Courtesy New Mexico State Records Center and Archives, Historic Santa Fe Foundation [HSFF] Collection, Neg. No. 20807)

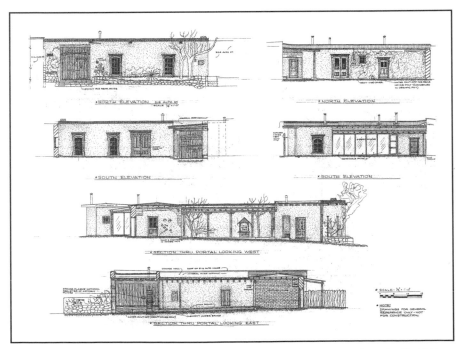

Elevations and sections, 518 Alto Street, 1995. (Drawn by Donna Quasthoff, AIA)

Hand-plastering by women from Cañones, June 1961. Mud-plastering and fireplace building traditionally were performed by women. (Courtesy Charlotte White)

St. Michael's College dormitory, c. 1890. Source of nineteenth-century doors and windows salvaged by William Lumpkins and installed at 518 Alto Street. (Courtesy Museum of New Mexico, Neg. No. 1402)

South-facing patio wall with Charlotte in doorway, November 1958. (Courtesy Charlotte White)

Newly plastered south-facing patio wall, c. 1962. A pile of stones marks the well. (Courtesy Charlotte White)

Patio *portal* under construction, 1961. (Courtesy Charlotte White)

Brickyard at the New Mexico Territorial Penitentiary, c. 1890. When the pen was torn down it supplied the bricks for paving the *portal* and the limestone blocks used for a low wall between the *portal* and patio. (Courtesy Museum of New Mexico, Neg. No. 15208)

Under Boris's patio *portal*, c. 1968. (Photo by Alan K. Stoker, Courtesy HSFF)

Neighbor children at newly installed south-facing patio door. (Courtesy Charlotte White)

Charlotte with Vixen and birds beside the completed well house. (Courtesy Charlotte White)

Benny dressed for his First Communion. (Courtesy Charlotte White)

Archie West plastering with adobe, June 1994. (Courtesy Charlotte White)

Completed south-facing patio wall, 1965. (Photo by Karl Kernberger, Courtesy Museum of New Mexico, Neg. No. 43373)

Olive Rush on horseback in her garden at 630 Canyon Road, 1930s. Charlotte's lily of the valley, violets, and crab apple tree came from starters from Olive's garden. (Courtesy Museum of New Mexico, Neg. No. 19270)

Sala, with door from St. Michael's College, Tommy Macaione painting *Falling Blossoms,* and window opening showing wall thickness. (Photo by Alan K. Stoker, Courtesy HSFF)

Boris's brother, the potter Warren ("Bud") Gilbertson, with some of his work at the fireplace later removed from the *sala,* c. 1952. (Courtesy Charlotte White)

Sala fireplace designed by Boris. (Courtesy HSFF)

Invitation to Boris's first New Mexico exhibition, 1962.

Shorebirds, bronze, 1972. (Courtesy Charlotte White)

Self-Portrait, Chinese brush
drawing, 1960. (Photo by
Erwin Jakobs, Courtesy
Charlotte White)

Chess pieces, bronze. Cast after Boris's death.
(Courtesy Charlotte White)

Tiffany Saloon, Cerrillos, New Mexico, c. 1977. Boris and Charlotte opened a gallery
behind the saloon in 1963. (Photo by Arthur Taylor, Courtesy Museum
of New Mexico, Neg. No. 111836)

Charlotte and her beloved Mau-Mau.
(Courtesy Charlotte White)

Boris with his Spanish mules.
(Courtesy Charlotte White)

Charlotte with Charlie beside a flowering apple tree.
(Courtesy Charlotte White)

Rear facade of back building, 1969. (Courtesy Charlotte White)

Boris constructing back *portal,* 1973.
(Courtesy Charlotte White)

Door to rear *portal* designed
and constructed by Boris, 1961.
(Courtesy Charlotte White)

Interior corner
of back building
before remodeling,
1978. (Courtesy
Charlotte White)

View of the kitchen, same corner,
1994. (Photo by Hope A. Curtis,
Courtesy HSFF)

Charlotte's "new" secondhand
stove installed in 1965.
(Photo by Hope A. Curtis,
Courtesy HSFF)

/1959

Journal

of House in Santa Fe

July 28ͭ -- Arrived yesterday, at six from Illinois
alto — with the little jeep's
arse dragging from its 1000
pound load, among which
was Bain's grandfathers
workbench that he had made
many years ago and is
prized among all his (B's) possessions — it is eight feet long
so naturally hung out making
it necessary to leave the tail
gate open — we had also
an 8 foot piece of plate glass
we hope to use for a sky
light in the bedroom eventually
— and tools — and clothes —
charcoal stove — cooking basket.
cots — sleeping bags — air mattresses etc etc — we were very lucky
for which I am most thankful +

The first page of Charlotte's journal, July 28, 1959. (Courtesy Charlotte White)

July 12, 1965–October 3, 1967

"Boris's work finally recognized"

July 12

I'm so happy sitting here under the *portal.* Rain dripping down, wonderful blessed rain in this country. We have had lots of it this year. The country, which is usually dry and brown, is actually green-looking, like Wisconsin or Illinois. I'm looking out over my beautiful, lovely patio—a sanctuary almost. I'm not working this summer, and it certainly agrees with me. Get up in the morning and have a calm breakfast under the *portal.* Taking care of my birds and Vixen, the flowers and the garden. Stopping perhaps to read outside under a tree with Mau-Mau squatting beside me and Vixen. To stretch out on my back, to look up through the leaves to the sky—this is living. Boris and I are ever grateful for this wonderful old house, our good friends, and that his work goes so well.

September 19

We had a busy and social summer. Continuous company, but enjoyed it. It has gotten depressingly cool. Such a short summer; hate to see the end of my beautiful flowers, which seems imminent.

Boris has so much work, I wonder how he will do it. Have had a marvelous month of selling, and I don't have to go back to work. No flower shop for Christmas; I can hardly believe it. So grand not to be tired all the time but just stay home and live.

Went to an opening at the Art Museum last night of Leon Gaspard's work. What painting. A real artist and a great man. We feel very fortunate to have known him. *[We met him in Taos, where he lived. He died shortly after we met him.]*

Have sold more than $2,000 worth of art from the house this year. Also Gallery A sold Boris's magnificent *Before the Wind,* five birds in flight, for $2,500 to a Mr. Moore in Denver, along with many other things. *[We had no further contact with him.]*

The new Volvo we got in March is a joy, such a pleasure and so inexpensive to drive. Had delightful trip to San Antonio early in the summer to pick up two pieces. Gallery closed. It was very hot but enjoyed the river with its park and restaurants. Went to the zoo and down to the border, which is always fun. We hope to get down to Mitla again before the winter is over; have made many runs to Juárez this summer, bringing back rum, coffee, limes, and so forth.

Have decided to just make the kitchen up here. Am getting a secondhand Chambers stove—gas—I hate cooking with electricity. *[That's the same stove I have here now.]* We do entertain quite a bit, and it's not exactly easy on two burners. *[I had just a two-burner electric plate up in front in the corner. When I got the stove, it went into the front room in the same corner where the hot plate had been. Later we moved it back here.]*

Boris has to have a better place to work in the back when it's cold. When the weather is nice, of course, he has a wonderful place to work outside. So he plans to push out the south wall and put plastic roof and walls up. *[He never did that.]*

October 14

Most of the flowers have survived the frost a few weeks ago; the vegetables are gone. We are having our usual gorgeous October. Warm, brilliant days, cool nights. Cottonwoods radiantly gold against intense blue sky. The aspens on the top of the Sangres froze before they turned, so they aren't golden this year.

Next Thursday we are going to El Paso. There is a big decorator show where Boris's work from the Marberg Gallery will be featured. He is frantically busy getting two large pieces finished: a beautiful, big giraffe, which Bob and Marty Brodkey have bought, and a couple of birds. I suppose the last few days will really be hectic getting them finished. Gallery A has sold out all but small things, but no time now to make more—next month.

Have all my cabinets in the "kitchen" *[over in the corner of the front room]*. What a joy to have more storage. Get my stove in a couple of weeks. Can hardly wait. We both had some horrible bug, but it's gone and we feel so happy and well. I don't have to go back to work, not even Christmas, and can't believe it. I have plenty to do here and love it.

October 17

The ground is white and the snow falling. Boris had to move inside today. It took most of the day. Too bad the lovely weather couldn't have held out until his work for the twenty-first was finished. Every minute counts.

October 28

We had a wonderful time in El Paso. Such gracious, cultured people. Everyone loved Boris's work. Sure they'll sell soon. I was very proud of him. He has been asked to submit a sketch for a piece of sculpture for the temple there. Marta and Aly Schlusselberg couldn't be nicer. We are very fond of them. *[She was the director of the Marberg Gallery.]* Boris is busy at it. So much to do, and he wants to get his greenhouse studio up before the bad weather. I'd hoped to get to Mexico after Christmas.

Most of the flowers are gone after the early frost and ten inches of snow, except some in the patio, which look a little sad and tired. When I water them it makes me think of a woman in her forties trying to hang on to some glamour for just a little while longer. That it will pass soon is inevitable; but we try, and I'm in my fifties still working at it.

November 3

Boris took off for Denver. Felix Labunski is there—the symphony is playing one of his works. Boris thought he should go since Felix was so insistent, and obviously it would mean a lot to him. I couldn't face the trip. I feel exhausted. There are still some flowers in the garden. Days are lovely; nights very cool.

November 4

Boris returned this A.M. from Denver. Had an interesting and enjoyable time. *[Of course, he loved to get away.]* Even though he had some sleep, he feels unwell and is lying down most of the day. Wish all this success had come ten years ago when he was younger and stronger. I'm afraid he can't handle the work now; he has too many days that he can't work. I do worry about him, but he refuses to see anyone or do anything about it.

November 6

Have my stove! I'm in such a state of shock that I can't think of anything to bake in it. It's been so long since I've done any. Will have to readjust my thinking. I'm so delighted.

November 10

We are having overnight guests for two nights. A funny, fun, way-out student at St. John's College, whom we have bumped into at the movies there, and a friend. Girl or boy? For some reason they have to be off-campus until Friday. We'll find out later why. Want to sleep here in sleeping bags, so it will be fun.

Which reminds me of the two hitchhikers we had a few weeks ago. Somewhere outside of Albuquerque, Boris picked up a young, supposedly twenty-one-year-old (but I'm sure not over seventeen) girl and boy (said he was twenty-two) along the highway. Discovered they had no money. Had had their sleeping bags stolen, so they said. Had spent four days in jail in San Diego for vagrancy. On their way to New Orleans from Seattle. Boris gave them dinner and money for a motel with the parting words, "If you get to Santa Fe, stop by." Those weren't famous last words, as I knew they wouldn't be.

The next afternoon they arrived in time for dinner. The girl was tall and thin, bleached blond and rather cute; the boy, very nice. She had on a dirty sweatshirt, a pair of shorts made from cutting off a pair of tight, tight stretch pants, and broken thong sandals. No wonder they had troubles. Her favorite expression was "Man, that's groovy." They slept in the back in our sleeping bags. Gave them breakfast; had visions of their being "guests" indefinitely.

As far as we could find out, they had no experience as to jobs. I thought if I could just get him some kind of a job to get enough money to get them on their way, I must; so I took him around to supermarkets to see if he could be an errand boy or something. No luck. He decided to call his uncle in New Orleans, collect, from a public phone. Whether he really did or not, we'll never know. Anyway, he said his uncle had a job for him on a shrimp boat when he got there.

Well, I was so delighted to know we weren't stuck with them that I took Judy, bare feet and shorts, downtown. Bought her a skirt, tennis shoes, and a shirt. Packed them a lunch and drove them fifty miles to Route 66 so they would have a better chance at getting a ride. Gave them $10 and sent them on their way. She looked quite pretty dressed, and her remark was "Bob will flip when he sees me in a skirt." Whether they were telling the truth we'll never know. Haven't heard a word. If they come back this way, we're going to be *very* busy. Had to leave town or something. *[We never heard from them again. No thanks; no nothing.]*

The birds we took to El Paso were sold for $1,200; $800 is for us. How marvelous to have that money. So much to do with it.

The few blooms left in my garden have become treasures. How I hate to see them go. Soon, surely, we will be having a real frost. Next week we go to Denver for Thanksgiving and are looking forward to it.

December 5

Had a grand time in Denver. A party of thirty people. Boris is working like a demon to get all of the small pieces—truly gems—done that Marta Schlusselberg wants before Christmas. *[She had the gallery in El Paso.]* They are magnificent: horses, ballerinas, birds; wish I could keep them all. Then the gallery wants the four pieces they ordered. Paid cash, but I don't see how he can do it all. Local friends and acquaintances want to see, and no doubt buy, them all before they go. It is amazing and wonderful to have Boris's work finally recognized and appreciated.

We have been invited to the wedding reception for Louis Ballard and his bride. He is the most talented composer and teacher at the Indian school, a Cherokee Indian, a large handsome man. His ballet, *Koshare*, will be performed in Paris next month. Mrs. Udall, the wife of the Secretary of the Interior, will be there. We are honored to be among the few who have been asked *[to the wedding, that is]*. He is a great admirer of Boris's work. Who isn't, everywhere we go?

December 15

Today is my birthday again. It's cold. Flurries of snow. We are going to the Kitchens, which I look forward to. *[They were friends of ours. He was an architect; she was from Venezuela, I think, or maybe Argentina. They went down there later, and I think they think I'm dead because she never got my letters.]* Mother is very close to me today. She always made so much of my birthday: little tree, chicken pie, peas, ice cream and cake, a beautiful gift; always thoughtful. Somehow she always found her way to me on the fifteenth, loaded down with the decorations and the makings for dinner. What a wonderful mother she was! If it were possible for spirits to return to earth, she would be here.

December 27

We had a very pleasant Christmas this year. Lynda and John Sargent were here for ten days, darling young couple. *[The Sargents were younger friends of ours and old friends of Boris's son, Eric. John had gone to school with him. He was a forest ranger up in Tres Piedras; eventually they moved down to Santa Fe.]* Had a big turkey to celebrate having a stove. Boris is still getting orders, mostly for flying birds, which everyone loves. They symbolize freedom to everyone's soul, I think. He seems to be feeling much better this winter, for which I am ever thankful.

Bought a Tommy Macaione painting. He lives in poverty and filth with his three dogs. *[There were many more later.]* A really great guy. *[I probably met him on the street. He was always out painting. He was an admirer of Boris's work. I bought two of his paintings, and I also have a self-portrait that he drew for us.]*

1966

January 2

The Kosickis and Florence Khedroo were here for dinner last night. *[Florence Khedroo was also a physician and a friend of the Kosickis. She was a real character and a lot of fun. She moved from Santa Fe when they wouldn't let her practice in the hospital because she refused to take out malpractice insurance.]*

Very cold today, even though the sun is out. In spite of it, Boris is working out by the back wall in the sun on a mobile of crazy birds and owls for the Marberg Gallery. *[Before we had the greenhouse, he'd work out there on that south wall.]* Thought Ginger Neveau and Don Stevning, who have the Desert Gallery in Palm Desert, were angry because we still haven't sent them the four pieces they ordered to be bought outright for delivery in December, but we received a lovely box of citrus from their grove with a note saying that any time we could come, we were always welcome. *[Ginger was the director and Don was the owner of the gallery. Boris did very well with them. Don also had large orange groves.]*

Boris and I are really lucky to have this great old house; his work is going so well and we're so happy. So many unhappy souls about, including too many people we know. We wish we could spend several months a year in Mexico; maybe live there.

The symphony is on; the canary is bursting with song. He sings constantly. Each day I think I won't let him out of his cage, but I see how happy he is—sitting in the sun, eating my plants, scratching in the dirt, throwing it out on the floor—I can't resist. He is more important than the mess. The parrots like the music, too, especially Pancho, who softly whistles to himself. Little Vixen has developed into even more of a personality. Everyone adores her, and she is beautiful.

January 25

A wonderful surprise this afternoon. Who should appear at the door but Malcolm Alexander! He has been in Spain for two years and is here on business. A great person. *[He was a painter; now he is a very good sculptor.]*

January 30

The day is unbelievably beautiful. Spring is in the sun and the air and the song of the house finch. Hope the worst of winter is over. Hopefully, next year we can get away from the worst of it. Boris's breathing is bad again. It worries me terribly, and I'm sure it does him; but he refuses to see a doctor. He prefers not to know what's wrong. *[This is sixteen years before he died and all the work he got out. It's unreal.]*

February 10

The news is most unsettling, this Vietnam business. Could become really serious, involving most of the world. Hope they can avert such a horrible catastrophe.

Boris has gone out to Suzie Henderson's to see the mules or try to see them. They are free now and try to make the most of it. *[We didn't have enough space for the mules and had to get rid of them. Boris couldn't part with them, so they kept moving. At this time they were boarding on Suzie's land near Cerrillos. Eventually, he sold them to someone in Wagon Mound. They could be free out there. Suzie was a friend and neighbor of Marc Simmons in Cerrillos. She had a lot of land that she later sold to a developer to the great dismay of the neighbors.]*

He got the four pieces off to the Desert Gallery. Now to get started on all the other things. It's strange for him to have so many demands after so many years.

I'm still loving my stove and the leisure to use it. I've been baking bread and delight in turning out really good meals.

February 13

Is there anyone like Boris? With all the work he should be doing—phone calls from El Paso wondering when the model for the temple will be ready and when will the man have his giraffe; cards from Gallery A clamoring for more things—he's completely relaxed, carefree, as though he had nothing to do. Today he sits all day surrounded by his jars of all colors of powder, bits of copper, making enamel Valentines for me. Birds in cages, hearts, and so forth. What can you do? He has the heart and soul of a real artist. I really envy him his temperament. It must be marvelous.

Cold and miserable today. Two buds on the white orchid, and the orchid cacti are covered with buds.

March 3

Very cold and terrific wind. When winter comes, can spring be far behind? Hell, yes! It's forever. Tomorrow, Frank Woods is coming to make a tape of me—subject: the house. They are doing a taped radio broadcast on the plaqued houses.

March 28

Returned last week from a wonderful, and what will be a most profitable, trip to California. The gallery in Palm Desert is really a fine gallery and promises to be great for Boris's work. They really have connections, and money seems to be no object. Everyone who is anyone spends their winters there, many collectors and patrons of the arts. Spent three most pleasant days at Ginger Neveau's going through her and Don Stevning's citrus and date groves, packing house, and so forth. They also own a gallery. They had a show of Fremont Ellis that Boris shared. Then we went up to Altadena to spend two days with Merton Rapp in his lovely house built way up in the canyon in the trees. *[Merton worked for Harcourt, Brace, the publishing company. He bought some of Boris's pieces.]*

May 4

Boris's son, Eric, was here for a week with friends. Boris is still busy with many things on the verge of being sold but are not. Gallery A is doing nothing. Perhaps later things will perk up.

Getting the garden in. The fruit trees were lovely. Now the fragrant, sweet lilacs are in bloom. Each year the place gets more beautiful, and I can hardly wait to get my patio all decked out with pots and tubs of growing, blooming, and dripping things.

Boris had his fifty-ninth birthday last Monday, the second of May. Dr. and Mrs. Kaplan from Denver took us to La Fonda for dinner. *[They were just passing through. I don't remember them.]* In the afternoon I took them over to see that remarkable and wonderful old gal, Eugenie Shonnard—eighty. An unforgettable day in her studio in the old house. Still active and working and utterly feminine.

May 25

An unbelievable day. No moisture for months. Constantly watering the place. It's gorgeous; more beautiful every year. More work, too, but worth it. I'm at it most all day, every day.

Took some slate carvings to Gallery A, but they want and need a large impressive piece. A charming, delightful couple was here from Yugoslavia on a Ford Foundation grant. He is a sculptor and she is a darling little thing—Peter and Lillian Boskoff. *[I don't remember them.]* The Palm Desert Gallery is closed until November, and Gallery A hasn't done very much.

June 6

A check for $1,500 from Marty in El Paso. *[That was from the manager of the Marberg Gallery.]* A lifesaver! We've been making it, but just; living is so expensive. I'm sure groceries alone come to $100 or more a month. We don't eat extravagantly; we do have company once or twice a week, but I still don't go all out on it. In summer the water is $8 to $12. *[It's $60 now.]* And the gas and oxygen *[for Boris's work]*. A week ago Boris was going to spend two days cleaning up where he works in the summer. He's still at it. There is no one like him. One thing leads to another until now he's sinking a stock tank for a pool. Gravel will be spread, and he's landscaping it, too. Fish in the pool, of course. That's why he does the work he does, but it will be good to have him at his own work again. He has a lot to do to get ready for his two galleries this fall, two winter galleries. Taos is just beginning now, and they also should have some more. So it goes.

June 15

Fritz Vertogen from Belgium left today after spending five days with us, a young, most handsome, and pleasant sculptor who is in this country on a cultural exchange. A few weeks ago Kate Cullum asked us to come and see her fabulous collection of Randall Davey's work. He left them to her, his sister-in-law. Most exciting work. Boris's pool is lovely. Each morning with his coffee, he turns the fountain on and sits out there enjoying it. He has started on a large piece for Gallery A, which promises to be wonderful—abstract birds swirling around a rock.

June 19

Went to an opening of Ernest Badynski, a sculptor and a promising and charming young man. *[I don't know what happened to him.]* How I love my animals; warm devotion and love without sex. I couldn't love a cat, though, too independent; could never trust one.

August 1

Yesterday was a day. Last night my night-blooming cereus bloomed. Purest of pure white, gigantic, unbelievably beautiful, fragrant blossoms.

We needed to go to bed, but we knew they would be gone in the morning. Two more tonight and then that's all. You can't imagine their beauty, so fragile, so white, so exquisite. We called the Rothbergers, who are here from Colorado, to come over; they were thrilled, too. They had been here in the morning and bought several things, and that, I can tell you, was a windfall we really needed. *[They were from Denver. I don't remember their names.]*

Glorious summer. Very warm, but I love it. We really enjoy the *portal* and patio. Even in the evenings, which are unusually warm for here.

August 23

All our company has gone. Mornings and evenings very cool. Pouring rain at the moment. Hate to see winter come, but perhaps that is why I love and appreciate my flowers and garden so much; can't take them for granted. The corn from the garden is delicious. Haven't bought vegetables or salad stuff all summer even with constant company and even having to give some away, which is one of the great pleasures of a garden.

Dear old Olive Rush died a couple of days ago. As far as I'm concerned, she was gone years ago when she went into the hospital and became a vegetable.

Have been to the Santa Fe Opera several times, and it is always an occasion. We seem to have constant streams of people dropping in. It is very flattering but hell on Boris's work. I don't see how he'll finish. The gorgeous birds are ready to go to Taos. Six of them balanced at one small point, to hang free to move around a pole. It's really beautiful. The gallery has been selling this month so has little left.

August 27

The air is redolent with green chile cooking. From door-to-door they go with their lard pails full. Soon it will be strings of red chile and apples. We are enjoying our own corn from the garden and all the other things, so delicious. Felix Labunski and his wife were here for dinner last night. *[We hardly knew his wife. He usually came to New Mexico for the summers alone.]* Monday we finally take the birds to Taos. Hate to see them go; they would look so beautiful in the patio.

103

September 10

Fall is on its way or is already here. Cool nights and mornings and days if the sun hides itself. Went to an opening of Georgia O'Keeffe in Albuquerque. She must be a cold person. An artist's work usually reflects its creator. I was disappointed.

The Art Museum here has invited Boris to show in its sculptor show in November. He's going to put in the big birds. Also the *Western Review* wants a picture of his work to be published in its art section. So he is becoming known.

September 30

Boris's beloved mules are going out to Pecos tomorrow to be trained with Brownie Hall—great guy. I'm glad. *[He was an amateur painter who had a place in Pecos with a corral.]* It's a shame to have such beautiful and intelligent beasts wasted by just standing in a corral year after year. Don't know how we will pay him; it's tough now just getting by. But Boris is always the optimist. He has just finished a really magnificent figure of a woman washing her hair. I hate to part with it, but it goes to El Paso next week. *[Actress Greer Garson's husband bought it for her.]* Vixen, Jean Buchanan, and I went up into the aspen today. Had lunch in a lovely meadow. So far no frost. Unbelievable. Hate to see it come, but it is inevitable. *[Jean moved to Santa Fe for her health about the same time I first came. We had apartments next door to each other at El Zaguán and remained friends.]*

October 8

Such a poignantly beautiful day. Temperature like summer, but all the brilliant colors and smells of fall. Birds singing like in spring. Vixen and I went for a long walk through the piñon and down the arroyos out by the Folk Art Museum.

This A.M. we went out to Pecos to see the mules, who are being trained by Brownie Hall. In a week's time only, he has them come to him to be bridled and saddled. Always before Boris had to chase them around like wild things with a lasso, rope them, and tie them. I think it was a game they enjoyed, but now they know they can't get by with it. I'm looking forward to riding them when I feel I can trust them. We are supposed to go out for a ride in a week or so.

Delivered some things to El Paso last Thursday. Left at 4:30 A.M. and got back at 10 P.M. Had a nice lunch with Marta and Aly Schlusselberg there, whom we both are very fond of. One of the things we took was the female figure, which is magnificent. How I hate to part with it. Marberg Gallery is really elegant, simple, good taste. Gallery A seems to have deteriorated in the last year. They aren't selling Boris's work much either.

October 17

Snow on the mountains this morning. A killing frost just a few nights ago. How sad to see the castor beans black and limp; the tomatoes and peppers drooping, black and dead. My flowers, my beloved garden, are gone. The patio looks sad, deserted, and empty. We have moved all the pots and tubs into the little greenhouse, and my windows here in the house are stuffed with greenery. *[We changed the greenhouse back here several times.]*

So begins the winter, which, to me, like my plants, is to survive until again we can be put out into the glorious sun and air of spring. Boris has been having trouble with his right arm. Our dear friend Dr. Florence Khedroo says it is a muscle spasm that will pass. Soon, I hope. *[She was a character. She came back to Santa Fe, and the last I heard she was very ill with cancer.]*

November 2

Boris's show, through the Marberg Gallery in El Paso, brought a great deal of notice and enthusiasm. I think most of the things will sell. The six large mobile birds will be at the Art Museum here in a sculpture show November 13 to January 8. If they are not sold, they will go to the show in California the first of February. His arm is much better. Dot and Treet arrive at the end of the next month. How good it will be to see them. Dot will stay with her daughter Karin; Treet with Kay.

November 21

Treet and Dot have left. So good to see them. Dot, Karin, and I went to

Juárez. Thursday I woke about 5 A.M., November 17, 1966, looked out my window at Sylvia's *[a hotel]* in Juárez to the northeast, and saw a star fall, then another. For an hour I watched a veritable shower of stars, thousands, like rain; like watching snowflakes under a streetlight; never stopping, on and on. Thought surely the sky was falling, like Henney Penney. I was indeed lucky for I found out later that this happens once in a hundred years, and it wasn't visible here at all.

Bern Keating, who is doing an article for the *National Geographic*, was here Saturday for dinner. Most interesting guy; been everywhere. Took pictures of Boris Sunday with Vixen and *El Tigre*, which Boris is working on. *[That's a life-size jaguar. A doctor in Albuquerque bought it.]* Took Bern out to Pecos for a mule ride. He is doing a write-up on Santa Fe; I'm anxious to see it. *[I don't think it ever appeared; at least, I never saw it.]*

Boris's birds in the show are receiving a great deal of praise; the best thing there, obviously. Lynda and John Sargent arrive tomorrow for Thanksgiving weekend. It will be fun having them here.

December 16

Yesterday was my fifty-second birthday. *[Was I ever that young?]* Seems impossible. I feel a little different than twenty years ago. We went out to Pecos for a quail dinner with the Halls. In three hours we leave for Denver by plane. I am so excited; it's the first time Boris and I have flown together. Dr. John Fleming, from there, sent us round-trip tickets so Boris could see where the piece will go that he wants him to make. Isn't that wonderful? Such gracious people. *[We met the Flemings through Gallery A. They bought a piece and came down to Santa Fe to find Boris. Dr. Fleming was the head of the hospital radiology department in Denver.]*

We are planning nothing for Christmas. Lots of work. Seems incredible. I'm working two or three days a week to make a little, to get us through the month. We have so much, though, and shouldn't ever complain. As long as Boris has his health, which I do worry about at times (his short wind and large diaphragm), and he doesn't overeat. *[He worked like a demon all that time; the sixties were the most productive time of his life.]*

Christmas

Beautiful sunny day. Would have been fun to have snow, and how we need the moisture. A wonderful quiet day, just the two of us; a little piñon tree that Boris cut, candles and greenery. Jean Buchanan is coming for a standing rib roast dinner. Vixen can have the bones. Always wonder what the next Christmas will bring. So thankful for everything.

December 26

It's trying to snow.

1967

January 19

Still no snow. We've had a lot of very cold weather. Two weeks of around zero at night. Boris has been able to work outside every day against the back south wall in the sun. The thirtieth we leave for California, Palm Desert, for his show opening February 2. We hope it will be lucrative; we need it. Don't know just how we'll manage the trip, but we've got to. We are going on up to San Francisco to case the Maxwell Gallery and stay with Ray and Miralotte Ickes, whom I haven't seen for ten years. *[Ray was a very old friend of mine since high school. I met him when I was seventeen on the beach on Glencoe, Illinois, where we both went swimming everyday in the summer. His father was Harold LeClair Ickes, President Franklin Delano Roosevelt's Secretary of the Interior during the New Deal in the 1930s. They were both very dear friends of ours. Miralotte and I had gone to the same girls' school. I saw a lot of them with my first husband Hal. After Miralotte died Ray remarried.]* I'm looking forward to it so. Have borrowed two beautiful suits from my niece Karin to wear; just don't have the proper clothes to wear for the big town. Lynda Sargent is coming down from Colorado to stay here and take care of the animals and plants.

February 18

Arrived home the fourteenth. A marvelous holiday in spite of the wicked, ghastly smog, especially in Los Angeles. Sinful. Don't see how plants or people or anything can live in that much longer. Show a great success.

Sold a few small things; enough to get home on and pay all the bills with some left over. The large pieces will go, I am sure. Such gratifying praise, and what wonderful friends we have everywhere we go.

We stayed with Ginger in Palm Desert, George Keelerik in Big Sur, Merton and Elizabeth Rapp in Altadena, and my old dear friends Miralotte and Ray Ickes in Berkeley. *[George was an old friend of Boris's. Later he moved to Ireland.]* Everyone is so absolutely wonderful to us. It makes you feel all warm inside. The car was loaded to the top on arrival home: fruit, dates, lava rocks, barrel cactus, goodies from Japantown in L.A., and Chinatown, San Francisco. *[Boris always collected everything.]* To top it all an old saddle Boris spotted in Cottonwood, Arizona.

All the family fine. Lynda did a great job. All so delighted to see us. Good to be home. As usual Boris has too much work to get out; Dr. Fleming in Denver wants his birds by September and Gallery A is depleted. Nothing here at 518 for sale. But we should complain?

Glorious warm day today. Worked outside all day watering and so forth. How I wish we would have a big snow.

March 4

It's been like spring. The plants pushing up through damp earth. We had a nice rain and wet snow a week or so ago. Robins twittering in early morning; house finches honoring us with their rippling song. Sun really hot; it's glorious. Have been working outside all week.

April 5

Still having summery days. Roses in full leaf. Peach, cherry, apricot blossoms almost gone. Santa Fe is a bower. My lettuce, spinach, and beets are up; sweet peas starting. Must hold back planting more. Surely, we'll have cold weather again this month. The place really looks beautiful; each year more so. Boris is busy mornings and evenings beautifying way in the back. Think I'll get one of the little boys to water that area this summer.

This weekend my neighbor Eloisa and her boyfriend are helping me paint walls and floor. Will be glad when it's over. I dread the mess and Boris's mood over it. He feels such things are unnecessary and foolish; but how nice when it's done. Have put Woodlife *[a wood preservative]* and linseed oil on the patio windows and doors. Want to get all this taken care of before the summer outside work really gets going.

Having dinner with our dear friends, Ann and Alan Vedder, tonight. *[They were very good friends. We met a lot of people through them. It was Alan who interested the Historic Santa Fe Foundation in the house. He got Myra Ellen Jenkins to do the original research.]*

In a few weeks we are going out to Palm Desert to pick up the birds. They may be sold by then. A woman from Cincinnati interested at $6,000, but even so, guess Boris would deliver them instead of packing and shipping such a big and complicated piece. They sold the nude, $1,800— I wept, such a magnificent piece—to Greer Garson's husband. Also two other pieces, smaller. So, as Boris says, "We're rich!" But not really. He has it spent ten times already before we get it. We have so much, so much. I wish I didn't let his attitude about his work bug me. After all, he's like that because his work is like that; and everyone loves him and his work.

April 13

This morning, when I went out with Vixen, it was like a funeral of dear and beloved ones. The temperature went down to sixteen degrees last night. What greeted me! Apple blossoms frozen solid—brown and dead now. My beautiful bleeding heart, which yesterday was a joy to behold, flat and limp, gone. Lilacs almost ready to bloom, drooping and lifeless. I wept; such a tragedy, and to think of the poor souls with orchards gone. Hope a few things will survive. Boris is busy planting a veritable orchard way in the back. If I can keep up with watering it, it will be lovely.

Decorated last weekend. What a mess. Don't believe I could ever face it again. Martine did the top of the walls, cleaning the *vigas* as he went; Eloisa the windows. I did the bottom part and floor. It looks lovely. *[This is the front room where we were living then. The back wasn't even finished.]*

April 27

Boris leaves Saturday for California. The birds are sold to the Reverend Waller of San Antonio for $4,500. He'll deliver them next month. Lynda arrives tomorrow to be with me. George Keelerik was here with Mickey, his seven-month-old shepherd, adorable. *[That's my Mickey. I ended up with him when George moved to Ireland and couldn't take him. I adored that dog, as I do all of them.]*

Last week Vixen met her equal; they played for days. It stays cold and the garden stands still—water, water—so dry. Mau-Mau's beak is growing crooked so it will have to be trimmed. It worries me so; poor little bird. She has had so much trouble, and she's such a wonder of a bird. Suppose she will have to have an anesthetic. I dread thinking of it. I don't see how it can be done any other way. *[I did it myself. She let me do it. She lay in the palm of my hand and I got her used to the clippers by say coochee-coo and scratching her stomach with them until she wasn't afraid of them and then I trimmed her beak. I was scared to death that I would get her tongue or something.]*

May 23

Summer is here! The gardens are in. Patio planted. Twelve fruit trees way in back. We have been working like maniacs. It's beautiful. More so each year; we adore the old place. Wish we could get the part of it next door. It could just be. *[I don't know why I said that!]* Eric and Claire hope to come next month. *[That's Boris's son and his wife.]*

Will be glad when Boris can get settled down to his work. It's been weeks. There is so much he wants to do outside, and, I must say, what he does is great. The place really looks elegant—a dream come true. For the first time we don't have to live from day to day. What a glorious feeling. And more work to do than he can do. It is indeed a good life. Still no rain. It's serious; hope the water holds out.

May 29

A few small showers but even that makes a difference. Boris still hasn't gotten to his work. Every day it's tomorrow. He really should, or should he, live in Mexico. Surely tomorrow will be the day. Having the Vedders, Myra Ellen Jenkins, and Suzanne for dinner tonight. *[I don't remember a Suzanne.]*

June 5

The skies have opened up and given us some blessed rain. What a difference it makes! The growing things are so happy and beautiful. All the watering in the world doesn't do the same thing. Eric and Claire arrived yesterday.

July 6

Party for Brud at Kay's tonight. He's sixty but looks like he could be my younger brother. My night-blooming cereus is going to bloom tonight. Only five blooms this year. Almost got killed last winter. Didn't think I'd have any. I love it even though I hate the watering twice a day.

Boris is still doing birds; everyone loves them, and he can't keep up with it. They get more and more beautiful; I hope one day I can keep one myself. He has been without a voice for almost two weeks and refuses to see a doctor about it. Seems laryngitis would be gone by now. It worries me, but what can I do. He feels fine otherwise and is getting a lot done.

July 16

Boris has a paralyzed vocal cord. X rays show nothing wrong in the lungs, chest, and so forth. Taking tests from spit. So far negative. Such a handicap for him; he loves to talk and has so much to say.

August 1

Boris still has no voice. Feels fine. May have been a small blood clot. Must get better. My brother Brud coming back tomorrow. Our lovely opera burned to the ground last week just after we had seen the American premier of *Cardillac.**

[That finishes the first volume of my journals. It was a busy and interesting time. We had people here from all over the world—artists; and we did a lot of traveling because by that time Boris had galleries in different places—in California, El Paso, and so on.

---

*Opera fire: Theater completely destroyed on the night of July 27, 1967, by a fire of undetermined origin. The season's scores were destroyed along with all costumes except those at the cleaners, as was the set of *Cardillac,* by Paul Hindemith (1895–1963), still on the stage from its American premier. The season continued in the Santa Fe High School gymnasium the very next night with *The Barber of Seville.* Igor Stravinsky served as honorary chairman of the National Emergency Committee to Rebuild the Santa Fe Opera.

[As you see, this is one of Boris's old sketchbooks. I used books he had around that he had perhaps done some studies in, such as animals at the zoo. At the back I kept lists of things we sold and, also, a list of what we paid for things for the house, which is very interesting now, I think. Unfortunately, it doesn't give quantities. Eighteen dollars for gravel—that was probably a truckload because I had the truck come in and spread it. These great big vigas back here, $228.81. You'd pay almost that much for one of those now. Adobes, $70 per hundred or 10.5 cents each delivered. Had the roof done for $146. I spent $82.50 for a secondhand refrigerator.

[A burglar alarm—when Boris left he put a burglar alarm wire all around the roof so that if anybody came over the wall I would hear them. The only time the darn thing went off was when there was a storm or when the tree would catch into the wire, so I finally just disconnected it.]

August 1 (continued)

Starting a new journal on Boris and 518 Alto Street. *[I used an old sketchbook of Boris's that had just a few drawings in it.]* It seems momentous for some reason; almost as though it meant there would be some great change or occasion. Things are going so well, even though we never seem to have any money ahead. When we are scraping bottom, somebody always comes along and buys something. We've had to raise prices because of materials and the cost of just living. It bothers us for it seems like so much money, but money goes nowhere these days; since everything is relative, I guess it doesn't seem like so much to those who have a lot. *[I see money rears its ugly head again.]*

Felix Labunski is taking us to the opera Friday evening. They are playing at the Sweeney gymnasium for the rest of the season because of the fire.

August 11

Boris is in the hospital in Denver to see what is really wrong. He is in excellent hands and with his friends *[both doctors]*, who have a personal interest. Will know tonight what's up, I hope. So thankful he got there; he never would have done this another way. *[Boris died in 1982, but you can see that his troubles started way back in the 1960s. It was a long time before the doctors figured out that his problem was emphysema.]*

Lots of rain every day or all night. All is lush and dripping. No waterng for days. Have had luscious corn three times from the garden—delicious.

August 20

My Boris returned the fifteenth and had every kind of test—three hospitals, five doctors, dozens of X rays—to find nothing except that he is amazing for his sixty years. They wouldn't believe him. It must be a nerve thing that may pass, which I think it is doing. His voice is better already. It may be we don't get to Mexico this year, but his health is the most important thing in the world.

Miralotte and Ray Ickes are coming to visit for two weeks. Can hardly wait; we are both so fond of them. The Indian Market is on this weekend, and I enjoy it more than anything we have here.* It is like a foreign market; the Plaza on all sides crowded with colorful Indians selling everything from bread baked in mud ovens to $1,000 necklaces, pots, and so forth.

Have had rain almost every day for more than two weeks. Marvelous! It is cool and fall is in the air, which is depressing.

Boris's work goes well. Mrs. Locke from San Antonio, who bought the darling foxes, called before dawn. Has sent for the *Hungry Tiger,* which is also a beautiful piece. So guess we will be able to pay our bills. *Ebb Tide,* two birds in Taos, sold on time last week, and the Reverend Waller in San Antonio still owes us $3,000. Boris's show comes up September 30 in Taos.

September 1

First day of Fiesta. Miserable, dark, cold, ugly day. Do hope it changes. How much it means to so many people, especially those who participate. Santa Fe just isn't Santa Fe without the sun. You can't see the mountains and the

---

*Santa Fe Indian Market: Yearly juried exhibition sponsored the third weekend in August by the Southwestern Association for Indian Arts. Begun in the 1920s, it is now the oldest and largest such display of Indian art in the world. More than a thousand artists from about a hundred tribes show their work in more than six hundred booths. Strictly enforced quality standards assure thousands of visitors the finest in contemporary Indian arts and crafts.

sky isn't blue. Went to the melodrama with Jean Buchanan and Betty Hall last night. Very good. *[Betty was an old friend of Boris's from Evanston. She was an amateur painter and came out to Santa Fe almost every summer.]*

Boris is having a terrible time getting a show together. Pieces sell as he finishes them. If anyone wants any more, they will just have to wait until after the show. And we're complaining?

Boris's voice is back!

September 7

Ray and Miralotte left today. They bought a large owl that had been out by the pool. I miss it but am glad they will have it.

September 25

Boris is almost ready for his show at Gallery A in Taos opening October 1. I bet him $50 worth of his silver coins, which he hoards, that he couldn't catch up on all his odds and ends—polishing, signing, and so forth—in less than a week. He always leaves them all to the last frantic, hectic moment. I've never seen him get so much done in two days. He didn't even stop to drink coffee or watch the news. Needless to say, I lost; but in a way I've won for I won't have that horrible last few days to go through. The large jaguar is the only thing not finished, and that should be by Thursday.

Boris had a wonderful spread, a whole page in the Sunday paper, the *New Mexican.* He pretends to dislike publicity and won't read it. Perhaps it embarrasses him. But I know it pleases him nonetheless.

October 3

Opening a great and gay success. Even had guitar music furnished by Cliff Menz's trio. Wonderful. Eric and Polly Gibberd had us over and took us to dinner. Muriel Hutner, who flew in from Denver, was a big help at the punch table and a delightful friend and person.

The aspen are golden on the mountainside. We must get up there for a picnic this week. Vixen, too, would love it. The woodbine on the north wall of the patio is spectacular, all orange, yellow, and peachy red. *[That was where the ivy is now. We took it down because it wasn't evergreen, like the ivy, and it spread so.]*

October 14, 1967–October 19, 1968

"Working on the portal in back"

October 14

No frost yet. How lucky we are! The aspen are gone. We did get up there for a picnic. They were gorgeous.

Boris has been working on the *portal* in back for almost two weeks. *[That's this back* portal *where we are sitting.]* It is going to be a thing of beauty, as is everything he does. One thing leads to another, of course, and he will be at it for at least another week. He is now making a large door. We will cover the *portal* with plastic for the winter to serve as a greenhouse and a place to work. What a wonderful difference it will make. *[We haven't fixed up the back building yet or added on the room. As Boris built it, the back* portal *had an open ceiling to let in the light. Later I got tired of being cold and had Archie West add the ceiling boards and insulated roof. My great-nephew George Jackson, Karin's son, devised the plastic panels I use in the winter now.]*

October 16

Frost last night. It is inevitable but still sad. Greenhouse almost ready. Back room literally solid with plants waiting for their new home, which I hope will be ready tomorrow night.

October 21

Large birds at gallery sold—$3,600; we get two-thirds—to a darling young couple from Boulder, the Kendahls. It is really touching and meaningful when people like that buy something. It is a sacrifice, I'm sure; but they had to have them. The *portal* is done and all the plants protected. It looks lovely.

Boris is still working on the beautiful door *[to go between the back room and the greenhouse]*. He just must get at his own work. Hopes to Monday. He is really in the bird business. Everyone loves the feeling of freedom and peace that they have.

October 26

The greenhouse so full of plants there is no room for Boris, which was one of the ideas—a place for him to work when the weather is bad. So he's had to build an extension for himself; he's still working at it. *[He made the greenhouse twice as big by slanting it out to the south from the* portal.*]*

I spaded up the vegetable garden and have put a coating of manure on it, the flower beds around the trees (after planting bulbs), and the two little patches of grass.

This morning we had the Preservation Hall jazz band from New Orleans here for breakfast. A marvelous group of old-time musicians, great people. They got out the Indian drum and danced and sang. We had the most wonderful time. *[They were in Santa Fe to give a concert at the Greer Garson Theater.]*

October 29

Our first snow. It's a heavy, wet one and looks lovely. Picked the last of the nasturtiums, which were hiding under it. Have been covering a patch to keep from frost. Also some mint for the leg of lamb tonight. Just made a luscious lemon meringue pie—recipe from Ann Vedder. No thickening, just lots of eggs, three lemons, and sugar; egg whites mixed with sugar meringue on top. Can hardly wait for dinner. John MacGregor is coming. He did the very nice write-up of Boris for the *New Mexican.* Such a cozy winter day. Snow and cold outside, warm in here. Boris just finished his shop in time. He is setting it up today. Hope he can start on his own work tomorrow.

November 9

Boris left at 6 A.M. for El Paso. Marta of the Marburg Gallery wanted something for the annual decorator show so Boris took four small things (he's been working like mad for eight days) and the large jaguar, which will be back tomorrow.

Bought another Macaione yesterday—*Falling Blossoms.* I love it. It's spring itself, which I adore more than any other time. Saw it years ago and never forgot it. So happy to have it. Gave him $100 and $300 more as we have it. *[I still love it; it's hanging in the* sala.*]*

November 27

At last some moisture. It's snowing. Hope it continues for the day. How snug and smug Boris looks working in the greenhouse with cold and snow outside. He's so happy with it. When the first real snow of winter comes it's so utterly beautiful. So quiet, so cozy. I wonder if I really could live where they never have any. I would miss it, I know. Must fix up a better place to feed the outside birds—perhaps a board under the roof of the wellhouse.

December 4

If anyone had told me ten years ago that Boris and I would be together in a beautiful adobe house in Santa Fe living on what his work brings, I wouldn't have believed it was possible. But here we are, surrounded by pets, plants, friends, and happiness. It is really unbelievable.

Boris leaves this weekend for Palm Desert, California, with three beautiful pieces for the gallery there. I was hoping I could go, but because of those same pets and plants, I must stay to take care of them. I hate the thought of him being without me, but that's the way it is.

It is cold and still not much snow. Wish we would have a blizzard.

December 14

It's at last snowing hard. The birds, Vixen, and I are cozy with a fire in the fireplace. Boris is in California. Hope he'll be back tomorrow but have a feeling it won't be until Saturday. Tomorrow is again my birthday—fifty-three. Can't believe it. If I can live to be old and as happy as I am now, I'll not mind. This is indeed a good life. Will be glad when Boris is safely back home.

December 16

Boris is still stranded in Tucson. Called yesterday noon. Can't get through because of the snowstorm—roads impassable. It's bitter cold. Ten degrees tonight. So far I've been able to keep the greenhouse from freezing. Wish he were safely home. When will he be?

My brother and I went to the Chinaman's for my birthday dinner last night. *[Remember the New Canton Café on San Francisco Street? We always just called it the Chinaman's. It was there forever.]*

December 27

Boris arrived safely the seventeenth. Had a great Christmas with Lynda and John Sargent; went calling to the Vedders and Kosickis. Dinner a delicious turkey and so forth. Yesterday Boris became very ill with bronchitis and flu. He is in bed sleeping all the time except when I wake him for liquids and pills. He's really sick. Never have I known him to stay in bed. May it pass as quickly as it came. *[Boris is ill again. The way he worked, ill or not, was incredible. That period of his life, from 1965 to 1975, you can't imagine. Not only did he work on the house but he turned out beautiful sculpture for three or four galleries. He worked in here with the* portal *closed in plastic. I took off the partition that he had built to make it bigger because I was tired of being cold in the wintertime.]*

1968

January 17

At last Boris feels well again. Thought his devastating cough would never leave, completely exhausting him. He again is eager to get at his work and is full of his usual devilment. It looks as though we will really get to Mexico again after dreaming about it for four years. Gallery in California sold a large bird, and Lynda says she will hold down the fort when we go, which should be in another month.

Boris has finished a figure, a prophet for Aly Schlusselberg *[the husband of the woman with the gallery in El Paso]*. He certainly should get a start on Dr. Fleming's birds. It sounds too wonderful to believe. We will go back to Mitla after stopping on the way in Mexico City to see the fabulous archaeological museum and in Taxco, which I love.

Still snow on the ground but melting fast and now the mud. Vixen is filthy. Sun getting warm and a promise of spring in the air. Got carried away by a seed catalogue and "planted" my garden last week *[in my imagination, that is]*.

January 31

Can't believe it but we plan to leave for Mexico two weeks from today. Saw a butterfly—a mourning cloak—and heard a robin sing, but it is still winter except in the middle of the day when the sun is out. Dug the last of the carrots yesterday. Imagine! Boris has been working on the truck all week. Built a box for the back that we can lock. What fun it will be. Hate leaving Vixen and Mau-Mau, but what can you do.

March 21

Arrived home March 14, cold and as dismal as when we left a month before. The day is bitter and snowy. We had a beautiful trip—the nicest one we've ever had. Spent two weeks in Mitla, which we still love. Now dream of building a small place there on the edge of town. Lovely hot sun, flowers, and singing birds. Most enjoyable meals—three a day. Was sure I'd come back fat, but for some reason even Boris, who ate like a hog, lost some of his paunch. Perhaps it's because he was active, walking and climbing big hills in search of bromeliads, of which we brought back many, causing a twenty-four-hour delay at customs while they inspected and fumigated every single one. Got down almost to the Guatemala border, San Cristóbal de las Casas, way up in the misty mountains. Fascinating Indians and a lot of tempting goodies.

Vixen and Mau-Mau fine, bless Lynda; overjoyed to see us. If it hadn't been for them, believe I would have just stayed in Mitla. Such peace and serenity.

March 29

Into summer. Warm weather days. No coats, sweater, or stocking days, which I love. The apricot has started to bloom. Peach buds ready to burst. Crocus, daffodils, hyacinths, silla in bloom. Have started planting the garden. Dug around the fruit trees and put on fragrant, fresh cow manure. Hope to get some fruit this year. Put in $36 worth of gravel yesterday, out to Agua Fria Road, through the Vierras—wonderful neighbors. At least now we aren't trapped, if we have trouble on the other side.

April 5

Two nights of heavy frost after lovely spring weather. Think most of the apricot blossoms survived. Martin Luther King, Jr., was shot to death last night in Memphis. Now what? Could it lead to a civil war? Such troubled times. Must really get busy outside next week. So much to do. Have been sewing the things I brought back from Mexico because I knew I'd never get at it once the nice weather is here to stay.

April 19

Another freeze last night and tonight again. Will be a miracle if the blossoms are spared. Another year with no fruit. During the day a bitter, strong wind blows. It is truly miserable. Will this winter never end?

Boris is busy on John Fleming's birds and also a chess set that John wants in the style of Boris Godunov.* It is going to be gorgeous. He wants one side cast in silver, the other in gold. *[Dr. Fleming later sent Boris to the Soviet Union for inspiration. He did some models in wax, but Boris died before he could finish the set.]* Boris has to take the birds to Denver next week to try for size. He has three birds ready, two more to go. Then the commission for Vivian Fiske. *[That's* Elijah. *That commission turned into quite a story as you will see. Vivian was a friend of Alan Vedder's. That is probably how I met her. She was from Texas originally but was living on Hyde Park Road when I knew her. She was quite a collector of art and left an impressive collection to the Museum of Fine Arts.]* Then the American President Lines.** *[This was a large piece for one of their ships. The model for it is on the coffee table in my front room.]*

We have company coming again.

April 28

For two days now the air has been full of migrating painted lady butterflies in spite of the miserably cold weather. They must indeed be rugged.

---

*Boris Godunov (c. 1551–1605): Russian czar (1598–1605). Perhaps best known through the opera by the Russian composer Modest Mussorgsky first produced in 1874.

**American President Lines: A fleet of President ships was established in the 1920s by Dollar Steamship Lines, which became American President Lines in 1938. The company's passenger service was eliminated with the last voyage of the USS *President Wilson* in 1973.

How many perish on the way? They seem to be sucking the nectar from the fruit tree blossoms. They are called the thistle butterfly because their caterpillars live on thistles. Very beautiful and exciting to be surrounded by hundreds of them as you disturb them walking by the trees. *[It was fantastic! Thousands filled the air just that one year.]*

Eugenie Shonnard is coming for dinner tomorrow for her eighty-second birthday. Remarkable woman. Still beautiful and so feminine.

April 29

A glorious day made most exciting by even more butterflies rising in clouds around you as you walk by the fruit trees. Heard the whir of a hummingbird, but I didn't see it. Have feeders out.

May 5

Is there anything more beautiful than fruit trees in bloom—the delicate pink of the apple, and some are still in buds. The snowy white of cherry against the blue sky. The waxy pear among new, delicate green leaves; the hazy apricot, which we have so many of here in Santa Fe; and the brilliant peach. It looks as though we'll actually get some fruit this year. The lilacs are going to be spectacular. This is truly a city of lilacs. Never have seen so many or such lush ones. Solid bushes of lavender. Spring, how I love it! When I die I hope it is in the fall or winter, but then I would say, "Please let me see one more spring."

Boris still hasn't gotten off to Denver. No doubt another week. I'm working Thursday, Friday, and Saturday and dread it already. *[That was for Mother's Day, a big day at the florists.]* Boris had a nice birthday the second—dinner at Jean Buchanan's. He spent the day doing just what he wanted, which was to work in the greenhouse with his plants all day. *[He had bromeliads from Mexico; they are air plants from the jungle.]*

May 12

If it isn't frost, it's hail. It is pounding down. Had a glorious rain last night; still cold. Lilacs all over town are breathtaking. Solid masses of fragrant blooms. My cereus has bloomed three nights' worth, too; more flowers to come. Heavenly. *[There is an awful lot here about the weather. I could really write quite a weather log for all these years. It seems to me I was preoccupied with it. I think anyone who has a garden is very preoccupied with the weather—the freezing and the watering and so on.]*

I went to work for three days to help get through the month. *[Honestly, with all the things that were selling, I don't understand where the money went. I guess we just spent it all on this place.]*

The Reverend Waller came through with the last payment of $1,500. We're rich again for a while and it's a good feeling. Boris leaves for Denver a week from tomorrow. Three of the birds are done and are exquisite. The models for the chess set are exciting.

May 22

Boris got back from Denver at 4:30 this A.M. The Flemings were delighted with the birds and the beginning of the chess set. At last I believe summer is here. It's been warm now for three days and even the nights. A horrible gust of wind blew Dicky Bird's cage over in the patio today. *[He was a canary.]* He must have been hurt. All puffed up and eyes closed. There's always some darned thing. Mau-Mau's worst foot is worse. Poor little thing can hardly get around so spends most of her time in a basket. Her spirits are fine, and she accepts all her troubles. What a marvelous creature she is.

May 28

How quiet it is. How much is gone. My little Dicky Bird is dead. I guess why he sang so beautifully and so constantly was that he had to get it all into his short life. Four years of glorious song. How we miss him.

Summer at last finally seems to have arrived here in Santa Fe. We have had lettuce from the garden for almost a month as well as several batches of spinach. Everything is growing so fast.

June 10

Everything seems to be in turmoil. The world situation, politics, people— the unbelievable, senseless assassination of Robert Kennedy last Wednesday—and the weather. We never have had such a time with coughs, colds, and so forth. Miserably cold this A.M. Will it ever, ever be summer?

The gardens are beautiful and never have the roses been so profuse and lovely. It's all hell on Boris's work. He's feeling lousy, and it goes very slowly. I'm starting to be a McCarthy volunteer. Only a few weeks to go before nomination and, as far as we are concerned, he is the only one. Hope all the fantastically millions of people who were obviously devoted to Kennedy will be for McCarthy.

June 25

Yes, it's summer. In the nineties for three days; cooler today but tragically dry. Hose goes twenty-four hours. If you aren't complaining about one thing, it's another—too cold, too hot, too wet, too dry. The deluge of moths we've had has left lots of eggs, which are now caterpillars that seem not to be at all fussy as to what their diet consists of, devouring most everything.

Boris left last night for California to pick up the jaguar since the gallery is closed for the summer. The only thing they didn't take to Jackson because of its size. *[The Palm Desert people had a summer gallery in Jackson Hole, Wyoming.]* Hated to see him go alone, but he no doubt enjoys it. It is good for both of us occasionally since we are together constantly. His presence is certainly missed; he is such an important and large part of 518 Alto. He hopes to be back by Friday, the twenty-eighth. It's a hot drive.

What a mess the world is in. Riots, protests, war, assassinations, dirty politics, hippies, welfare, etc.

July 2

Boris arrived safely Friday. Had delightful news that our dear friends Ray and Miralotte are coming to see us. Something to look forward to.

It is overcast and rumbling with thunder, naturally—it is the opera's opening night. If we ever have rain it's during the opera. There must be a lot of frantic females who have been planning their costumes for months and just had their hair done. How we need rain.

July 7

Haven't watered for almost a week. Delightful, beautiful rain almost every day. My night-blooming cereus is covered with buds. One will open tonight, most tomorrow night.

July 8

The Kosickis are coming for a cereus party. We will sip wine and watch them open. Which is the most intoxicating? Four open tonight.

July 9

Six of the cereus are opening this evening, starting at eight, and they peak from ten to two or three in the morning. Hummingbird moths are attracted by the overpowering, heavenly fragrance. More to come—thirty-two in all. Such perfection.

July 14

I have a new member of our family—a beautiful, dear, sweet, intelligent, male German shepherd named Mickey. George Keelerik is leaving for Ireland. On his way, he has left his beloved Mickey with us. Vixen and he are great friends. It was indeed a sad parting when George left this morning. Mickey is still waiting for him by the front gate. However, he ate a good dinner and will adjust quickly. He will be two in September. *[He and I were devoted—he followed me everywhere.]*

August 31

So very busy with company and the garden. Lots of rain this year; everything lush and beautiful. Mickey has really settled in. An adorable animal, devoted and protective. It was so great having Ray and Miralotte here. Hated to have them leave.

Boris has gone today for a mule race in Socorro. No telling when he will return. I plan to take the model of the birds for the ship to San Francisco soon. Look forward to again being with Ray and Miralotte.

The Fiesta is on but no desire to go. Such noise, dirt, and smell. *[That's different from the first one, isn't it?]*

September 16

First frost; not a heavy one. Beans, squash, and tomatoes gone.

September 28

No more frost but have brought everything in so as not to have it all to do at once. So much stuff. Spent a day in Juárez with Jean Buchanan. Am having made a beautiful, long jacket suit of wool gabardine and a 100 percent camel-hair coat. *[Wow! We must be in the money. That was to go to San Francisco to take the birds for the American President Line's commission.]* After living in Santa Fe for so long, you realize that you have nothing to wear in a city such as San Francisco.

Gallery A is completely sold out of Gilbertsons and no time to make any. How I hate to see winter come. Aspen changing rapidly.

September 29

Waiting to take off for Taos for Malcolm Alexander's wedding. As usual Boris leaves everything to the last minute; we are late in starting and will no doubt be late arriving. I should be used to this but never will be. It takes the fun out of going anyplace for it is always so desperate and frantic getting off. We are taking the big jaguar up so that they will have something there. The price is $6,000, so it should be there a while. *[It sold to a doctor in Albuquerque.]*

October 13

Jaguar sold. It is all unbelievable. After all these years, now Boris will surely give the go-ahead to finish the back. That will complete my dream of 518.

No more frost. Boris is covering the *portal* for the greenhouse. I leave the twenty-third for San Francisco. Am so excited; looking forward to being with Ray and Miralotte. Whenever I fly anyplace I feel I'll not come back, which is ridiculous when you think of the thousands of people who fly everywhere all the time. I love it, though; I feel so elegant. Poor Boris, he has so much to do; he is overwhelmed by all this and so thankful.

October 19

Four more days and I take off. Am packed already, and, in spite of large suitcase, small suitcase, and vanity, I still can't take everything I want to. Fall is here, winter in the air, mountains white with snow. Garden is gone, greenhouse full.

November 14, 1968–January 10, 1970

"Adobes are going up fast for the new room"

November 14

Had two glorious weeks in San Francisco. Stayed the extra days so that I could go on the USS *President Wilson,* the sister ship to the USS *President Cleveland,* to see exactly where Boris's bird sculpture will go. The model was most enthusiastically received and, I must say, will do something for the ship that needs doing. It was exciting to go through it, having never been on one—like a big hotel, which is what they call it. The flights to and from were impressive, but I must say it was good to get back to blue sky and sunshine after the wicked smog, rain, and cold of the coast.

Was hoping to start the storeroom *[now my guest room]* this week—first step to fixing the back, but nothing is simple these days. Our contractor, of course, had to get a building permit. Couldn't get one because the new regulations are that you can't build within five feet from your property line. In this case it's ridiculous but has to go before an approving committee before they will OK it. So God knows when or if we'll ever get it done. Had to pay $45 for that plus whatever the permit will be. So it goes. They're doing all they can to take away all of Santa Fe's charm and individuality, making it like any other city. To hell with the lot of them, I say. *[I'll tell you how we got the permission. The board, whatever that was, came over and looked at the situation. I explained that being a common wall it would be ridiculous having that five feet sitting there. So he said it was all right if it was all right with the neighbors. So we got our neighbor Mariano García's permission. He said it was all right with him to build it right on the property line, which we did.]*

A cold, wet day. Should snow any day. Boris has been working on his shop in back for a month. He has to have a bigger place to work this winter with all the work he has to get out. Do hope he will finish soon. Everyone is breathing down his neck. Galleries have nothing, and the

126

ship job has to be done and delivered in March. We hope to get to Mexico after that. We never know. Still hope to buy some land in Mitla.

November 23

A month ago today I flew to San Francisco. A Mr. Jan Mitchell called from New York wanting to buy the jaguar, which he had seen in the gallery in Palm Desert. "He who hesitates doesn't get a Gilbertson." Also Governor Rockefeller from New York was delighted with the crazy sculpture *Candidate* that Boris sent back with Sally. *[I don't remember who this was. There were so many people; I don't know how we coped with all the company.]*

As it is, he can't seem to get two orders done that were taken by Gallery A four months ago. Today he has a bug and is in bed.

November 26

Boris still sick. Must be a bug. Can't work, of course. We are having company for Thanksgiving dinner. Please, may Boris be all right by then.

December 1

Had a wonderful Thanksgiving dinner. Boris is working some. Still feels rather punk. Today is very cold. Will be glad when Christmas is over. I really hate it. Roger the Lodger is still here. *[He was a friend of Eric Gilbertson's who came out with him and stayed and stayed after Eric left.]*

We are going to a gathering at Sallie Wagner's tonight for dinner for Peter Hurd, the painter, who has a show opening tonight at the Art Museum. *[Sallie was an old acquaintance of ours.]* From what I hear, he is really a fine guy, even though his work isn't my cup of tea. His wife is artist N. C. Wyeth's daughter.

Went to the meeting of the adjustment board last night. Have permission to build the storeroom on the property line. Still very cold.

December 5

The Hurds are wonderful. They seemed to like us, too. Came over this morning before heading for Lubbock. Loved the house and I believe will be future friends. His lithograph show is really impressive.

December 26

The birthday passed, also Christmas, both of which were the nicest of days. We were alone for a peaceful, quiet day, with the dogs playing with toys, a game to get them away from each other. Dinner in the evening at Jean's. My brother was there.

December 28

Had another gloriously beautiful walk with Jean and the dogs this noon. When I got home, the sculptor Alonzo Houser and his wife from St. Paul, Minnesota, were here. *[How strange, I have no memory of this at all.]* They are staying in Albuquerque and came to see Boris. Coming back Monday to take us out to lunch, if Boris will go.

1969

January 1

Today is like spring. Boris is working outside. Parrots, having had a bath, dry in the sun on the table. Mickey, of course, is here by me. Vixen lies in the sun in the patio. *[More people coming. It's amazing.]*

With Tricky Dick Nixon in for another four years, I would just as soon be somewhere else, say Mexico. The ghastly war goes on, trips to the moon—mighty impressive, but so what with all the unsolved problems on this earth.*

January 13

Can't believe it. They are going to start building the storeroom on the back. The cost is fantastic, but what isn't these days. Fortunately, we have the money—$1,885 plus $75 tax. Unbelievable. Almost half of what we paid for the whole thing. Just the cost of materials, no labor, for Boris's

---

*Nixon was dubbed "Tricky Dick" by Helen Gahagan Douglas, whom he defeated in a 1950 Senate race with communist baiting that included calling her "pink right down to her underwear." The Vietnam War, which had destroyed the presidency of his predecessor, Lyndon B. Johnson, continued during his first term, accompanied by violent protest and social upheaval. The six Apollo program lunar landings occurred during his first term.

shop was more than $1,400. So there you are, money means nothing. God knows what really finishing the back would cost. Wonder if we'll ever be able to.

January 21

The adobes are going up fast for the new room, and how nice it looks. Should be finished in a week. Then the job, and that will be a job, of moving all the stuff into it. Hope Boris will be able to part with at least some of it; like suits and shirts he hasn't worn for ten years and never will, beat-up suitcases, worn-out shoes, and so forth. There are boxes and boxes of old magazines and records that I had sent out from Illinois and crates of broken pottery that Bud *[Boris's brother, the potter]* brought from Japan. It will all no doubt be moved to sit there for the rest of time.

Anyway, perhaps we can get the back cleaned out and ready to go ahead when we can. It is very exciting after waiting so long. *[My guest room was built as a storeroom and then it became my bedroom and then it was Boris's room. We needed a storeroom because we had all our junk in the end of this big room in the back building—there was no place else to put it. Before we could start on the back we had to move all that stuff someplace, and so we built the storeroom. It's all like a game of chess. You have to do other things before you can do what you want to do.]*

The *perros malos [vicious dogs]* have to be shut in the patio. My sister Kay and I are going to take them for a long walk in the country this beautiful afternoon.

January 26

This time each evening, just before twilight, great flocks of birds—what kind? They soar, twist, turn, swirl against the sky toward the south. I can see them here from the window. It is beautiful.

February 1

The storeroom is almost finished. A misunderstanding about the ceiling; to cover up the two by fours will cost $100 more. Then decided to plaster the inside at $185. So that will make it $2,245. Seems absolutely unbelievable. Anyway, if we ever want to make it into an extra bedroom, all we have to do is to paint the walls. *[Steve Kestrel put in the window on the south and built a closet for that room. After Boris died in 1982, he and Cindi Kunselman lived in the room up front for a year.]*

Boris still hasn't started the birds for the American President Lines. They are supposed to be delivered in March; it will no doubt be April. Hope we can make a hurried trip to Mitla at that time. Days most pleasant, nights cold. Already thinking of vegetables and flowers I want to plant and where.

February 5

The room is finished. Looks great, as though it belonged. Really adds a great deal, and what a wonderful, warm, cozy corner it makes for sitting in the sun. *[Right out here.]* As soon as it warms up, I'm going to wet the walls down again and spray them with a product to preserve the mud. *[I never did this. The room has a nice overhang so the exterior mud has never had anything done to it.]*

February 14

Boris has drawn me two wonderful Valentines that were sitting on the table waiting for me this morning, all with owls, cupids, and so forth. No matter how much he has to do. Having a few in for dinner. Putting gorgeous camellias from the greenhouse and the first pussy willows on the table.

February 23

Boris is taking off for Palm Desert in a few days with long overdue pieces for the gallery. Some really magnificent ones—a handsome horse of silver and bronze, which everyone loves; the lovely giraffe, which I thought we were going to keep, alas; and an impressive female figure, which emerges from roots and a tree behind a part of it, little owls sitting on limbs, her hair hanging—silver and bronze—*La Bruja de la Noche. [The Witch of the Night. I don't remember that piece at all, and I don't know where it went or who bought it.]* Wish I could have kept that, too; unfortunately, we need the money. *[Always needing money; I don't know where we spent it all.]*

February 26

Boris left at 10:30 A.M. for Palm Desert. I've been painting all day, the bath and dishwashing room. I hate it but it has to be done. Just the floor left. *[For twenty-two years I washed dishes in the little room by the front bathroom.]* I can't do it when Boris is home. Puts him in a horrible mood, and he always wants in where I am for some reason. *[That's when we only had one bathroom.]* It is terribly empty without him. Hope he has a good time and a little rest, which he needs. He's been working so hard and coming back for more. If all that he took is sold, we will finish the back. When he left, he pointed to the pieces in the back of the truck and said, "That's our finished house." He is so happy and delighted that his work sells, and for once in his life he is a successful artist.

March 3

Boris had a wonderful trip and enjoyed his stay in California. They were thrilled and delighted with his work, and they should be. He, as usual, was tempted beyond his strength and bought me a gorgeous, and I'm sure expensive, Indian necklace. *[Much later I sold that for $1,000.]* There is no one like him. It makes him so happy to be able to spend money. Good to have him back.

March 10

Bitter cold and more snow.

March 16

At last a gorgeous, sunny, warmish day. Pruned all the fruit trees and grapes. Spread goat manure and planted my sweet peas. *[You always plant sweet peas on St. Patrick's Day.]* Had lunch out back with Mau-Mau in her wooden salad bowl that she likes to sit in. Marc Simmons stopped by. Such a darling guy. Tomorrow night we go to Los Alamos to hear a young pianist, James Dick. *[He has become very well known.]*

March 19

Beautiful performance by the young Jim Dick. A most talented boy and darling person. I went to Los Alamos and got him yesterday. *[I don't remember this at all.]* Catherine Rayne had us for cocktails and dinner at the Vedders. *[Catherine was Miss White's companion—Amelia White, that is.]* He was completely taken with Santa Fe and can hardly wait to return next summer.

March 25

A sparkling morning, sun on new-fallen snow. At last a blue sky; this winter seems like purgatory.

March 28

Have had two heavenly days—the kind we dream of all winter. Planted carrots and lettuce. I feel this morning as if I won't live long. I've had this cough for almost a year, and no one can find out why.

April 5

From winter to summer. It's all right with me. How glorious to be out all day in the sun in shorts, getting everything watered. Apricot in full bloom, sweet cherry starting. They are up by the house and protected.

Monday I start going from shop to shop in hopes of getting new members for the Historic Santa Fe Foundation. We need money! *[I was membership chairman, and I got a lot of members that way. I went up and down Cerrillos Road to the motels telling them that they count on the tourists and we help preserve things that make the tourists come here. It worked. I don't know whether they are still members or not. I was on the Foundation board for twelve years with a one-year break.]*

April 16

Having the biggest and wettest snowstorm we've had all winter, almost six inches already at ten A.M. Looks as though it will last. Seems so strange to hear thunder in a snowstorm.

April 27

Winter is still with us, although the glorious blossoms still go bravely on. Thursday, May 1, we leave for San Francisco with the birds for the American President Lines. We'll stay with Ray and Miralotte, visit the Rapps, and then to Palm Desert.

May 18

Back from a wonderful and successful trip. The American President Lines was absolutely awed by the gorgeous birds, as well they should be. Boris saw them installed and had pictures taken with the commodore. Then to Palm Desert to pick up the beautiful giraffe, which is here with us to stay, I hope. *[I'm not sure if that's the one I have or not.]* How glad we were to get back to sparsely populated and relatively peaceful Santa Fe. *[How it's changed.]*

June 1

Cool and cloudy today. Poppies in bloom. The house is on a tour of historic houses, which I've been getting together in an effort to publicize and increase membership to the Historic Santa Fe Foundation. Will be glad when it's over and will be glad to get up to Minnesota in July for a real rest and vacation. *[I visited my sisters, Dot and Treet.]*

June 9

The front has been mud plastered finally; waited two years. Had it treated with Pencapsula. *[That product that was supposed to preserve it for twenty years. I don't think we ever put that stuff on.]* Busy getting ready for the tour. Place looks lovely.

June 12

Miserably cold and dark. Rain last night. Please may it be nice next week.

June 20

Tour over. Two magnificently perfect days. Everything wonderful. Made more than $600 clear for the Foundation. Will no doubt do it again in August.

August 23

A long, steady rain at night; a beautiful, magical morning. Tonight is the last night of the opera *Tosca*. Hope Boris will go. He had a dreadful and frightening night. Had one of those attacks where he can't breath. It is all so mysterious. Is it the weather, allergies, fumes? Wish they could track it down.

August 28

Fiesta starts *mañana*. Glad when it's over. The noise and the filth. The Brodkeys are here from Columbus, Ohio. Dr. Fleming thinks maybe Boris's problem is asthmatic bronchitis. Gave us something to try. He's had stomach flu and *tourista [the runs]* for several days.

September 5

Brodkeys gone. Thought I could now relax, but Boris was carried away with nine baby guinea hens and Polish chickens at the feed store when he bought feed to take to the mules. I certainly don't want any more animals, but now that they are here, I worry and stew over them. Already I have one in the house who is, and was, being shoved about on his wobbly legs. I mixed some pabulum and milk, which he gobbled up. He was lonesome so I brought another one in to keep him company. Boris's idea is to take them out to Brownie Hall's later. We shall see.

September 25

Santa Fe's perfect weather, just as I first remember it. Boris is putting the greenhouse up *[for the winter]*.

September 28

Just returned from Taos. Went on a beautiful picnic. Aspen golden; wild asters and chamisa more brilliant than I've ever seen.

October 5 (Sunday)

Supposed to frost tonight; the greenhouse is up and ready. Boris goes the twenty-first to take twelve pieces to the El Paso Art Museum. They are mostly not for sale because we want to keep them for ourselves. *[We didn't, of course.]* He's having a show there starting November 2 for a month. He is now working in Corten steel.* It is much stronger, cheaper, and no doubt better for outside things particularly. *[It superficially rusts but doesn't deteriorate. They use it a lot for outdoor bridges.]*

---

*Corten: U.S. Steel trade name for a high-strength, low-alloy (0.09 percent carbon) steel. Particularly amenable to welding and tooling.

Mau-Mau has been very sick and has no control of her droppings and throws up most of what she eats. Her spirits go on; such a wonderful and beloved bird. Can't imagine how she can endure so long what she has gone through.

October 18

We had a very light frost ten days ago. Most things not hurt and still have carrots and chard from the garden. Mau-Mau better again—amazing creature. Put $100 down on a Toyota pickup on the strength of Vivian Fiske's commission for *Elijah*. Start the first part of November. A handsome, rather abstract figure with birds, sixteen feet high, in memory of her first husband in the cemetery at Fort Worth. It will be made of Corten steel, which is cheaper. Bronze would have been prohibitive.

October 20

Had a check for $600 for a bird that is being given to Governor Rockefeller, so we'll get the truck tomorrow. We'll give the old one to Brownie and Mary; they need one so badly.

October 24

Heavy frost last night. Boris left at 5 A.M. in our new Toyota truck for El Paso with his sculpture. Brownie picked up the old truck and the chickens yesterday. Mr. Paul Nelson, a banker from Denver, was here yesterday. Maybe another commission for a new twenty-six-story bank building. *[Boris didn't get it, thank God. He was so busy.]* John and Celeste Fleming are coming.

October 26

As usual, first thing I went out in back with the dogs to greet the morning. A glorious morning it is. You wouldn't believe you are in a city of forty-five thousand and only five blocks from the Plaza. It sounded like the country, with dogs barking, roosters crowing, and birds chirping.

November 9

Boris was thrilled beyond belief with the show. Said it was just what he had always dreamed of—his work being displayed. Sold several things, orders for others that were not for sale.

Miracle of miracles, Mau-Mau has again come through. Talking like mad. Tough little bird.

November 23

Won't believe it till we get there, but we plan to go to Oaxaca and Mitla for Christmas. Leaving the fifteenth. Ray and Miralotte are going to meet us in Mexico City.

December 3

Dark day. Looks like snow. Boris left for El Paso to pick up his things at the museum. It was a really impressive show. He will be back tomorrow. Leave for Oaxaca by plane. *[That's the only time we didn't drive the truck down.]*

1970

January 10

Arrived home from Mexico on the thirtieth of December. Seems ages ago. Lovely summer days there. Gertrude Frizzell begging us to come back to stay and oversee the place. It's a temptation, but I really believe I would like being here in Santa Fe in the summer. We'll see what transpires.

[Gertrude was an American widow who owned La Sorpresa *(The Surprise), a small hotel where we stayed in Mitla. She and her husband had gone down there to live in their later years. He had collected local Indian artifacts and had a small museum. At this time, Gertrude was getting old and was looking for someone to take over the hotel. She asked me if I would be interested in moving down and taking the job. Boris could do his work there and I would supervise the inn, but I decided against it.]*

Boris goes to Denver this week to deliver the birds for Muriel Hutner's grave. It's been a year. *[Later somebody stole them from the cemetery.]*

February 14, 1970–January 21, 1971

"I haven't had a minute"

February 14

Valentine's Day. Boris left the tenth for Palm Desert with some very nice pieces for the gallery. He is going to try it one more year. If they sell nothing, we'll pull out. Also believe this is the last for El Paso. The Carlin Gallery in Dallas would also like some of Boris's work. Believe it's a fine one.

When Boris is gone I can get so much done. Up at five or six in the morning and don't have to stop all day. I stained the ceiling and painted the walls of the new "storeroom." After moving lots of stuff into it, moved it all back into the mess of the back building. I'm going to make it a bedroom for me and for guests. Can hardly wait. Should be darling. Will use Mother's lovely old bed; have a closet built, a chest of drawers, and a dressing table. Will put one of my Mexican "dog roaster" fireplaces in for heat. *[This was Boris's pet name for our pottery fireplace from Oaxaca.]*

Spring weather is still with us. Already have a tan. Surely it can't last. Boris is supposed to be back today unless, of course, he should decide to take the scenic route home through various parts of Mexico. It is very good for both of us to be by ourselves. We are together so constantly when he is home.

February 23

Winter again, wet snow, which is great. However, four dark days in a row is almost more than one can stand. We are so spoiled: How well we remember the weeks and weeks back in Illinois. I am planning to go to Berkeley on the tenth for ten days. I already have my ticket from Ray in hand.

We are really broke, and to me the coming year looks ominous. Everything is such a mess, and Tricky Dicky Nixon is living up to his name.* And that Agnew, even the thought of him makes me ill.** No bedroom, no money, another dream shattered. *[I don't understand. We got all this money. Where did it all go? I think a lot of it went to Boris's materials. We set our prices; the galleries didn't tell us what to charge. Boris always said he was lucky if he made a dollar an hour. Those pieces took so long. He never cast anything. He built everything up with his torch. After he built it up, he had to grind it down and then polish it and put it on a base. Each piece took a lot of time and work. How he got all that stuff done I'll never know.]*

March 10

Snow and cold, but spring is on its way: all the bulbs green and fresh against wet earth and manure; apricot ready to burst into bloom; the birds singing these mornings; and the smells of damp earth all about. At 3:45 today I take off for San Francisco. You would think I never go anywhere, I get so excited. I'm always so relieved when that plane finally takes off. How I look forward to my visit. It will all be over too soon.

April 4

Arrived home March 23. My clothes have been tighter after two weeks of eating all sorts of exotic, delicious food. So now I'm counting calories for a while. *[I don't know why I said that; I never gain weight.]*

We've had more snow in the last month than all winter. It's really

---

*Richard M. Nixon had been in office for two years. The Vietnam War, which he had pledged to end, continued, although a phased American withdrawal had begun under the cover of the "Vietnamization" of the fighting forces. During the final months of 1969, there had been massive antiwar demonstrations in Washington, D.C. Nixon had vowed not to be swayed and had claimed that a "silent majority" supported his war policy.

**Agnew attained national notoriety attacking Vietnam War protesters, journalists, intellectuals, and liberals with such alliterative phrases as "nattering nabobs of negativism" and "pusillanimous pussyfooters." Later became first vice president to resign under legal duress. Pled nolo contendere to one count of failing to report income to avoid federal extortion, bribery, and tax charges stemming from his tenure as governor of Maryland.

coming down. Beautiful but would have been more so a month ago. However, the moisture is always needed. I have my sweet peas, lettuce, chard, and onions in. Have been preparing a bed for dahlias. The greenhouse is so pretty now. The orchid cacti are covered with great flowers and buds of magenta and scarlet. Gardenia blooming, as are cymbidium orchids, geraniums, and citrus. The tuberous-rooted begonias that I started two months ago are strong, rich plants and are doing well. If the time ever comes to put them out! The winter seems nonending, and it started so early.

Mau-Mau is much improved. Have been giving her gravel in her food. Looks as though our fruit may be gone again. Very cold nights, and buds out too far.

April 20

Still miserably cold and devastatingly windy. Great gusts, so destructive that the plastic on Boris's shop and some on the greenhouse is in shreds. Just hope most of it holds until the weather warms, if that ever comes. *[When he was in that greenhouse extension on the south, all he had covering the slanted roof was a heavy plastic. This was before he built his shop out back.]* Enjoyed my dear sister Treet's visit.

A cock robin has been fighting his reflection on the patio window for days. Hope he survives. There seems to be nothing I can do to discourage him. He's determined to kill or frighten his rival away but can't, poor thing. *[They do that all the time.]*

April 22

At noon forty-one degrees with a cold, miserable wind. Bound to be a killing freeze tonight.

April 27

Two glorious, warm, sunny days. Doors open, working outside in shorts. Heavenly. Supposed to get cold again today.

It seems the young people eight years and up are bent on destruction these days—breaking windows, burning up, destroying everything. Little boys have even pried off the copper coverings of the lights on either side of the gate. They constantly throw rocks at the gate and once in a while even at the front windows. They see violence and destruction everywhere. The ghastly war in Vietnam; television such an awful influence; newspapers; everywhere—a reflection of our times, I guess. Most depressing.

May 1

Two nights of twenty-four degrees. Even yesterday during the day it didn't get above thirty-two. Today, however, looks as though it may be clear. Will this winter ever end? Tomorrow is Boris's sixty-third birthday. You would never know it. He will never grow up; truly young at heart. He has requested a gigantic strawberry shortcake. Will make a chocolate cake, too. Jean will join us for dinner.

Richard Nixon, the Lion Heart, has done it again! He is now sending troops into Cambodia. He promised to end the war in Vietnam, and instead it gets worse and bigger.

May 4

Two lovely days. A man from Santa Fe City Planning came to take photos for the National Historic Sites—518 is up for that recognition. Wish we had the whole building as it was originally.

May 9

Last night thirty-four degrees. Don't dare put out flowers yet. Gorgeous clear blue sky and sun today. Am painting floor in the back "bedroom." Am going to put up the bed, even if I never have a closet. *[I did later.]* Bought two lovely old chests in Las Vegas, New Mexico. At least it is a start.

May 23

Have been so busy, I haven't had a minute. I'm in my bedroom, which I adore. It is really darling. What a job moving all the stuff into the back again, but how great and big this room looks now. *[The erstwhile new storeroom.]* Eric and family are arriving in a week for two weeks. *[That's Boris's son.]* Have rented Eloisa's little house in back for them to sleep in. Will be more pleasant and easier for everyone.

The gardens are lovely now. Wish we could just pick it all up as is and put it down in the country. The quiet and peace would be wonderful.

June 1

Eric and his wife are here with dear baby Mark. His first birthday is Wednesday. Will make a cake for the occasion. Got him a little rocking chair in Juárez last week when Jean and I went to El Paso to pick up Boris's things at the Marberg Gallery.

June 7

Up until this afternoon it has been cold and overcast. The mountains again white with snow. Next week my roses and Oriental poppies will be spectacular.

June 11

Bitter cold, dark, and windy. If it's like this next weekend, or rainy, think I'll shoot myself. Boris actually—I did the negotiating—sold his mules. They were so much trouble and expense, even though beautiful and wonderful animals. They will live on a big ranch in Wagon Mound. A Mr. Stewart McArthur bought them today.

June 20

A week of perfect summer weather—no rain, which we need badly, but glad it isn't today or yesterday for the Historic Santa Fe Foundation tour. *[So many people wanted to come, we had to do it twice.]* I had four busloads yesterday, one from the College of Santa Fe. Looks as though there would only be two today. Everyone wonderful. The place really looks beautiful. Roses spectacular. The weird, wild, night-blooming cereus is full of buds, only fragrant when it gets dark.

June 22

Poured yesterday. How lucky that it wasn't the day before. All the plants look so clean and happy. Boris left for Palm Desert this A.M. to pick up the *Owl Tree.*

July 6

Brud coming for his birthday dinner. Made a cake. Put wax on a water lily, hoping it will stay open, to put it on the cake. That is his birthday flower and favorite flower. Made a yummy sour cherry pie for lunch. First time we've had enough for a pie off of our little tree. Very warm and extremely dry in spite of the opera having started. Ray and Miralotte Ickes arrive on August 3 for a week.

July 17

How dry it is. I'm most depressed. My tuberous-rooted begonias are doing nothing. They are usually so gorgeous. Can't blame it on the weather. Next week Walt Hutner and his new bride, Barbara, will be arriving.

July 19

A real soaker. River running like a wild thing. Floods in *portals* and patio and Boris's shop. Afraid hail may have done some damage. Will see in the morning.

August 19

It seems I haven't had a minute. One batch of company after another. John Fleming is buying one of the giraffes, and how we need the money. Ray bought a small owl slate carving and the Mansfields a large one of horses. *[I don't remember the Mansfields.]* Somehow we keep going in spite of galleries not selling. Vivian Fiske's commission will be done by November. Something always turns up, it seems.

Boris has been doing some beautiful things this summer and seems to feel better than he has for years. His lotus is blooming—now two huge pinky yellow flowers on stems bursting out of the water more than two feet long. My cereus has had a series of blooms all summer. Have frozen lots of beans and twenty quarts of peaches. The vegetables have been wonderful this year but roses horrible—some kind of blight. I'm going to Berkeley again for Halloween. *[Halloween in Berkeley was a tradition. We turned out all the lights and had candles. I was the corpse lying there, and I'd jump up once in a while and scare the kids.]* Then in December we hope to go to Oaxaca. So life goes on in this beautiful old place that everyone loves. Countryside looks more like Wisconsin than New Mexico with all the rain.

September 7

Fiesta over. Fall is in the air. Horrid thought. When I think of all there is to do before frost, I can't believe it. Took cuttings of all my geraniums today, daisies, fuchsias, coleus, and begonias. Repotted a few things so it won't all come at once. Have many acorn and butternut squash put away. Still freezing beans. Off to Juárez in a couple of days. Look forward to the jaunt.

September 18

Still no frost. Still eating from the garden. The greenhouse is up and very elegant this year in spite of giving lots of big plants away. It will be crowded as usual. Boris used chicken wire and two thicknesses of plastic. Put brackets and nice shelves up instead of planks on cement blocks—really elegant outside of my bedroom door.

I'm taking Spanish lessons again and hoping some will sink in. We hope to take a jaunt to Guatemala when we are in Oaxaca this winter. Hope to leave here by December 10. I'm to spend two weeks in Berkeley with the Ickes for Halloween.

September 27

Light frost. Green squash, nasturtiums, beans, tomatoes, and dahlias gone.

October 4

Last week gorgeous, just as I first saw Santa Fe seventeen years ago. Today cloudy and rainy. Of course! I'm having the tour from Los Alamos. Boris installed one of those pottery "dog roaster" fireplaces from Oaxaca in a corner in my bedroom. It is darling, and it throws so much heat, really more than a fireplace—the whole thing gets hot. Boris hasn't been well all week. Everything he gets seems to go to his lungs. So no work and so much to do.

October 7

Cold and snowy. Summer has gone.

October 14

Really no aspen this year. Never saw that before. About half had turned, then we had cold, wind, and snow. The next day looking up to the mountains, it is bare—all gone.

October 15

Snowstorm. Another long winter with no fall.

November 7

Returned the second from a beautiful vacation with Ray and Miralotte. Now Boris is madly getting things together to take to Fort Worth. We have decided to give up the gallery in El Paso and try the Carlin Gallery in Fort Worth. His impressive *Elijah* is finished—sixteen-foot-tall, Corten-steel figure commissioned by Vivian Fiske to go to Fort Worth in February. It will be on display at the Art Museum until then. We leave for Mexico December 10. Boris is very tired, and we can hardly wait to get off.

Thanksgiving

Warm, springlike day. Having ten for dinner. Turkey, of course. The week seems to drag by before we leave. Boris is busy making a camper for the truck. Should be great for traveling and later for the dogs. They ruin the Volvo. Looks as though I may have to take Mau-Mau with us. She is ill off and on and I can't desert her after all these years. She counts so on me, especially when she isn't well, dear little thing.

December 6

Can't believe we'll be leaving in three days. Camper elegant. So excited. Thank the powers that be that we have had gorgeous New Mexico weather with so much to do. Come Thursday the tenth, let it snow.

1971

January 21

What a beautiful five weeks in wonderful Mexico. Only three and a half days back. One glorious summer day after another. Spoiled rotten by being served three delicious meals a day in the lovely La Sorpresa, with nothing to do but enjoy myself. Ray and Miralotte came for two weeks and stayed three. They are so enthusiastic that the four of us are dickering for some land.

While we were gone the temperature went down to twenty-six below zero for three nights and never crawled more than twelve degrees in the day. Many people were without heat or water. Many of our plants in the greenhouse froze, but Bobby had heat and water. *[Bobby Hughes was a very old and dear friend of mine from Glencoe, Illinois. He stayed in the house while we were gone. I'd known him since I was seventeen years old, through my brother. He was a clothes designer for the movies in Hollywood before he came to live in Santa Fe.]* The animals were all delighted to see us and all fine, which is the most important thing. Balmy weather since we've been back and we need moisture badly. Oh, for a good snow.

While we were at La Sorpresa, Mr. and Mrs. Norman Rockwell stayed there for three days. Absolutely charming people, great humor and fun. He looks like an Irish gnome, even though very tall and thin with a great mane of white hair. It's his sparkling pixie eyes, I think. His wife, Molly, is a darling. We got along fine, and I'm sure they will come to Santa Fe. *[They didn't come, but they sent us a lovely signed print of his.]* Also Frank Waters, the writer from Taos, was there briefly. Didn't really get to know him.

February 6–December 25, 1971

"We may finally finish the house!"

February 6

I'm so terribly excited. It looks as though we may finally go ahead and finish the house! *[That's a funny one. Nine years later it was finished.]* At least a starter with the bathroom in the back. Have known we would have to borrow to get it done and have decided it's now or never. So have gotten estimates and hope to go ahead in March. Also our dear friend John Fleming is coming down from Denver at the end of this month and will put electricity in my bedroom. *[That was the bedroom that started as a storeroom. I don't remember what I was doing for light.]* We have such a great thing in this old place, it seems wicked not to really fix it. How gorgeous it will be. Had a beautiful snow yesterday. Much colder today, beautiful sky.

February 24

The Flemings were here over the weekend and dear John wired my bedroom. It is like magic to just touch a switch and all is light. I really did love the candlelight, but it was impossible to dress after dark—makeup, hair, and so forth. Now I can sew or iron there or even have an electric heater. Such a friend, a great and wonderful guy. He plans to wire the back room when we get to it.

Hopefully we start the bathroom next month. Boris has decided to put up the walls around the bath instead of paying out $60 to $75 a day for a carpenter and the helper, which they always have to have. Had a nice check from Carlin Gallery in Fort Worth so at least can get the bathroom done without borrowing and perhaps we can manage the rest. How marvelous! The bath plumbing will run $1,200 to $1,500. That includes a forty-gallon hot water tank, kitchen plumbing, and fixtures.

Boris leaves with twelve-foot trailer March 8 for Fort Worth to take *Elijah*. When he returns I hope to make a quick trip to Berkeley.

March 13

Boris left yesterday without *Elijah*—to be delivered in May. He has to go to Fort Worth and then Palm Desert. Plans to be back Friday. I'm supposed to take off Monday the twenty-second for Berkeley. Still hoping to get the back fixed; not sure where the money will come from. Am having a hell of a time getting houses for the Foundation tour this year. Hope it works out. Refuse to have the same darn houses all the time.

April 10

Returned after two glorious weeks in Berkeley. Saw my first Greek belly dancer—wish I could do it. Had dinner last night with the sculptor Una Hanbury, whom we met several weeks ago. Then Manila O'Neal—she too is a grand person and I like what she does. *[She was just an acquaintance. I don't remember what it was she did.]*

We are in the midst of cleaning out the back room to make way for the plumbers Monday to start the bath and kitchen. Unbelievable mess and upheaval—wondering if it is worth it, if it is ever done. I'm sure it will be. It would be so much easier just to leave it, but as an investment it is the wise thing to do, so I guess we'll push on. Poor Boris is so damn tired of hard work. He hopes after this he can take it easy. After all, he'll be sixty-four next month.

When I was in San Francisco, I arranged for him to show at the Maxwell Gallery, which is in the middle of the city on Sutter Street and is well established—thirty years there. They are eager for his work. The director, Joan Wortsman, said it was very difficult to find competent sculptors. Do hope it leads to a more remunerative and easier life for Boris and his work.

It is dangerously dry. Snow almost gone on the mountains. Many things have been killed by the severe winter—pyracantha, butterfly bush, most of the roses—things that have taken seven to ten years to grow up. It is so sad. No peaches this year, and maybe nothing else.

April 12

It's started! I'm wondering if I would have done it if I had known what a mess it would be! *[This is putting in the back bathroom.]* A trench across the patio down through the *zaguán*—bricks, dirt, rocks piled high. Reminiscent of ten years ago when we first started the place—almost impossible to get to the bathroom *[up front]*. How complicated life has become with plumbing. How simple it was without it. Guess one's personal life wasn't simple, however. Anyway, when it's done, I'm sure it will be worth it. *[And it is!]* Of course, they have to take the plumbing all the way to the street because there isn't enough drop or something. So up goes the price. Doubtless it will run around $1,500 before they are through. Hope some money rolls our way before it's finished so I won't have to borrow. If all is paid that's owed us, we'll be OK. *[Owed from Boris's work, that is.]*

Had a grand time at Ann and Alan Vedder's Easter dinner last night.

April 13

Today's thrilling event: While digging to the sewer out front on Alto Street, the machine with the shovel broke the water main. Public Service turned off water, fixed rusty pipe, started to fill hole, and now it has broken again. La-di-da! Workman laughing as a fountain bursts up into the air. Where will it end and how much money?

The air hammer broke up a fourth of the cement floor in the back room to lay the pipes. Thick dust all over. To say nothing of what has happened to the floor. Don't miss tomorrow's thrilling episode.

April 16

In the meantime, the broken cement has been removed from the back room, ditch dug for pipes making piles of dirt, of course. Pipes being laid—naturally, sewer pipes and water pipes can't use the same trench, so here we go again across the patio and *zaguán* to the street. I should have waited until now to go away. Had to borrow $2,000 to see this through. Hope it will be enough.

April 17

Can't believe we're really getting started on the back. Horrible mess and ghastly expense. When we'll finish who knows, but it is a start. Monday the floor goes back, pipes are laid, then the fixtures. I even have an outside faucet in back now instead of just the one in the patio, which will certainly simplify watering. It will be in the greenhouse with a connection to the hot water heater so we can have warm water for the plants. Leave it to Gilbertson for fine touches. *[Actually, I never use it for that, but it is handy to bathe the dogs.]*

April 19

All is lovely and white with wet snow this A.M. Digging another trench—the same one, really, only deeper (against the law). Am walking a plank over it to the *[front]* bathroom. Each day I think it can't get worse but it does—also, a leak in the roof, burned-out valve in the truck, so it goes. Wonder what tomorrow will bring.

April 20

Today the whole front drive is up—piles of dirt, rocks, brick, and mud. Is there no end? They are hooking up the new plumbing to the meter instead of to the existing pipes of the front bathroom, so it's all new. In the winter we can drain the water and do away with the freezing. *[As it turned out, we never did that—I just turn on the heater.]*

April 21

No one showed up. Still walking the plank from this room *[sala]* to bathroom over deep trench and piles of dirt.

April 22

Laid pipe to front and filled in trench—thank God! Don't know when poor Boris will get the drive in front relayed or bricks in *zaguán*. Poor guy! He has to put up the new bathroom walls so they can install fixtures. Paid George Richey, the plumber, $1,296.91 for rough-in. The rest will be around $600 to $700. Good thing I borrowed $2,000.

April 23

Cement was poured, and floor in back finished today.

April 25

Boris has been relaying drive out front. Good thing he is so strong; no one else could do it to suit him. New gravel in patio and the patio will all be put back together again. I worked on the outside all day in the glorious sun.

May 2

Boris's sixty-fourth birthday. He certainly doesn't seem or look it; but the older we get, the younger older age seems. He is doing only things he wants to do today, which is "horticulturing." Had a coffee cake for breakfast and tonight a giant strawberry shortcake with candles.

May 8

Ordered bathroom fixtures and kitchen counter at Sears today.

May 17

Ordered two lovely doors from Decor in Juárez *[for my bedroom]*. Also bought tiles for around the tub—five cents for plain and fifteen cents for decorated. Had a nice holiday, beautiful drive. Left at 5 A.M., back at 10:30 P.M. Boris still not at his own work. Front finished but everywhere I look there are things to be done. If that back ever gets any further, I'll be surprised.

May 18

Cold, dark day. We are again in the spring purgatory. New gravel all spread in back; looks wonderful. All awaits decent weather to get the plants out of the greenhouse and annuals put in. Tired, so tired. Tired of never getting things done, tired of all the things Boris never does, tired of Pancho screaming, tired of everything.

May 19

There was ice on the birdbath this morning. There was frost on the grass. Poor birds.

May 23

Dark and cold again, nerve-wracking wind. I guess we will just all blow away with the dry land.

May 30

After emptying the greenhouse, tonight we haul everything back in, and that is a job. Going down to the thirties tonight and we can't take a chance of losing everything. Just hope what I planted will survive. Still no moisture. What a year!

May 31

It didn't frost. Hope it is over with. Glorious summer day today.

June 6

Believe summer is here; greenhouse down; all looks lovely. Just hope we have water to keep it alive. It's serious now. Our country is burning up. A huge fire out of control in the Jémez—so far three thousand acres. Sky hanging with smoke.

June 8

After burning five thousand acres, the Jémez fire is under control. A reporter and photographer from the *Albuquerque Journal* took pictures for my tour tomorrow; *New Mexican* the same. Should bring the people in. Hope all goes well. It hasn't been easy this year; 518 Alto not on it, thank God.

June 17

Still no rain. A week from today is the tour.

June 25

It's over and a great success—120 people each day—all delighted. Netted $886 on tour. No rain, very hot.

June 28

Still no rain. Beautiful summer days. So dry.

June 30

Twelve thousand acres burned in Pecos Wilderness. The fire is still burning. So tragic.

July 2

For three days now, there have been heavenly afternoon thundershowers. So welcome.

July 13

No more rain. Very hot. Boris left for Palm Desert last night to get the large bird. Hopes to be back Friday. I slept in the patio last night where it was cooler. Could hardly get to sleep because looking up at the stars was so fascinating and provoked many thoughts.

July 16

No rain. Still hot. Boris expects to be back tonight. Have loved being alone this week. It's good for what ails you to have solitude occasionally. The water shortage is critical.

July 19

Can't believe it—it's raining. The fragrance of it, the sound, the feel! Such a wonderful relief.

July 21

Shower last night again, and now another one.

July 30

No rain for several days. John Fleming is here with us. The dear is wiring the back building in preparation for the walls to go up for the bath. Can't believe it is going ahead. Have hired the walls and ceiling done. Will start hopefully next week.

We're planning to rent Eloisa's house to sleep in because Ray and Miralotte are coming. After Ray and Miralotte leave the Hutners arrive. *[The company never stopped; between people and trips, fixing the house went very slowly.]*

August 2

Bathroom goes on. Carpenter arrived this A.M. It's all so great. Cutting the window in the wall *[for the bathroom]*.

August 3

Again I say, is it worth it? The mess and the expense? The worst thing is cutting the window in my vine and the Solomon's seal crushed. It will come back next year, I know. Now I wonder why we just didn't have a skylight and vent, yet a window is nice. *[To put that small bathroom window in they had to cut the vine that was on the outside wall.]*

Walt and Barbara Hutner arrive tomorrow.

August 10

Carpenter's work, practically all, has to be done over. Unbelievably unsatisfactory job—insulation in wrong; window unfinished; door hung wrong; a mess left behind, along with breaking the ceiling fan.

Today the plumbers arrive and it's a shambles again. Knocking places in the wall for gas. Another hole in the roof for the water-heater vent. Really, if I had known, I wouldn't have had the courage to do this. And the expense!

August 12

Bathroom will be functioning. Hot water, too, but not finished—tiles, floor, wallpaper, etc. *[left to be done]*. Monday the sixteenth Ray and Miralotte arrive. It looks as though we would have Eloisa's house. She has cleaned it all up nicely. This morning I awoke to a phenomenon for us— fog! Thick fog, and all so beautifully quiet and still.

September 6

Ray and Miralotte have been here three weeks and we have loved it. Many people have come to see us this summer, including the Spanish opera star Mirna Lacambra, a great gal from Barcelona. She starred in *Yerma*.* Also a husband and wife piano team, the Babins.

---

*Yerma: Opera by Brazilian composer Heitor Villa-Lobos (1887–1959). Written, 1950s. Based on play by Spanish poet and dramatist Federico García Lorca (1898–1936). World premier, Santa Fe Opera, 1971, with Spanish singer Mirna Lacambra.

October 9

Still no hard freeze. Boris has finished the Corten-steel giraffe. It goes to Maxwell's. Just returned from an opening at Randall Davey's Gallery. Such a perfect place—perfect peace, quiet, beauty. Kate Cullum is a really great person. Davey was a wonderful artist. His work is beautiful. *[Kate Cullum was his sister-in-law. He left the house to her. She sold it to the Audubon Society.]*

October 17

Boris won't get off until the nineteenth. His things are truly beautiful—the large Corten-steel-and-bronze giraffe and two large birds, which are different than any he has done. They are absolutely perfect, simple, and thrilling. Also, his shorebirds, small owls, and small birds, and even the little mice, too, are adorable. *[This was for the Maxwell Gallery in San Francisco.]* I'm trying to get a brochure together. It is almost next to impossible to corral Boris to tell me what to say; always some excuse, but I am determined to get it going while he is gone. He hates this but, unfortunately, it is necessary.

October 19

It's been really cold for two nights now. Boris plans to leave tonight. He's also taking some of our friend Malcolm Alexander's work, who is having a show at Maxwell's next month. Then I plan to get on my broomstick and go to Berkeley for Halloween.

October 22

Poor, dear, tired Boris. He was so looking forward to a peaceful, pleasant trip. The truck broke down in Williams, Arizona, and had to be towed in. No parts. Toyota in Los Angeles would only send them to a dealer who was in Flagstaff, a hundred miles away. He was still waiting yesterday and decided to rent a truck, reload, and be off. I wired him $300. Why do such things have to happen? Thank God for the $3,000 Ray and Miralotte gave us in September.

Santa Fe is getting so big. Traffic at all times is awful. The Hilton Hotel is going up only one block east of us. Model Cities is going to pave

Alto Street.* All the charm of the whole town is going fast. Will even have smog before long, I suppose. Everyone is running away from it in other cities and will bring it here. Too bad.

October 23

A beautiful, warm rain all night. Dark today. Boris called yesterday. He's waiting to leave today and take the parts with him. Hope they have them. The truck he was supposed to get from Flagstaff broke down before he was to get it—thank heaven for that—so they sent him a large Pontiac with automatic transmission, which he never could cope with. Always stepping on the brake, searching for a clutch, throwing everything at the windshield. However, he made it, and I'm sure he will make it back to Williams.

October 26

The story isn't finished yet. Boris left San Francisco yesterday unable to find the part he needs for the truck. Not even salvage yards. He plans to leave the truck and come back by bus unless by some miracle a part appears. What a mess. I really have no business going to San Francisco; maybe I won't. Just picked a bouquet of calendulas in the snow.

October 27

Boris arrived in Flagstaff to find that the parts, all but one small important one, had come, but since the owner's wife had shot him—not dead but seriously—the night before, no one knew where they were. They finally found them in a box marked "windshield wipers" but without the other part, so nothing can be done. If it comes by tonight, he will wait for it to be fixed. The train to Lamy arriving tomorrow afternoon. Will I still get away? *[I don't understand that. I usually flew.]*

---

*Model Cities: Urban redevelopment and renewal program aimed at revitalizing central-city areas by attacking "urban blight" with massive federal financial aid, late 1960s, early 1970s. In Santa Fe the program was undertaken at the western edge of the downtown area. Large sections were cleared of small old buildings and replaced with larger new ones. The Hilton Hotel, a three-story, split-level building at 100 Sandoval Street, opened in January 1973. The historic Ortiz Houses, around the corner on San Francisco Street, were remodeled and incorporated into the new hotel.

November 20

Boris did get back with the truck. I took off on the twenty-ninth; arrived home November 15.

December 4

Had a most pleasant evening with the Vedders. Eliot Porter, the photographer for the Sierra Club, and his wife, Aline, were there. Nice couple. *[Eliot was an old friend of Ray Ickes. They were both from Winnetka, Illinois.]* Also the Liebersons, who are great people. *[Mrs. Lieberson was a ballet dancer; Vera Zorina was her stage name. We met them through the Vedders. She may have performed at the opera.]* Unfortunately, we will not be going to Mexico for Christmas; perhaps not at all.

December 14

Tomorrow it's fifty-seven years for me. Seems absolutely impossible a year ago tonight we slept in the truck on the road to Oaxaca, unable to find a place to stay, and was it cold! Christmas Eve at the Vedders.

December 19

Had a pleasant evening at Eliot and Aline Porter's. What a lovely home, tucked away among old cottonwoods in Tesuque. Thirty-seven years ago today Hal and I were married. Another world, another lifetime. *[He was my first husband, Harold Marks.]*

December 23

Boris is having his yearly collapse. It seems each year around this time he gives out. Hope rest will restore him, which he has been doing nothing but for two days.

Christmas Day

Boris feels much better. Rest was what he needed. Today is like a perfect spring day. Took a long, beautiful walk among the arroyos and piñons with the dogs. How they loved it, and so did I. Mau-Mau has been better this last year than she has been for years. Sure it is the gravel I put on her seeds every day.

January 4, 1972–January 19, 1977

"One thing actually finished"

January 4

This is a winter! More snow last night and ten degrees below. Now only ten above at 3 P.M.

January 23

Boris feeling fine, thank God. John and Celeste Fleming are here for the weekend. John finished wiring the bathroom fixtures, switches, and so forth. Boris working on tiles. Hallelujah! Maybe it will get finished one day. I'm leaving for Oaxaca, Mitla, the second of February. Boris insists I go to stir up the property deal. He is so anxious to get going on the place there. Ray and Miralotte are taking me to the Yucatán—Mérida—the last week of our stay to see the Mayan ruins. We will fly from Oaxaca. And then the first part of April, Jean is taking me to Majorca to see her sister Kitty. How can I be so lucky? This is my year, I guess. Have waited all these years to travel; then—poof!—all at once.

February 1

Off tomorrow for Mexico. Albuquerque to San Antonio to Mexico City overnight to Oaxaca first thing in the morning. I'll believe it when I get there—it's all like a dream.

March 4

Home again a week ago. It all seems dreamlike—such a glorious trip. The ruins in the Yucatán are impossible to describe—the grandeur, the proportions, the settings. The land deal goes along slowly; hope by Christmas it will be settled. Robins are twittering and we are having glorious spring weather, but will it last?

Boris hopes to leave with *Elijah* in a week or so—Wolf! Wolf! Then when he returns Jean and I take off for Majorca.

March 8

This glorious unseasonable weather has brought the apricot out full bloom. Hundreds of bees buzz around it. *[We have so few bees anymore. It's scary.]*

March 18

Jean brought over my tickets today. How exciting. I have a stomachache over the prospect.

March 21

Elijah is loaded in the van. It fits. Hallelujah! Boris wants to finish a giraffe before he takes off. Carlin Gallery has done so well he wants to take at least three pieces there.

March 23

Six A.M. and it's raining. How perfect that I got all of the goat manure on everything yesterday. Peach trees a haze of pink; apple buds all pink. Daffodils and tulips out. Nothing like spring—it's so very beautiful. Boris left yesterday.

March 27

Cold and overcast. Supposed to be a hard freeze tonight.

March 28

Boris arrived home this morning at 12:30 bearing a huge bunch of lilacs gathered for me along the way. He is tired, and his wind is bad. Now that *Elijah* is set, he'll be able to relax and feel better. I have a feeling this breathing problem is pressure and/or emotional. It is going to be eighteen degrees tonight. How cruel!

April 3

Can't believe it—day after tomorrow Jean and I take off for Spain.

May 5

Majorca is indeed a paradise—the old stone houses tucked among the terraced olive groves. Was a sore temptation to just stay.

May 19

This never-ending wind! Boris's work goes very slowly.

May 26

Alto Street and 518 are never going to be the same. We will be living in the middle of a big city. Horrible Hilton Hotel is going up a block away. Urban Renewal—the worst thing that has happened to Santa Fe—is going to blacktop Alto Street. That alone wouldn't be bad, but, alas, they are putting in curbs and sidewalks. Guess this is supposed to be progress and elegance. No sense of their heritage or ethics. I'm fighting to keep the parking space in front and not to have curbing or sidewalks in front. Hope it won't be a losing battle. *[It was. Alto was blacktopped, with curbs and sidewalks. However, I refused to give them enough room to make the sidewalk. It's not more than a foot wide at the west end of my property.]*

May 29

Rain! Mickey is very sick because I gave him a bone last week. *[He recovered.]*

June 12

Boris left at 1 A.M. driving to Illinois. *[Time meant nothing to Boris.]* He dreaded the trip and I hated to see him go, mainly because of his breathing difficulties. I know it frightens him when he is away from home alone. Want to get the walls washed and the floor painted—a job I dread.

June 17

Floor done—looks lovely. Should have painted the walls also; it's like putting on dirty underwear after a bath. But now with the furniture back and the floor so pretty, I don't notice the walls. Tomorrow the publicity for my house tour is coming out in the *New Mexican* and the *Albuquerque Journal.* Have my fingers crossed; will be glad when it's over.

June 22

Today is the day! A lovely morning even though we need rain desperately. Hope we won't have any until Sunday or at least after 4 P.M. tomorrow. Have four buses full for today—turning people away. Also for tomorrow.

Great publicity both here and in Albuquerque. Boris called Tuesday. Sounds as though he is having a marvelous time.

June 24

Tour over and a great success. Netted more than $1,000—308 people all together. Had a half-hour rain after it was over. How lucky can you be? *[Another house tour for the Foundation.]* No word from Boris.

June 27

Boris arrived home yesterday before noon. Everyone glad to see each other. He brought back some absolutely magnificent Korean and Japanese ceramic pieces—old and exquisite—also Chinese scrolls, many of his drawings, a beautiful stone bowl that he did many years ago, and the original bison slate carving. The truck, as you can imagine, was bulging. *[The Korean and Japanese pieces had belonged to his brother, Bud, who had studied in Japan. I sold those to keep going and to get the book printed about Boris's work. I sold an old Korean scroll for $1,000. Of course, it was all after Boris died; he'd never sell anything no matter what.]*

July 17

Boris takes off tomorrow to get the rest of the tiles for the bathroom.

Yesterday I had a notice from the State Planning Office that 518 was on the State Registry of Historic Buildings. Today Dr. Myra Ellen Jenkins from the State Archives, who documented the house, called to inform me that it is also on the National Registry—so now we are a "monument."

August 27

Busy, busy. Ray arrives today.

September 1

Fiesta starts tonight. Thunderstorm is going on. It doesn't mean a damn thing to me. Boris home tomorrow, to return to Denver in a week for another check. His lungs are in bad shape due to years of smoking and also the fumes from his work. He is to do exercises and use a machine four times a day to pump oxygen into his lungs. Thank God for Medicare.

Had a call from Mitla offering me the job of managing La Sorpresa. Most flattering but doubt very much that I will take it. I don't believe we'd want to live there permanently, and it would be most confining.

September 4

Boris is feeling so very much better for using this oxygen machine several times a day. Hope he sticks with it. He returns to Denver the sixth for further tests. Again, thank God for Medicare. Boris has finally consented to my getting rid of Pancho, the screamer. Now to try and find a good home for her. Can't just dump the poor bird.

September 10

Pancho is gone—for a try, anyway—to a gal here who has a house built around her animals, Marjorie Gold. Pancho seems very happy, she says, because of all the other birds. She is a bird's bird. *[Pancho should have been Pancha. She was a parrot that was not interesting, not tame, and happier being with other birds.]*

October 7

Boris still has no real verdict or cure. Took oxygen from a machine four times a day but decided he was worse for it. Stopped and feels better. Supposed to go to Denver this week, but he may say to hell with it since they do nothing for him except charge great amounts of money.

Urban Renewal, damn them, is fixing the García house next door on the west, and it looks like hell. Alto Street is changing character so fast. No street paving yet but curbs are in. Of course, two cars can't pass because of the curbs, which was obvious to me. It will have to be a one-way street. *[It isn't.]*

October 15

Boris arrived home last night. He's still sleeping so I haven't talked to him. Talked to Dr. John Fleming on the phone yesterday, and he seems quite encouraged over Boris's health. The enlargement on his lung hasn't grown over four years so he is sure there is nothing to worry about there. The lung damage, though, can't be repaired; but he feels that with medication the spasms can be controlled so he won't have much pain.

November 20

Never have we had so much moisture. It hasn't stopped since it started in early August, and now we are having a blizzard after eight inches of snow two days ago. We are having eight here for Thanksgiving; that is, if everyone isn't snowed in.

Boris hopes to leave for Denver Saturday the twenty-fifth to have a checkup. Then he is to fly with John Fleming to San Francisco to get his sculpture at the Maxwell Gallery, which has been the biggest disappointment in our lives, as far as galleries go. John is having the big pieces crated and sent air express to Denver to be there when they return Thursday. Friday he is having a party for Boris and expects to sell most of it. Such friends we have!

Speaking of friends, Ray expects to come for a couple of weeks next month while Miralotte is with Andrea when she has her baby. *[Andrea was Ray and Miralotte's daughter.]* Boris is feeling much better since he uses the oxygen machine several times a day. His work is almost nil, though. He can't seem to get into it. Sidewalk curbs and blacktop in. Street much narrower; looks horribly civilized.

December 6

Ray arrived a week ago and plans to be here until the sixteenth. Good having him here. Boris was in Denver. He and John Fleming flew to San Francisco to get his work from Maxwell's and also the big birds off the USS *President Cleveland* because the American President Lines is giving up passenger service. *[Dr. Fleming bought those birds and still has them in Denver.]* At John's party, they sold all but one piece of the things they brought back so that is most encouraging to Boris. He still doesn't feel too well.

December 15

Another birthday—fifty-eight today. Am finding it impossible to believe. If I never looked in the mirror, I wouldn't believe it. *[Was I ever that young?]* Received many cards and presents. Boris gave me a gorgeous, old Afghanistan silver necklace, like a belly dancer might wear. It jingles when

I move and is permeated with exotic incense. Love it! Little Vixen is nine today. Still full of life and health but looking a bit old around the face. Who isn't?

December 22

Never have I felt or seen such a lack of Christmas spirit. Of course, I haven't liked it for years, but who could, with this tragic hate and destruction going on. The goddamned people who believed that lying bastard Nixon about peace before the election! It's worse now than ever with the whole world hating our guts. Russia and China are threatening to cancel all relations with us. Sometimes I am so ashamed of being an American.

It looks as though we would leave for Mexico January 25 and meet Ray and Miralotte in Mitla. Hope to get something going on the property. A Mrs. Joiner will stay here for $25 a week. *[Now I pay $20 a day for a sitter!]* Nell will take care of my dear Mau-Mau, whom I am loathe to leave. *[I think Nell's name was Campbell. Later she married my brother.]* Sister Dot is here with Karin. Has decided to buy into El Castillo retirement apartments and will move back in May. It will be good to have her near.

Christmas

What a farce! What a void! Absolutely no hint of feeling on this day. Just another holiday. The Vietnam War goes on endlessly, it seems. No amount of protest helps. Nothing helps. Those bastards in Washington do as they damn well please. I tried to go through some of the motions by putting *luminarias* across the roof and wall in front, wreaths on the windows, roping around the gate. It did look so sweet and lovely last night with all the candles flickering in the brown paper bags. Went to the Vedders for dinner.

1973

January 1

Last week, Eugenie Shonnard, Dot, and I went to San Ildefonso Pueblo to see María *[Martínez]*, the potter—a friend of Eugenie. A man, a son, no doubt, came to the door and informed us that María was in California.

We were so disappointed, but it seems María was sitting where she could see who it was and we were welcomed in. What a beautiful, wonderful, simple person she is—eighty-six and her mind is sharp. You wouldn't believe she has been honored all over the world for her work. It was truly a wonderful experience to meet her.

May decide to take Mau-Mau with us to Mexico. Hate the thought of leaving the dear thing. She is so dependent on me. She's going on eighteen—all those years together. Poor little crippled bird. She dozes here at my elbow as I write.

January 15

Ray arrives tomorrow for a couple of days. He is offering his legal knowledge to an organization in Albuquerque that defends the Indians. Such a wonderful cause.

It has finally decided to warm up. Mud is everywhere. Boris and I have both had ghastly and tenacious colds. Never had such a one. Have decided to take Mau-Mau over to Nell's. Will take her there tomorrow for a couple of days' trial run. Nell has a lovely, sunny solarium with a parrot. Mau-Mau will be very happy.

We plan to spend three weeks in Guatemala—two, really, three from time we leave Mitla and get back. Just the thought of the markets with their fabulous textiles is amazing. We will be driving our good old faithful Volvo all the way. It has forty-five thousand miles over one hundred thousand. Seems in beautiful shape. *[That car still runs; it is sitting out back.]*

March 17 (St. Patrick's Day)

Arrived here yesterday after seven weeks traveling seven thousand miles in the good old Volvo. No mechanical trouble, just tires—had to buy four new ones. An interesting but exhausting trip. The lush green jungles of Tikal with the Mayan ruins; spider and howler monkeys swinging in the treetops; dozens of gorgeous parrots; and many other exotic birds. Three days on the tropical island in Rio Dulce was a great experience. We had the adventure of seeing volcanos erupting near Guatemala City—shooting black clouds of dust thirty-five thousand feet and covering everything with layers of evil-looking, black lava dust. It was such a depressing sight.

The house in Mitla will be under way soon if all goes as planned. How it will all work out only God knows. Ray is financing the whole thing for we can't—so it won't be ours. We can't even finish the back at 518 Alto, and it doesn't look very hopeful that we ever will. The dollar is worth very little now. Prices are unreal, and no sculpture being sold. Fortunately, Boris has orders (same ones he has had for years), so if they ever get done we will have some money coming in for a while. The future doesn't look all that bright. Boris felt much better on the trip; hope he continues to.

Vixen and Mickey are fine—delighted to have us home. Nell took excellent care of dear little Mau-Mau, who thrived on all the attention and good care.

Weather, while we were gone, was ghastly. I am eager to get at the outside work, of which there is plenty. Should have gotten my peas in today but will have to wait till next week. *[I always tried to plant my peas on St. Patrick's Day.]*

March 24

Yet another snowstorm, another and another. Going on since Halloween. The only good thing about it—since I don't ski—is that the moisture has actually reached the subsoil. These dark, cold days are depressing. They go on and on but maybe will keep the trees from blooming too early and there will be fruit for a change.

The mess out in front is still as the Urban Renewal left it last fall: rocks piled up in the drive and parking space; walls half torn down; ditch so the parking space can't be used; survey stakes still not replaced. It looks like hell and I'm pretty damn sick of it. Seems everything is wrong, so won't go on.

March 26

A glorious, brilliant, shining day. Beautiful sky and sun! Will be able to work outside today. Maybe even plant my peas. *[You can see, it's the cloudy weather that depresses me. My spirits rise with the sun.]*

March 27

Did get my peas in. Today cold, dark, and snow.

March 30

Still snowing.

March 31

6:30 A.M. The sun is shining; the sky is blue; a robin sings; and so do I.

April 3

The last two days have been the usual cold, dark, and snowy. Miserable, horrible storms. Floods all over the country. *[That's interesting; the same thing happened this year, twenty-four years later in 1997.]* This A.M. is still cold—twenty-five degrees—but the sun is out and the sky is blue. May it last!

April 5

Still clear but cold. Spread manure; started to clean up outside. A year ago tonight, Jean and I were in Barcelona. Seems impossible.

April 8

Sunday, 6 A.M. Four inches of fresh snow on the ground, fifteen degrees. Will it never end?

April 13

The last two days have been beautiful. Worked outdoors. Daffodils and tulips budding. Greenhouse lovely. Magenta cactus and red ones blooming.

April 15

Cold and snow flurries again. Have lettuce and carrots in; the rest wait until who knows when.

April 18

Turned cold after two lovely days. Dark as evening at 2 P.M. with a terrific wind raging, blowing up a dust storm. *[How can there be dust after all that snow?]* They are at last fixing the walk in front.

April 21

After more snow, temperature dropped to twenty degrees. Everything literally frozen solid. It is sickening to see the daffodils and tulips lying on the ground. Suppose all the buds got it, too. Delphinium leaves are solid ice. Will they survive? How cruel on the poor little birds. Tomorrow is Easter, and I am working at the flower shop today to get my mind off this ghastly, sickening weather.

May 1

Cold, windy, and cloudy. Expect snow. Heard a hummingbird zoom by two days ago. Where, oh where, is he and how can he survive? Poor creatures and blossoms.

Boris is taking off for the scenic route to and from Juárez tomorrow, his sixty-sixth birthday. He bought a new truck, a red Datsun. The Toyota needed a lot of work and in Mexico they don't have Toyotas. Are there Datsuns?

Gertrude Blom, an anthropologist from San Cristóbal de las Casas in Mexico, is coming over this morning. She lectures here tonight.

May 5

More rain last night. Ice on the birdbath this A.M. Had an estimate yesterday from two women from El Valle to do the adobe plaster. Front and two walls of patio. More than $500. It would be $100 a day for two of them and maybe would take more than five or six days; so we'll forget it. If we can, we'll do it ourselves. The electrician will fix the wiring for $161—a new circuit box and so forth that must be done.

May 13

The river is exciting, beautiful. As a result of all the snow last winter, it is roaring. You can hear it from here. For weeks now it has been running. Each day getting higher and swifter until now it is almost up to the top. It is raining and has been all night, which will add to its contents. And the blossoms—I've never seen them so utterly gorgeous. It's almost more than one can stand, the beauty of it all.

Busy on the tour. A lot of work, but guess it is worth it. June 21 and 22—Olive Rush, Eugenie Shonnard, the Randall Davey, and the Van Soelens. *[Those are the houses on the tour.]*

May 21

I'm not waiting any longer to finish the bathroom. Boris has too much to do anyway, so today some men are finishing the tile and floor. Then I'll get someone to put up the wallpaper. Can't believe it! One thing will be finished. Gorgeous weather; greenhouse almost emptied. *[Because it was May, we emptied the greenhouse and took the plastic down.]* The place has never looked so beautiful. Blossoms fantastic. Such a wonderful place this is.

May 22

Very cool, fifty degrees, windy, dark, and storm-threatening. How quickly it can change. If we should have frost this place would be a catastrophe. All my plants are out from the greenhouse, annuals in. Please . . .

May 27

Cruel, cruel nature. After a dark, cold day yesterday, with a ghastly wind tearing everything to bits, it went down to almost freezing last night. Poor birds and plants. How does the dear, sweet little hummingbird survive? Just saw him at the feeder. When will it stay warm? I am so sick of cold.

June 10

Summer at last. Lovely warm days, balmy, starlit nights. Gardens beautiful, even though annuals have done nothing. Oriental poppies ready to burst, roses covered with buds. Castilian and Austrian copper are breathtaking. *[These roses started from little shoots that Olive Rush gave me. I moved the shoots all over the garden. They are especially magnificent this year.]*

Tile up. Floor in, in the bath. No wallpaper yet. Wall has to be fixed and sanded, so no telling if and when it will get done. It looks great, though. Almost finished. *[We went to Juárez for the tile.]*

Water the garden constantly in spite of all the moisture. River still tearing along.

June 18

1:30 A.M. My dear, sweet, wonderful Mau-Mau is dead. *[Even now I can't think of it; I don't think I'll be able to read this.]* Long live Mau-Mau! This house will truly be haunted now. Her sweet, clear, little voice and whistle will still be everywhere. There will never be another Mau-Mau. She couldn't eat yesterday, but even so her spirits were good. I put her in her basket for the night and at one o'clock I got up to see how she was. She could hardly move. I picked her up and held her in my arms; it wasn't more than five minutes. She tried to flap her wings, made a small sound, and was gone.

June 26

Still expect to find my precious little Mau-Mau when I come home. There are so many things that I say that she said; things that I do that she commented on. I've learned a great deal from that little bird in eighteen and a half years. Her acceptance of all her illness and deformities, her endless, beautiful spirit through everything. In death I have really seen that when life or soul has left the body, it is no longer the person or animal. It could have been any parrot—Mau-Mau was gone. I put the little thing in her cozy little basket, which she always loved, and we buried her under the tamarisk in the patio.

The tour as usual was a great success. Sold out days ahead. Turned people away. Netted more than $1,000. Four full buses each day. Perfect weather.

Eight P.M. We are having a glorious thunderstorm. Sitting under the back *portal* watching the green trees bending and waving in the wind against a black sky. Jagged lightning in all directions, thunder cracking and rumbling constantly, rain beating down on the roof. Beautiful. How happy all the growing things must be. It has been very hot all week— of course, I love it.

July 5

Still no break in the heat. No rain. I water all day. Boris took off for Denver this A.M. delivering two pieces. The one for the Kochs is exquisite—four bronze birds—and Dr. Pfister's two Corten-steel birds. *[The Kochs and Dr. Pfister were clients from Denver who bought a lot of Boris's work. We didn't know them personally.]*

169

July 19

A phenomenon. Fog at 6:30 A.M. It is beautiful and something we rarely see. Everything is dripping and laden down with moisture from all the tremendous rains we have had.

July 21

Again to the exact day, the rufous hummingbirds are back. More downpours; haven't watered for a week. However, the hail yesterday made a shambles of my vegetable garden.

August 12

Paper hung in bathroom. Looks wonderful. One thing actually finished. The Flemings and the Bartons are here. Have been for a week. Staying at the Hilton. *[Dr. Barton was a physician from Denver. He and his wife were friends of the Flemings. The Bartons often came down with the Flemings for the opera.]* Such wonderful friends we have. Ray Ickes arrives a week from tomorrow.

September 1

It has been cold and rainy for the last two days. Such a short summer, it is depressing. Hope the weekend is clear for all the people who are counting on Fiesta.

September 10

Gloom and sadness hangs over 518. There will have to be a change somehow. Think I will have to get a job. For one thing sure, there will be no Mexico this year.

September 15

My strange carrion plant, or starfish cactus, is in bloom. Ten buds. Fantastic flowers—huge and smell like something dead. Flies by the dozen swarm all around them.

Boris and Bob Brodkey are going to start putting up the *vigas* in the back building tomorrow. We've had them out back for twelve years—well seasoned, I must say. A good thing, for even if we could find them now, we couldn't afford them. They *[Bob and Boris]* are in the back room now. Hoping to get it going to save fuel this winter since by all reports it will be scarce and expensive. Doesn't look as though we would go anywhere for some time. Boris's work, the house, the *dinero*.

September 17

Six *vigas* in. Can't believe it. Absolutely perfect weather as it was twenty years ago when I first fell in love with Santa Fe.

October 2

Still no killing frost. Perfect fall weather just like it's supposed to be. Am working a couple of days doing dried arrangements for Flor-Al. She wants me part-time all winter; so does Dressman's at $4 an hour. I may do it after the freeze. Busy freezing applesauce, green chili.

November 6

Still picking daisies in the patio. Most things in back have been nipped by frost, but no really cold weather yet. Returned last week from my annual trip to Berkeley for Halloween. The children these days see so much horror and violence at the movies and on TV that it is almost impossible to frighten them, so it was sort of a bust. Had a grand time, though.

Boris hopes to get Mr. Johnson's birds for Boettcher School in Denver finished this month and delivered. *[I think Mr. Johnson bought them for the school.]* We have had practically no income for months. Living on $200 from Mrs. Koch and drawing from savings. Nothing from galleries. Will start work again a couple of days a week to help. Ashamed to say, I hate it.

November 12

Still no frost in patio and still picking daisies. Have my cuttings all potted. Seems so ridiculous when it is still like summer outside to be potting up plants for next spring. Must have fifty or more.

An archaeologist is coming for lunch tomorrow to see about digging out the well. My fingers are crossed. Hope he thinks it would be worth the bother. Another unbelievable, gorgeous, warm day.

November 23

Had Thanksgiving with Nell and Brud. We are still having such beautiful weather. Man from museum has not come. Probably won't. Our dear friends Ray and Miralotte may be here for Christmas. Don't know what we would do without them. Ray, of course, has financed all of the Mitla house, which we can hardly wait to get to—hopefully in February—and for the last two years has saved our lives by presenting us with $3,000 a year. This year he sent $2,000, but I have returned $1,000. We'll make it. Our friends, especially Ray and Miralotte, are so much more devoted and helpful than my family. I never receive anything from my two rich sisters who could easily help and, I think, with pleasure. It looks as though they are closing in on Nixon.* I certainly hope so. This energy shortage is crucial.** It looks like gas rationing.

December 15

Another year and I'll be sixty. Impossible. Had a nice quiet day. Instead of going out to dinner, Boris bought a two-and-a-half-inch steak for dinner. Boy, was it good. He goes to Denver day after tomorrow, with the birds for the school. Should be back the twenty-first or the twenty-

---

*"Closing in on Nixon": President Richard M. Nixon had won reelection in a 1972 landslide over Democratic, antiwar candidate George McGovern. In May 1973, a Senate panel began hearings into Nixon administration efforts to cover up efforts to spy on Democrats during the election, the scandal that began with the discovery of a break-in into Democratic national headquarters in the Watergate complex. By November incriminating audiotapes had been discovered and a new special prosecutor named. In the summer of 1974, facing almost certain impeachment by the U.S. House of Representatives, Nixon became the first president to resign.

**"Energy shortage": In October 1973, Middle East oil-producing countries imposed an embargo on shipments of oil to the United States to protest American support of Israel, vowing to steadily cut production and sales until Israel evacuated the lands captured in the 1967 war. The retail price of gasoline was expected to top fifty cents a gallon.

second. Looking forward to comet Kohoutek, which we should be able to see at the end of the month; also to Ray's visit.*

December 22

Boris called from Denver saying he would be a day later, naturally. He said he is bringing me a bird, a canary. I am so worried—that long trip, so cold for it in a box. Why doesn't he come? Our creatures are so dependent on us, such a responsibility. Please may the bird survive.

1974

January 2

Snow a foot deep. Beautiful but confining. With chains on the truck we can take the dogs walking and it's truly beautiful among the piñons and the junipers. Boris brought back two birds, and they both sing all morning. Had to put them in separate cages—being male, they fought when together.

January 8

Forgot to note that Nell and Brud were married December 26. It's great. Nell is a grand and wonderful gal, and they seem so happy.

January 20

Snow almost gone. Have had some lovely, sunny days. We hope to take off for Mexico February 4. Thelma will be back to take over here. She is the perfect house sitter and loves the dogs. Even lets Mickey share her bed, as I do. *[He was the biggest dog I ever had and the only one that ever slept on the bed with me.]* Hate leaving them so long—six weeks—but we must see about our little house in Mitla, where we hope to stay.

February 1

I am pleased to hear from John Fleming about Boris. Today Boris is hav-

---

*Kohoutek: Comet that was unusually bright when discovered out beyond Jupiter. Visible to the naked eye from end of November 1973 until late January 1974. Although touted as the comet of the century, didn't live up to expectations.

ing a prostate operation in Denver. He flew up there four days ago in great pain. This has been bothering him for a year. Of course, his breathing problems complicate the whole thing. Poor dear, how he loathes anything like this. It always seems strange around here when he is gone. He is so much a part of it; more so than I. May all go well. No telling if, or when, he'll get off for Mexico. We're so looking forward to it.

February 7

Boris leaves the hospital today to spend seven to ten days with our dear friends, the Flemings, then will be home. He is feeling fine considering the cold, miserable weather. Have painted front bath and now am sewing.

February 14 (Valentine's Day)

Boris has been home two days. He's in good spirits but still bleeding. We still hope that by March 1 we can leave. Just have to wait and see.

February 18

No bleeding since last Thursday. We will talk to the doctor and hope to leave the twenty-eighth. We'll believe it when we are gone. Boris feels so well and in fine spirits.

April 20

Mother's birthday. Taking violets over to Brud. Weather cold after a glorious week of working and planting lettuce, chard, radishes and wearing shorts; hummingbirds here. We had six really hot weeks in hot Mexico.

1976

October 4

[I didn't do much journal writing for a while, it seems. Two and a half years between entries!]

Dear, beautiful Vixen is gone. Like my wonderful Mau-Mau, there will never be another Vixen. She was thirteen and had lost control of her bowels and back legs. The horrible decision. Dr. Witcher came to the house for she hated the vet so. She seemed to know and accept. She just lay there on the floor in my arms. So quick; wish I could go like that. We are despondent over losing such a wonderful creature.

1977

January 19

Have purchased a new "child." Chica is her name. Three-quarters wolf and a most charming creature. Four and a half months old, beautiful, fearless, a mind of her own. Hope dear old Mickey accepts her and in time will be devoted to her. *[Which they were; they loved each other.]*

June 5–December 19, 1978

"Wish we had never started the back"

June 5

[Another year and a half between entries.] Can't believe it. After how many years, we are again having some work done on the house. The back wall under the *portal. [It was all just raw adobe brick.]* Windows put in. I haven't had any since we've been here. *[In the back building, Boris made the window sashes, and we put up these old frames around them.]* Walls plastered and painted. Boris says I'm being impatient—only nineteen years. Maybe I'll start a third journal now that things are going on here again.

[My third journal is in a sketchbook that Boris had used to start recording his impressions on a trip to Russia in 1975. Dr. John Fleming of Denver had commissioned him to make a chess set in the style of Boris Godunov, one side gold and the other silver. He sent Boris to Russia to get the feeling of the onion domes and the landscape. I don't imagine he ever had such a wonderful time in all his life. He was carried away by it all; of course, he was part Russian. I find what he wrote very moving, and I would like to include some of it here. The part about my sister shows his humor, which he kept through all of his troubles to the end of his life.]

May 26, 1975 (Moscow): The clouds part and there is the Russian landscape reaching up to you as though from Dostoyevski, Gogol, or Chekhov. Pine forests interspersed with small meadows watched over in the hazy distance by the glitter of gold onion domes. From the Missouri River, saw your sister as we flew over Kansas City. She was in the backyard. Would have missed her if she hadn't stooped over to plant something. My how she carries! *[She had gained weight.]* To London over clouds, great massive ones. First glimpse of the world and English countryside zipping by at four or five hundred feet as we touched down at Heathrow

Airport. Small bits of the Baltic, Denmark, and Estonia appear now and then like an old movie house with a constantly breaking film. After an hour in London, on to Moscow, Kremlin, Pushkin Museum, and innumerable other treasures. The second day we ride about broad avenues as well as nooks and crannies even more intriguing. Old log houses with beautifully carved windows, fine old buildings as well as gigantic new ones.

[After a couple of days Boris got so busy he didn't write anymore. He only used a few pages of his sketchbook, so I started my third journal in the same book.]

June 6

It's been years since I've kept a journal, only very occasionally jotting down an important event. However, now the back portal is actually on its way to being finished. Won't believe it till I see it after all the years. *[The back* portal, *without the ceiling boards, had already been put up by Boris; Archie West laid the bricks under the back* portal *and plastered the south wall of the back building. It was just crumbling, bare adobe until then. Archie laid the brick floor inside the back room also. Boris laid all the bricks under the patio* portal *but not back here. He just couldn't do as much because of his illness. I am always amazed when I think of how much he was able to do even under those conditions.]*

Of course, Boris claims I'm just being impatient. He has no sense of time and believes life goes on forever on this earth. Archie West, our dear friend, is working on the *portal*—and how lovely it will be. This, along with our new roof, which we desperately needed in the front, will be deducted from the property tax in the name of preservation. This is because the house is on the National Historic Sites list. This has been approved by the Cultural Properties Commission.

The weather has gone mad. A hailstorm last week destroyed my vegetable garden and most of the flowers. Have started over hoping we don't have another. Had a storm last July that was almost as bad. Sometimes I wonder why I keep on.

Boris was in the hospital a couple of weeks ago for more than two weeks. His lungs are in bad shape, dear guy, and he isn't able to do much anymore. His fantastic spirits and physical strength keep him going, and no doubt will for a long time. He has to take oxygen twelve hours a day and is on medication.

Chica, the wolf dog, now that she is a year and a half, is finally more or less calmed down and is developing into a beautiful, lovable, loving, interesting animal. Dear old Mickey, who is twelve and deaf, is still a marvelous friend. He is so good and patient with Chica, who adores him.

Have been working part-time since January at the Guadalupe Chapel, which has been restored. Now that summer is here (Will it ever warm up?) I'm only working on Saturday because I have just too much to do here. Will miss that extra *dinero*. Will be open here on Mondays since I have to be open twelve days a year to get my property tax deduction. *[For several years you could get a local property tax credit for a historic property if you opened it to the public on this limited basis. I put a sign out that the house was open and had to stay home all day. Not many people ever came.]*

June 21

First day of summer, even though we have been having hot weather all week. Very, very dry. Water, water, and hate to think of the cost, but how can I let anything go without it? Have let the two small plots of grass go. Hated to.

Archie is gone for a month to break a couple of horses. Brick work one-fourth done. *[That was the floor of this greenhouse.]* The wall looks so elegant. *[He had plastered this back outside wall.]* And hope I don't break my silly neck tripping over the step-up from bedroom and back room. We had to raise it because when we get a hard rain it all runs into the house.

Boris sleeps a great deal during the day so not too much gets done. Guess it is just as well for he shouldn't do much anyway. The gardens and watering, the house, shopping, and cooking seem to take all of my time. Then Saturday I am gone all day, which really plays havoc with my chores, especially now that it is so dry. How I dread being open Mondays! Wonder if it is worth it.

Mickey is failing fast—how sad and depressing—what a wonderful creature he is. Dread the thought of not having him beside me, as he has been for eleven years.

June 26

A heat wave! Betty and Dana arrive July 2 for a week. *[That's my niece and her husband from Oregon; Treet's daughter.]* Wish it were for longer. Love having them here. Boris is not at all well today. So discouraging for both of us. He naturally becomes most depressed over it. Unable to do much but just watch. He'll outlast me, though I'm seemingly in A1 shape, outside of arthritis and knee joints. It's his attitude, his faith, his hopes, his indestructible spirit that have kept him going all this time.

July 11

The heat continues, but I'm not complaining when I think of the long winter ahead. Have had lovely rains and can hardly keep up with the vegetable garden. It's outdoing itself. Have started freezing beets. Soon the beans will have to be picked and frozen each day. So wonderful having lettuce, chard, peas, onions, soon carrots and zucchini. Hated to see Betty and Dana leave; loved having them here. How comfortable they are and so much help. Dana can do anything; and in the kitchen and garden, Betty is unbelievable. Had a little party for six.

Was open yesterday with a sign out front but had no takers. Eric *[Boris's son]* arrives this weekend. In a way Boris wishes he wouldn't come to see him when he is having troubles. Hope he will be feeling well while Eric is here. Today is lousy for him.

Archie should be arriving next week to finish the brickwork. *[That's the greenhouse/portal floor].* Maybe he will be able to do something about finishing the back room so we can camp out there this winter and turn the gas off in front.

Love sitting here under the *portal* looking out on the beautiful, gay patio with Mickey sleeping at my feet. A cool breeze blowing through even though it is still hot.

July 13

Boris is in the hospital again. Weak and breathless.

July 23

Eric left this A.M. after a very pleasant week. He and Boris were together every minute and enjoyed each other so much. Eric cut us some piñon, which will be great to have this winter. He also fixed some things for Boris and did some cleaning up for him in his shop. It was a pleasure to cook for him; how he loves to eat.

No word from Archie. Where, oh where, is he?

July 30

Archie arrived back this A.M. to finish the brick. Think it will take him the week to do it. How lovely it will look. Boris has done nothing about the windows or anything else. It's all he can do, I guess, to get up and go to bed. He's done some straightening up in back, but that goes on year after year. *[It was always a mess, but he knew where things were.]* Betty Hall left yesterday. She bought an owl that has been under the *portal* for a couple of years. How that will help. It's very difficult for me to understand why Boris won't consider selling a few of the old baskets or other treasures that he never looks at. You would think he'd be so delighted to think he could help in some way to meet the expenses of his medicine, doctor, or so forth; or just to help do things around here. *[In a lot of ways, I am delighted he didn't because after he was gone I had them to sell so I could live and publish the book about his work and do the other sorts of things that needed to be done.]*

August 1

Today is another day and another mood. Sometimes I wonder about my sanity, I have such extreme moods.

Archie will finish the brick tomorrow. He will then start on finishing the ceiling in back and, if money permits, finishing the walls. We still hope we can camp out back there this winter and turn off all the gas up front. I can go back on my electric plate and electric skillet and leave the stove and fridge up here. It would save an awful lot of money.

August 9

Brick finished. Ceiling finished. *[That's the back interior ceiling of the back room. The beams were already up when Archie and I put the ceiling up between them, so the boards are just sitting on top of the beams. Next we blew in the insulation from the outside.]* Now for the walls, can't believe it. Should be very cozy.

Bought some peaches to freeze. Soon I will have to start the freezer in the back; I have so much stuff; the front one is full. Cool weather, like fall. I hate that it portends winter.

August 11

Boris has decided to have Archie brick the passageway between the patio *portal* and the backdoor. *[This is the back of the* zaguán.*]* What a difference it makes and will be cleaner, too. How lucky that we had all those penitentiary bricks bought nineteen years ago when we fixed the house. We could never afford to buy any today, and they would be all new looking and look like hell in this old place. Archie will take a week or so off. Meanwhile, we'll figure out the wiring in the back when John Fleming comes down from Denver. *[That was the doctor who commissioned Boris to do the chess set. He was a fantastic electrician. That's how he worked his way through medical school. He came down from Denver with a huge box of tools and wired the back.]*

August 21

Had the shattering news last week that Miralotte, of all people, has cancer. Unfortunately, it has spread. How quickly things happen to change or destroy your life. The older you get the more you see of this. As Kay says, "Treet and Dot managed it very well," both suddenly just popping off. *[My two oldest sisters died of heart attacks very quickly.]* May I be so lucky.

August 28

Archie is back. John Fleming, dear John, spent four frantic days wiring the back room—wall plugs, switches, and a new fuse box. We didn't realize how complicated it was or how extensive or we would never have brought it to his attention. It was embarrassing, to say the least, but how gracious he was and claims he was glad to do it. *[He did it for nothing. Of course, Boris gave him sculpture and made jewelry for his wife.]* Anyway, now Archie can go ahead with the plastering of the wall. He's working this week in exchange for my old Gibson guitar, which I haven't touched for twenty-five years. It's like new for I never did much with it, and he's always wanted a Gibson, so that's good. *[At one time I thought I would be the life of the party and learn how to play the guitar and sing. That didn't last long; I found I wasn't born to do that.]*

We have had the driest summer in twenty years—lovely big old trees are dying off. I can't even keep up with this place; we're losing many things, too. Boris seems to be feeling quite well and is very active and helpful.

August 31

If I had known what a ghastly mess it would make and how much work the back was going to be I don't believe I could have faced it. But once it's started, there's no stopping. Like Macbeth: "I am steeped in blood so deep returning would be as tedious as to go o'er." Each day I think it can't get any worse, but it does.

To make room for the refrigerator, a large piece of wall had to come out. Then I had the bright idea of moving the door where the fridge would have gone, which we all agreed would be much better but more mess and more work. *[There was a door where the refrigerator is now. It would have been a mess to have a door between the refrigerator and the sink. So Archie filled in the original doorway and installed the present door in the opening first created for the fridge.]* Archie and I constantly say what a marvelous decision that was, how awful it would have looked to have them the other way. Archie made a space to fit the fridge where the original door had been. He is such a good sport. I am sure we never could have found anyone who would put up with what he is putting up with. He is working this week in exchange for my guitar, but I think I'll give him a bonus. God knows he deserves it.

This town is drying up. How haunting it is to see trees and shrubs dying all over town. People have let everything go because of the price of water. We've had no moisture this summer and little snow last winter. It's tragically serious—it will be desert if something doesn't happen.

September 1

Our dear friend Miralotte died yesterday. Dear Ray; all he must decide and do. Hope he will come out here to live. He's been wanting to for years. *[Instead, he eventually married Janet.]*

September 4

Wish we had never started the back. The mess and complications are unbelievable. Boris is in a horrible mood over it, and poor Arch is plugging away under terrible obstacles. What Boris will do with all his stuff is beyond me. His shop is stacked already; you can hardly get into it with the stuff. *[This is the shop out back. He was a pack rat. I think many men are. To me it's a sign of being insecure.]* He's taken over the bedroom for the duration.* It's a mess and full of things. Wonder if it will ever be finished and organized. I doubt it at this moment. I hope one day to look back and say it was all worth it. *[Believe me, I have many times.]* Not sure the money will stretch to finish it. Never thought it would be such a project.

September 6

These days are just so beautiful—just like when Kay and I first visited Santa Fe twenty-five years ago this October. Hope the cold weather holds off until we at least get the back closed in, greenhouse and all, for there are no windows yet in the window openings. Have been waiting two years for that. The door to the passageway has to be put in, and the alcove for the refrigerator is still open. When Arch gets through with the plastering, I'll paint the walls while he works on other things. Hope we can get the fundamentals done by the fifteenth.

September 18

Archie has returned just in the nick of time, I must say. It's getting cold and the greenhouse isn't started. Boris couldn't possibly cope with it alone. Wish I could afford to keep Archie for another month but I fear this will be the last week. We hope to have him put up the insulation in the back

---

*"For the duration": A phrase that gained currency during World War II, meaning "for the duration of the war."

part to save heat. Also, he has to plaster the outside of the refrigerator space *[in the* zaguán*].*

September 19

Archie, bless him, is here again this chilly morning. It's down to around forty degrees. Any night there will be frost and an end to my beautiful patio. Oh well, it's good to go when you are still loved, still beautiful, and still wanted.

September 21

Archie and Boris are putting the insulation above the ceiling of the back room. Nasty job. How good to have it done. Should save lots of heat. *[Boris went to Albuquerque to get great huge bags of insulation.]*

Boris is going to make a little alcove for himself back there so he can get his bed out of sight—ugly hospital bed—and fix up the back living/kitchen area to look nice. *[He never did the alcove. He was sleeping back here because he was so ill and up so much at night. We were living up in the front.]*

This will be Archie's last day except now and then if Boris needs a hand. So good to have someone we can count on. Down to forty degrees last night. Greenhouse up, all but the door. Wall mud plastered in the passageway. *[That's behind the refrigerator in the* zaguán*.]*

An archaeologist was here to see if he thought the well was worth digging out. He thinks it is and will see what he can figure out. *[He came back with what it would cost—thousands of dollars—and it was much too much for us to handle, so we never did it.]*

September 25

Yesterday morning we had breakfast by the first fire of the season in the fireplace with rain coming down outside; so cozy and fun.

October 3

Since my last writing it has been like summer during the day. Today, however, there is a bite in the air that portends a change. It will frost tonight—it is late this year.

Heard that friends of Vivian Fiske are going to buy *Elijah*—which Vivian loaned to the Fine Arts Museum before she died—and present it to the museum in her memory. I'm delighted, for it should stay there. *[She lived in Santa Fe up on Hyde Park Road, but she was from Texas originally. She had commissioned* Elijah *for her first husband's gravesite in Fort Worth, where she was to be buried also. But, as it turned out, the sixteen-foot, Corten-steel statue attracted too much of the wrong kind of attention. First somebody tried to steal it, so they bolted it down to a piece of granite. Then someone sawed off the top bird and took it. After that a group of young men painted gold crosses on the front and back and held meetings at midnight dressed up in tails. Finally, after the night watchman who tried to chase them away was fired upon, the cemetery manager wrote to Vivian that though they loved* Elijah, *they just couldn't cope with the never-ending problems. They offered to send him anywhere she chose at their expense, and so he came back to Boris for repairs. After Boris put a new bird on top—he could still use his torch then—and took the crosses off the back and front, Vivian loaned the refurbished* Elijah *to the Fine Arts Museum in Santa Fe. He was in the patio there for years. When Vivian died there was no provision in her will for* Elijah, *so her friends purchased him for the museum in her memory. Now he is out in front of the land office building on the Old Santa Fe Trail, where he looks marvelous.]*

Wonder if the mess around here will ever be sorted out. If Boris just didn't have so many things; sometimes it drives me mad. I would love to live simply with few possessions—so free and easy and unencumbered—but it's piles of stuff everywhere. I'm off to work now.

October 8

Still no frost. Amazing, gorgeous days. Aspen almost gone. On my walk in the morning through the piñons, down the arroyos with Mickey and Chica, the air is full of bird song, just like in spring. Dear dogs they are. How they enjoy that time. All the delightful smells and running free. Chica bounds through the trees and floats up and down the banks of the arroyos, digs in the gopher holes, and has a gorgeous time. Dear old Mickey plods along.

Boris still hasn't gotten the door on the greenhouse. *[That must be*

185

this big one that he made from the kitchen into the greenhouse.] Lucky we aren't having cold. Poor guy, it takes him so long to get anything done these days.

October 25

Ray left yesterday after a most pleasant visit. Unfortunately, all hell broke loose while he was here. Everyone decided to come to Santa Fe—friends, friends of friends, sister Kay and her husband Ced *[Cedric Gifford]*. Rather exhausting, to say the least. As a result, I have tons of cleaning and yard work and . . .

Still haven't had a minute to work on the back. The greenhouse is all tight, door and all. The Mexican door is on the back room. *[Between my bedroom and the guest room, or maybe it's the one from the bedroom into the living area. We bought those two doors in Juárez.]* Want to get some woven stuff for the plywood wall, paint the floor, lay the tile on the windowsills, and so forth. *[The walls surrounding the bathroom here in the back are just plywood. I never did get anything woven.]* Doubt that we'll get the kitchen moved this winter—knew it all the time. Still have had no frost, but the last two nights have been close to it. Mickey is not very well.

October 29

Mickey seems to be fine again. I am sitting out in the patio without a sweater on—glorious hot sun. No killing frost yet; and the flowers are still lovely—tuberous-rooted begonias dripping down in a profusion of blossoms; gay, bright geraniums and petunias—incredible. We're going to visit Benny and Carla Jaquez this afternoon and see their new baby boy. He is working at Los Alamos as a mechanic, and Carla, too, is there in an office. *[That's little Benny, the neighbor, who was such a wonderful child.]*

November 3

Believe I have never seen so much rain—almost steady for twenty-four hours—at times really coming down. *[It's one extreme or the other.]* The river is roaring and it is getting very cold. If this keeps up we may have snow by morning. *[I have a complete report of the weather here for the last thirty-four years.]*

Boris took off for Juárez, taking his box of oxygen. He just has to get off once in a while. He goes early and gets back the next morning, sleeping along the road. He loves it. The car always looks as though he was going for a week, all the stuff he has to take. Then his return—powdered coffee, which is less than half of what it is here; glorious steaks, hamburger, and stew meat, which are much less; and, naturally, a few treats such as a fancy lock, paper flowers, masks, and so forth. It gives him a lift for days.

While he was gone I planted my geranium and fuchsia cuttings, with the parent plants still blooming in the patio. Made two kinds of bread; washed and cleaned. I, too, enjoy an uninterrupted day alone.

November 7

Can't believe I still have geraniums blooming in the patio. Picked chard for dinner from the garden—delicious.

November 15

Below freezing last night. Ray plans to come for Christmas, as usual. He loves going to Indian dances every day.

November 23

Never in New Mexico have I seen so much dark, dirty, wet weather. Tomorrow is Thanksgiving, and my dear friend Jean Buchanan will be here for dinner as well as Nell and Brud.

November 27

Still another dark, dreary day. Yesterday morning I gathered greens for the pots in the patio. How beautiful the juniper looks covered with blue berries. Chica loves eating them—the wolf in her, I guess. *[She did a lot of things like that instinctively that my other dogs just didn't do.]*

November 30

Went to the see *Folklorico* dancers last night—a treat from my dear brother. I was ecstatic—the colors, the light, the excitement. How homesick it made us for Mexico. Many times we have sat under the *portal* of La Sorpresa listening to guitars and marimbas, glorious hot days with the sounds and smells of Mexico. Another sadness of getting old is to realize there isn't any time left to know and see these things. *[How many years ago was that?!]*

Boris got along fine; didn't even take his "breathing machine"— portable oxygen that he carries with him around here. However, all he did was sit; and if he doesn't move he is fine. Dear guy, it is so difficult for him. Do wish we could get to Mexico once more together.

December 8

Pipes frozen—five degrees last night—supposed to be worse tonight. Even Los Angeles had freezing weather.

December 10

One degree below zero. How do all the creatures survive? It is ghastly. Not only cold but a strong north wind.

December 15

My sixty-fourth birthday. If I didn't ever look in the mirror, I wouldn't believe it. Feel great and how flattering and wonderful to have so many remember. Boris made me a pair of gorgeous twenty-two-carat gold earrings, just like I wanted, a little larger than a quarter. Love them; feel so elegant. *[Of course, I never wear them for fear I'll lose one.]*

December 17

Whatever would we do without Ray? Again he sends us a check. Anyway, I'm going to lay in a supply of food, drink, and wood so he won't have many expenses while here. Wish he would get out of that big house and his lonely life. Dreary, dark, cold day.

December 19

If I had stayed married to Hal—which I'm glad I didn't (think of all I would have missed); dear Hal, wonder if he is still around—this would be my forty-fourth anniversary. *[His Social Security is what I am living on now. Isn't life strange?]*

January 4–November 9, 1979

"Poor Archie, poor Boris, poor me"

January 4

This is all very depressing. I'm in a mood. *[I guess it is the weather again. I'm nervous about everything and depressed.]*

January 12

More snow, many dark days. Boris isn't at all well. He has some kind of a bug. Sleeps a great deal. Don't see how he could get to Mexico or how I could leave him to go by myself.

January 16

Fourth cold, dark, dismal day. The pollution has something to do with it. Definitely decided I can't possibly leave Boris to go to Mexico, and he will not be able to go this year. *[I don't think he went again.]* Have started sewing summer clothes, for surely summer will come.

January 19

Another overcast day. Gas bill was $60. Boris has been having a tough time with his breathing.

January 26

This seems to be a journal of the weather. You wouldn't believe what it has been doing. Nothing but cold, dark days.

February 3

As much as I resent the house finches when the fruit is ripe—taking a bite out of every peach, apricot, and apple—I adore them in February for they are the first to sing; and it makes me believe that spring really will come. The sun has been out for three days. How glorious it is not to freeze. Have made reservations for Chicago to see my dear friend Gerta. Boris seems to be getting along well, so I don't feel guilty leaving him. *[Gerta Humrich was an old friend. I knew her since I was seventeen when she was going to art school in Chicago. She visited us in Santa Fe from Illinois a number of times.]*

February 11

All ready to leave on my Chicago adventure. Not taking anything that won't fit in my little overnight bag. Boris seems to be feeling very well and getting a lot of work done. Weather lovely, the feel and smell of spring. The frost is coming out of the ground, snow melting from the roof.

February 25

Back again and how good it is to see bare ground. Chicago is unbelievable. *[They had three feet of snow; there were walls of it on either side of the roads.]* Today was gorgeous, sunny and warm. I did some transplanting and started my tuberous-rooted begonias. Camelias still blooming like mad. Citrus covered with buds. I'm going to start working at Flor-Al again one day a week. Will make $36 a day. Boris and I live in a world years back.

March 28

Boris has just finished some beautiful bronze shorebirds for John Sargent, who is trading his old truck for them. I feel that John is getting the best of the bargain. Boris plans to sell the Datsun truck and with the money fix up the dear old Volvo. He also plans to go up north this summer to meet Eric and his family and bring back his Model T pickup. The back will look like a secondhand salvage yard. Wish I could have a neat little new car—just a little one. Afraid if Eloisa is unable to, I may have to do all the cleaning and fixing up outside as well. *[She did housework for me.]*

April 17

At last I think spring has sprung. The bulb flowers are so sweet and beautiful. Apricots almost gone, some frozen. If we are lucky, we will still have apples, peaches, and cherries. Nothing like the fruit blossoms. Ah, spring! This year I am hoping to get everything that needs doing done. It should last the rest of my life. Strange thought, isn't it—the world going on without you? Ten years or twelve or maybe not. Who knows? I hope to get this place fixed up so I can forget it—either to live in and enjoy or to sell and enjoy the profits. Boris goes into fits whenever I mention death. Strange, for I would actually welcome it, but he cannot accept it.

April 26

6 A.M. Here I sit out back by the pool, surrounded by beauty and Mickey and Chica. Suddenly spring has burst into all its thrilling glory as if by magic. The lilacs are covered with big, fat buds. The tree in the patio— radiant crab—is a cloud of dark pink blossoms. There is nothing like spring. The first joys of love are similar, but you can count on spring. It never disappoints.

It will be beautiful for the tour Sunday unless it freezes or rains, of course. Washed down the *portal* yesterday and cleaned the greenhouse. Eloisa comes tomorrow to wash windows, floors, and so forth. It's good I have these things done occasionally; otherwise I'd just let them go. Now I'll sit back, drink my coffee, and bask in the wonder of it all.

May 2

Boris's seventy-second birthday. Dark and raining but not too cold. Glad I got my vegetable garden started yesterday. The tour was a great success. Glad it wasn't on a day like this. A great group—Harris County Heritage Society from Houston, Texas, thirty-nine of them. This was one of four places they went.

The next tour is June 1—the fine arts committee of a university museum in Texas. Hope they will buy something. This month is Boris's last payment of $200, so our only income will be Social Security at $167 for me and $204 for Boris, which isn't enough these days. The money Ray sends is for the house, and God knows getting that done will mean a great deal. Archie still hasn't shown but hope he will this month.

May 3

The scarlet tulips under the tamarisk in the patio are blooming over where dearest Mau-Mau is buried in her cozy little basket. They are just the color of her tail. *[I don't remember planting those, but for years they came up just where she was buried.]*

I am reading what I think is a very worthwhile book—*Four Arguments for the Elimination of Television.** I've hated this damned thing ever since Boris got one. *[He was addicted to the thing.]* The horrible damage it is doing, especially to children and young people, is frightening. People are actually addicted to it, like alcoholics; they'd go berserk without it. What TV does to the minds and bodies of especially children is ghastly to contemplate. One of the worst evils of our time, I'm sure. This book is most enlightening and thought provoking; unfortunately, like most books written on controversial subjects, it is never read by the mob who should read it but only by those of us who already agree.

May 6

A glorious spring day—lilacs in great masses all over town, abundant.

May 9

Rain, snow, and sleet. Boris pooh-poohs my idea that the moon has a great deal to do with the weather. If it's going to be cold, it is when the moon is full, which is in two days. We'll see. This violent year has seemed to me as though the elements were trying to rid the poor old earth of all the nasty and evil polluting man has done. Chica is beginning to grow up some, actually trying to be good and usually succeeding.

May 10

All is covered with white frost—birdbath frozen, tender, sweet new leaves stiff and frozen, as are all the blossoms. How cruel; no fruit again.

May 14

Glorious three days. I sat out by the pool with my coffee, Mickey, and Chica yesterday early morning. So lovely and quiet; nothing but birds singing, chirping, and winging by. Counted ten different kinds. Betty and Dana arrive the twenty-fifth.

Four Arguments for the Elimination of Television (New York: Quill, 1977): Written by former advertising executive Jerry Mander.

May 19

Weather still glorious; two good rains. Poor, dear Boris was so sure his truck would sell immediately—no takers. He had planned just what he would do with all the money and even spent some of it already. We spent hours cleaning and shining it all up—looks great. I hate to sell it.

June 3

We're rich! Glad I quit my job. Boris sold his truck for $2,100, and Betty and Dana bought a small slate carving of a horse. Boris intends to fix up the Volvo—new fenders and so forth—and to restore his Model A, which he hopes to go and get at the end of the month. That will all take more than the $2,100, but it is fun to have it at the moment.

The tour is over and they all enjoyed it. A group from Texas Tech at Lubbock. The Rio Grande has flooded its banks and the vegetation is lush—just so we don't have hail. Boris may make shutters, and I am determined to order grilles for them.

August 12

Hope we can get the back fixed before it gets cold. Archie arrives Monday. He came last Monday but my back was out. Could barely move so we decided to put it off yet again for a week. We have to have a new roof, which is a project. We'll put a slight pitch on it and use tin instead of gravel. Hope it lasts for our duration anyway. *[Instead of just continuing to patch the flat roof in back, which was always leaking, Boris decided that we would have Archie build a frame with a slight pitch. Instead of roofing we used corrugated tin and haven't had any trouble with it at all. Flat roofs are absolutely insane. The front has a lake on it when the snow melts.]*

August 13

Dear Archie arrived. An overcast day, so working on the roof won't be so hot. *[It was hot up there. I helped him put that stuff up.]* No one, no one would do this work but him—and for $5 an hour. What a friend.

August 14

Raining hard; poured down most of the night, naturally. Archie started on the leaky roof yesterday and is the roof leaking! Couldn't stand listening to it all night so slept up here. Too bad the joy of hearing it come down has to be resented. Wish he could have waited just one more week. Archie couldn't have come today anyway. He called early to say one of his neighbor's bulls got hit by a car last night and had to be taken care of. Guess they'll shoot him and dress him for meat—poor old thing. Dear creatures; how helpless and defenseless they are against the damn automobile, which is causing problems with energy and pollution.

August 15

Still raining. Hasn't stopped for two days. A very large lake on the back roof that is draining down through the ceiling. Please don't let the bedroom spring a leak Wonder when Archie will be able to work. Naturally, he didn't come today. Maybe tomorrow will be better.

August 17

Archie got a good day in yesterday in spite of several showers. It's trying to clear. Hope it makes it.

August 20

A glorious day. Blue sky and burst of cumulus clouds. Archie is hard at it. I put the wood up to the roof where he can grab it. It's getting there. The materials alone will be more than $1,000. Staggering. May it be a roof to end all roofs! Almost done with apricots and beans; next peaches. *[I froze lots of fruit in those days.]*

August 21

The hole is in for the skylight *[in my bedroom now]*. How glorious to have the sun and light flowing in.

August 22

If I had known, don't believe we would ever have started this project. *[Sound familiar?]* Boris feels terrible so naturally is in a dire mood about everything, which makes it twice as hard. Poor guy is really in bad shape physically and emotionally. Wonder if that roof will ever be finished; the skylight is really delaying it by several days, to say nothing of the cost. I hope it will be worth it. The roof alone with skylight will run around $2,000. *[That's nothing today. We have insulated glass in that skylight, too. I'm talking about money again; it's always money, money.]*

August 23

Skylight finished. Boris got insulation in Albuquerque yesterday to put in before the tin goes on. We should be as snug as bugs. Will help Arch with that and getting the planks on this afternoon.

August 24

Poor Archie, poor Boris, poor me. This roof, figuring out the drainage, the pipes, and so forth—more and more material, more and more money. Will it ever be done? Have been up there hammering, lugging, putting goop on the seams. The old gray mare she ain't what she used to be, but the show must go on.

August 25

Archie worked this morning, which gave me the afternoon off to clean and freeze peaches. He is working also tomorrow, Sunday, to get the darn thing done. What a guy! Of course, none of this would be possible without Ray, who is financing the deal. The roof may be finished tomorrow.

August 27

Archie and I worked on the roof all day yesterday and almost finished it. I really did work—putting goop on the edges and bringing the sheets of tin for him to nail. We had quite a system. We will finish today with flashing, gutters, and so forth. Thank heaven the rain has held off. Hoping Archie will take a couple of days off before he starts on the back. *[That's the inside of the back room.]* I'd like a couple of days to catch up on my garden and freeze the lovely, ripe peaches.

August 31

Oh where, oh where has the summer gone? It seems so short and winter so long. Archie took off until September 4. Thank God I can do things to get ready for Bob and Carolyn Brodkey, who arrive Labor Day, the third. *[Unfortunately, Bob and Marty Brodkey had divorced and then both had later remarried.]*

September 4

Took Boris to the hospital last night. He is still in intensive care but is better. Had a violent attack. Thank God Bob is here; such a help and comfort. Archie arrives this A.M. to start on the back room. What a mess. Bob, bless him, is able to help with things I would have no idea how to cope with. Off to see Boris.

September 7

Boris came home yesterday seeming OK. Ceiling is done. Archie is working on the partitions to divide the back into rooms, Bob on the wiring. *[The partitions that created the bedroom and bath are plywood. Our dear friend, Bob Brodkey, finished the wiring that Dr. Fleming didn't quite get done.]* It will take me the rest of my life, if I live that long, to get this place cleaned up and put together. I am so weary, so tired of the mess. It is really a disaster area.

September 9

Tomorrow dear, faithful Archie starts on plastering the walls *[inside the back building]*. When that mess is over, perhaps we can start getting things put back. That is, if anyone puts in the closet and the cupboards above it. Hope to keep Archie a week after plastering to catch up on some things I know won't get done if he doesn't do them. I am really enjoying having Bob and Carolyn here. I'm glad that we will have company from now until November 1 in spite of the work. It is stimulating and relieves the monotony.

September 14

Winter is coming. Winter is here. Already I'm tired of winter this year. Have our first fire in the fireplace. Greenhouse not even started. *[I think this means putting up the plastic as we did each fall.]* No windows or doors in back. Just hope it doesn't frost. Plastering done and I'm almost, after mixing and hauling all day. Dear Elizabeth, Archie's wife, relieved me of it for two days. Not sure I could have done it for five days running. Now I must paint the walls and do something to the floor before we can move in. The closet has to come first so we can get things out of the way.

September 21

Archie working on closet. Can't believe I'll have a place to put things. Greenhouse not up yet. Hope frost holds off. Herbert *[a German friend of Boris's]* arrives tomorrow; staying here. So does Betty Hall *[another friend of Boris's from Evanston]*, staying at La Posada.

Getting cool. My flowers are beautiful. Have been making and freezing applesauce and making pies. My freezers are bulging.

September 26

For several hundred dollars the closet is finished but not painted. *[That's the clothes closet in my bedroom. It never did get painted.]* It is a great disappointment to me—ugly but will serve the purpose of stuffing in all the stuff—worthless, useless stuff that can't be parted with as far as Boris is concerned. Because of the huge, heavy doors, you see the junk on the shelves above every time you open it. Anyway, as Ambrose Bierce says, "A year is 365 days of consecutive disappointments."*

September 29

Herbert is gone; Gerta not coming. Great disappointment but just as well because Eric is arriving; also John and Celeste Fleming, who won't be staying here. John is coming just to finish the electrical work on the "new" room. What a friend! Weather still glorious. Eric will be a big help. Boris is looking forward to seeing him. Doubt that Boris will take off for northern Wisconsin. *[He wanted to bring back that old Model A Ford.]* Mickey gets feebler and feebler but still loves his tennis balls.

---

*Charlotte has slightly embellished his definition: "YEAR, n. A period of three hundred and sixty-five disappointments."

September 30

It seems Boris does little else but sleep day and night. So much to do that I can't do. Glad Eric is coming. Hope he will help.

October 6

Still no frost. Eric is a pleasure to have around, to say nothing of all the help with cutting up and piling wood, greenhouse, and so forth. How Eric loves to eat. It is fun to cook for him. Boris is so indifferent to food, except desserts, of course. Eric leaves Monday. Ray and Janet arrive Wednesday. *[That was Ray's new wife.]* After Ray leaves, we can get to work on the back. The cost of everything is staggering. Wonder how we'll get kitchen cabinets. Have had an estimate of $2,000, which is out of our reach. We will see about ready-made ones. Boris says he can do it, but I don't see how. He feels rotten most of the time and carries oxygen with him. *[But he did—he made them out of birch plywood from Russia. He did so much after he was ill, and he never gave up. He couldn't do anything that was dull, so he carved little creatures where all the knotholes are on the doors of the cabinets.]*

Dear sister Kay is not coming; she doesn't feel well. *[My sister, who had moved to Santa Fe before I did, later moved to Kansas City to be near her son.]*

October 20

Still no frost. Fuchsias and geraniums still lovely in the patio. Have pulled up the vegetable garden and started spading. Have picked most of the apples but not the pears. *[I had a lot of fruit that year.]*

We bought a ready-made door for the bedroom that Boris is cutting down and taking out panels for glass. They wanted $250 to make one, which probably wouldn't be much better. *[That's the door in the bedroom that goes out to the patio. In place of a window, I had a door put in there.]* Have started painting the floor so after Boris glues the bed together—we had to wire it to keep it from falling apart, poor old thing—I can start moving in. *[That's the bed in my bedroom. I was born in that bed.]*

Ray, bless him, gave us the money for the door. They left Monday. Hope he will be happy. He married a young woman named Janet October 3. Couldn't face being alone and doing all the chores.

Having sold the Navajo chief's blanket and the Japanese screen Dot left me, think we'll make it fixing the back; that is, if Boris does all he says he is going to do. Hope so much he will be well enough. *[Dot was my oldest sister. I don't know how Boris ever consented to sell that chief's blanket.]*

Greenhouse together, plants and cuttings in. Any day now winter will burst in on us. Wonder if and when we will finish the back and be able to cut off the heat up here. *[Evidently, I was writing up in the front room.]*

October 22

This morning there is ice on the birdbaths—first frost.

October 28

Summer days for several days now. As far as I am concerned, it can stay this way, but I know it isn't fair to the growing things. The bulbs will no doubt think it is spring before long.

Have the floor of the new room painted. *[That's my bedroom now.]* As soon as Boris hangs the door and glues the bed we can start moving. My neck and shoulder haven't been the same since all that plastering. Ah, these golden years—baloney!

October 29

Again, my dear friend Gerta can't make it.

November 9

This is the day Gerta was to arrive. Glad she isn't coming. We have had a cold, nasty rain for two days. This morning half snow and cold. A lovely rug is being delivered for my bedroom *[from Sears]*. What luxury—so warm and soft on bare feet. Maybe it is foolish, especially after painting the floor twice, but I am determined to have at least one place that is lovely and a joy. The rest of the back is still a hopeless mess. Must find an interesting project for the winter. I know I should be happy and also grateful that I have a place to live without rent, as well as the other things I have.

November 10, 1979–August 20, 1980

"The kitchen is a joy"

November 10

I slept in my bed in my beautiful new room. Never thought I'd see the day. One of these days I really might also have my kitchen. Today I'll clean my old bedroom and start getting it ready for Boris to move in to. *[The "old bedroom" is my guest room now. We built it as a storeroom but I decided to make my bedroom out of it. Boris's stuff went into his shop and I moved into it. Boris had his hospital bed in the back room. Here I am moving into my present bedroom and Boris is about to take over my old room. So that added room went from storeroom to my room to Boris's room to my guest room now.]*

November 25

A month from today and then the whole mess will be over. It is such a chore to get done just the few things I must do for Christmas. It's too bad that I feel this way when it used to be such a beautiful, magic time. Now it is just something to get over with and know that spring is that much closer. The darn merchants had all their trimmings out before Thanksgiving. If that doesn't take the thrill and excitement out of it, I don't know what would.

When I was a child, there wasn't a sign of Christmas until about ten days before. Then the secrets of closets and knowing smiles would appear and how thrilling it was. Then to go down Christmas morning into a wonderland. The tree—a big one that touched the ceiling—all glittering with tinsel, ornaments, and lights. Where it was hidden, I never knew. The fire crackling in the fireplace and the music box playing. Was there ever anything as beautiful?

Have been having lots of fun cutting and painting butterflies for my closet doors *[which I had on for years but have since taken off]*. Also painting a little bedside chest *[which is still there]*. That room is a delight.

When the doors between the rooms are on, I can sit back and enjoy. Haven't gotten Boris's room fixed yet. He hopes to work on the kitchen cabinets next week.

December 10

Ray and spouse are not coming for Christmas. They can't find a house/dog sitter. Ray, I believe, was truly upset, and we are very disappointed. It will be the first Christmas he has missed in years.

Weather continues cold but not as beastly as before. Glorious sun warms the whole back. If we were only back there. Still get a huge thrill out of my new room. *[I still love it!]*

Have been reading biographies and writings of Maurois and Maupassant and realize all the more how damn rotten unfair it is that men at any age can have exciting, romantic affairs with younger women but not so for females. Nobody wants to get excited over a wrinkled, gray, old woman. How unjust. We feel the same inside, but it's the look that counts to a man.

Boris seems to be feeling better and works every day. Sent off the shorebirds that Andrea will have for Christmas from her father. *[That's Ray's daughter.]* He plans to start the kitchen cabinets soon.

December 14

Tomorrow I will be on Medicare. The only good thing I can think of about being sixty-five. Can't believe it. Don't feel nearly as old as that sounds, but for the first time I see signs of age in my body. Boris, Jean, and I are having lunch at my very favorite restaurant, La Tertulia, where they have the best Mexican food and sangria. Have been looking forward to it all week. Boris, in honor of the day, has hung one of the doors to my room.

No more snow, which we could use and it would be pretty. As a child I always hoped and wished very hard for snow on my birthday. Dearest Mother always made much of that day—like a preview of Christmas, with my little decorated table tree, a party for my friends (who received presents), chicken pie, ice cream, and cake. Even when I was grown, she often appeared with the tree and chicken pie. What a woman! Wonder what the next year will bring. Hope completion of the back, anyway.

December 22

Have painted the walls and the floor of my old bedroom, which is now Boris's room. As soon as he gets a ceiling light in, we can move him in and hopefully start on the kitchen area. *[Up until then he was sleeping in the mess back here, in his hospital bed, near the bathroom. He had the pot-belly wood stove and his television. This was his place.]*

His Russian birch plywood is in Albuquerque. It will be $800 for the kitchen cabinets but cheaper than pine. He plans to make them so maybe by summer it will be done. *[Boris had ordered the wood for the cabinets from a place in Albuquerque—I don't remember the name. Can you imagine, imported from Russia and it was cheaper than pine.]*

December 29

Bitter cold after a light snow. The little birds really appreciate the seeds I put out twice a day. Fortunately, the sun is out today so it will heat the back. Wish this front room could be closed up—maybe next year. *[I wanted the back finished so that we could live there and close the front room in the winter. It was so expensive to heat.]*

We went over to Karin's the other evening for a buffet supper. *[She is my niece, Dot's daughter, who married Dave Jackson.]* All the kids were home with friends, and son George put on a magic show for us. How he does some of these things is amazing.

Boris went for the wood for the cabinets so will be eager to see his progress. They should be elegant.

1980

January 3

Here I sit in the lovely, warm, beautiful greenhouse, surrounded by blooming bougainvillea, camellias, azaleas, Christmas cactus, and gerani-ums—gardenia ready to burst open any day, along with lemon and orange. *[I can't imagine I had all that. I don't have nearly that anymore.]* Even on this cold day—ten degrees last night—the back building here is hot from the sun. How very lucky we are to have this place. God knows we could never pay rent anywhere these days. Just a one-room apartment runs anywhere from $125 to $200 a month. *[After all my complaining, it's nice to hear something positive about money, isn't it?]*

Gold was up to $620 an ounce, silver $40—unheard of. A silver dollar is worth $27. Boris hoarded away silver coins when they started making copper-filled ones, and he must have several hundred dollars worth of them. A thousand dollars worth of silver coins will bring $27,000. *[Where did I get that information? President Johnson had said not to hoard money, and that was all Boris needed. I later turned his coins in for quite a bit.]* None of this makes sense, and our money is worth very little. Thank God, too, that I still have a lot of frozen fruits and vegetables from our own place. Bought some broccoli yesterday for dinner; seventy-nine cents a pound. Guess we will stick to our beans, beets, and squash. Unfortunately, my carrots are gone from the garden. The ones from the store taste like sawdust by comparison.

Boris is busy on the cabinets. Can't believe that I will have a kitchen yet. Am eagerly looking forward to Betty and Dana's visit February 9. Only a week, though; they never stay long enough. So thankful Boris is feeling better and in fine spirits. He still hopes to take off for Mexico next month. Don't see how he can; but knowing him, he'll find a way. What a guy!

I am reading one of the most fascinating books I have ever read, Van Gogh's letters to his brother Théo. What he has to say about art and life is certainly thought-provoking. He really meant what he did from his very guts and that is why he is great and his work lives and why what passes as art today has no substance, is nothing. I can't leave the book alone and yet I hate to finish it.

January 4

The world situation is frightening. The United States casting stones at Russia when the United States is far from sinless.* The propaganda and

---

*"Casting stones at Russia": On December 31, 1979, President Jimmy Carter had accused Soviet leader Leonid Brezhnev (1960–1982) of not telling the truth about the Soviet invasion of Afghanistan when he asserted that Soviet troops had been invited by the government that subsequently fell in a coup that Carter accused the Soviets of engineering.

brainwashing going on to build up more hate for Russia is disgusting—
just so everyone will hate them and we will be willing to go in with all
four feet if necessary to destroy them. This business of cutting out food
for them is criminal; after all, they are people just like us. God knows I
would hate to be judged by what our government represents.

January 18

Another dark day—there are so many and so little moisture. Lack of snow
almost everywhere making up for last year, I guess. There is a feeling of
spring, though; can't come soon enough for me.

Boris still busy on cabinets. Have him moved into the old bedroom,
which he seems to like. He is feeling well so I'm going off for a few days
to see my sister Kay in Kansas City. She is delighted, and it will be fun to
fly off for a bit. I sold a piece of sculpture to pay for it.

The greenhouse is so gorgeous. Never have I had such magnificent
camellias. Have sold some to the florist for $2 each. Gardenia loaded with
buds ready to burst. Azaleas a riot of glorious blooms. Gold more than
$700 an ounce. Gas more than a dollar a gallon. Finally giving up on my
bursitis and going to the doctor next week, it's so painful. *[I got that from
mixing all of that plaster when I was helping Archie with the back room.]*

February 18

Betty and Dana have gone after a wonderful week. How I hated to see
them leave. Wish they lived closer. Had two great days in Juárez. Bought
tiles for the kitchen and $60 worth of groceries—so much cheaper than
here. The bulbs are popping through and the birds beginning to sing, so
spring *will* come!

March 4

Eric *[Boris's son]* arrives tomorrow for only three days. I spread eleven bags
of steer manure on the garden and trees.

March 7

Eric, bless him, has been working ever since he arrived, getting plumbing
connected, sink in, electric plugs changed, gas in for the stove. Hope he'll

move the stove and refrigerator to the back tomorrow. It will be a mess for a while, but eventually, I hope, it will be all settled and something really good. Such a great guy he is.

March 17

Dad's birthday. *[That was always a big day in our house when I was growing up, a big celebration. I think of it every time the date rolls around. Mother and Father's anniversary, too.]*

The front looks truly gorgeous as one huge room *[with all the kitchen moved to the back].* I spent all last week cleaning and painting the floor. The heat is off so we will really save on gas for it is still cold. The sun heats this back room because of the greenhouse, which is bursting with lovely things. *[We also had the wood stove and the panel ray for heat.]* Can't begin to say how elegant it is to have a real kitchen, though piles of things yet to do.

If we—Boris mostly—ever get done all the little things that need doing, the place will be *muy elegante.* Want to get the vinyl for the floor, which, of course, means taking off all the doors and shaving them off on the bottom. Have a Mr. Roybal and *primo [cousin]* from Tesuque lined up to do the mud walls. It will cost around $1,000 just for the front and the north patio wall, which is in very bad shape. Boris is not well; on oxygen all the time—carries it around with him. Mickey is terribly feeble. It is all so depressing.

March 21

My dear loving, beloved Mickey has finally been relieved of all his pains and confusion. It had reached the point where he could barely navigate, and his nights were filled with fear and pain. Took him over this morning. With his head on my lap and my arms tightly around him, he was put away quickly and painlessly. How tragically sad it is to lose a close and devoted friend. I hope dear Vixen and he are romping together somewhere, as they did joyfully many years ago. Part of me is with them, as it is with my dear Mau-Mau and Chou. *[Chou was my first dog when I married Hal.]* If I lose many more things, there won't be any of me left. Maybe that is what dying is.

March 25

What a joyous sight and sound. Came home from shopping this A.M. and was greeted by a big flock of robins—in the trees, on the ground, flying, drinking water, singing, and twittering. There must have been more than fifty. I suppose they are on their way north. Having a hell of a time trying to decide what to put on the floors back here. These constant decisions wear a girl out.

March 29

Mother used to have nightmares about going to heaven with a dishrag in her hand. She hated washing dishes. It seemed endless, and it was. Think I'll start having nightmares with a paintbrush. Except I do believe it's almost at an end. I've painted every wall and floor in this whole place in the last two months. Decided to paint the plywood partition around the back bathroom white. First I had to spackle all the holes and cracks. And what cracks! Then I discovered that it bled through the textured latex so I had to put on a sealer. Now I can paint it.

All this could and should be fun since the back is finally getting done—but it ain't. Boris is feeling so lousy that he gets nothing done and is in a vile mood. So it is a chore and an effort and a hell of a lot of work. My bursitis doesn't help. Have had more winter the last week than during the whole season.

April 8

Finally, the ghastly wind has stopped. The wall finally done. *[I had to paint it four or five times. The plywood bled, and then the sealer, which was silver colored, showed through so I had to paint it again.]* Boris is putting shelves in. *[Where do you suppose that is—kitchen cabinets?]* I will paint the woodwork and the door dark green and maybe the window parts. *[No, I didn't paint any of them green except the door on the north side of the back room.]* The tile on the windowsills could have been done better. I am not by nature a tile setter. *[Knowing nothing about how to do it, I put Mexican tiles on the sills of these two back windows into the greenhouse so that I could set pots there.]* Still waiting for the floor guys. *[We had the vinyl floor tiles in the kitchen and living area of the back building professionally laid.]*

April 16

Slowly we progress, at least my end. Still painting, but the end of that is in sight. As soon as they put the floor in, which I hope will be next week—I dread the mess—we will be presentable. Still no windows or shutters or more cabinets. In time, I hope.

Boris shot his wad on a stereo system and speakers. He gets such pleasure out of expensive, impressive things. Oh well, he can't travel or do much, so it gives him pleasure.

May 14

The two Mr. Roybals from Tesuque have started mudding the walls at $5 an hour each. Unfortunately, it looks like a storm. My back is still very painful. Painted woodwork back here. Windows almost ready to paint. Will have them glazed and then hung. Wow! *[Boris made these two windows into the greenhouse and I had them glazed.]*

May 19

Mudders are back, and my back is better. It has been raining and snowing up until yesterday.

May 22

The walls in the patio are done. Just hope new rain won't hurt them. Now to clean up. Never saw such a mess.

June 7

The house tour is over—it was a group from a craft and folk art museum in Los Angeles. It was a great success. The place never looked so beautiful. The weather was perfect. Can't get over having a real kitchen—thought I'd never see the day—and real windows (no latches yet) that Boris made. *[So you see, we finally finished in 1980—just twenty-one years after we started.]*

June 30

The end of my third journal. For what it is worth, I will start number four.

June 30 (continued)

Boris is busy—it is all such an effort—putting shelves up in his room for all his things, of which he has an abundance. How he can stand all the clutter is beyond me. We have this year what I think is a pair of Bewick's wrens. What a joy it is to hear the sound from morning to dusk. Many robins, too, busy with their young. *[I don't have robins anymore. I just don't understand what's the matter; there used to be so many.]*

July 5

Bob and Carolyn Brodkey arrived from Ohio. They have an apartment for two months. Here for dinner last night. Still very hot; no relief in sight. Boris's medication runs about $50. What luck we sold that land in Pecos. *[Boris had been given some land by a friend of his.]*

July 29

Still feel great. Haven't been so relaxed and happy for ages. Love my new home and especially the kitchen is a joy. Beginning to freeze my produce. No rain yet; have to water all the time.

August 4

Made a deal next door with Mariano García. We are to pay him $15 a month for the use of his driveway as long as we live here, after using it for more than twenty years. Could have gone to court and maybe won getting a legal easement, but also we could have lost and that would have been the end of it. I'm a weak sister but preferred it this way. *[I still pay him. He sued me for that easement, but it was settled out of court. Later the city surveyed the property around here gratis so the poor people who were living here could sell if they wanted. It was stated there that this property has legal easement to fifteen feet with Mariano García and ten feet with Eloisa. It is part of the abstract of title. After the survey, I wrote to Mariano saying that although I didn't have to because I now had a legal easement, I would continue paying him in appreciation. After all this Eloisa blocked my easement. Because of the way the legal system works, you can't just arrest someone for doing that. You have to take it to court to prove that you have a legal easement. The Historic Santa Fe Foundation paid for that, and, of course, we won.]*

August 20

Gerta has come and gone. Great to have her here. Starting to get ready for winter. Nights and mornings chilly. Greenhouse will have to go up soon. Nectarine tree in patio loaded with beautiful dark, reddish fruit. Brodkeys leaving Monday. Hate to see them go. Sister Kay hopes to get out in a month or so. Hope she makes it this time. Betty and Dana will be here in October. So look forward to that. Boris not feeling too sharp. Weather gorgeous.

September 15–October 29, 1980

"You can't help admiring his spirit and guts"

September 15

The dear little hummingbirds have been gone for several days. I miss them so much. *[They don't come anymore. I don't know what has happened to them.]* The greenhouse must go up soon. Any night it could frost. Karin and I are going to Juárez next week. Will get meat and coffee. Also I need new glasses. All these things are half as much there. I always enjoy Karin's company.

September 29

Had a great time with Karin in spite of the weather—poured most of the time. Prices have gone up there, too. Boris still working on his truck and plans to leave next week for Wisconsin and his Model A. He is on oxygen all the time and plans to put the big tank in the bed of the truck and bring the hose up to the cab. Hate to see him start out. Don't see how he'll do it.

October 2

Jean and I just returned from a most spectacular and beautiful day in Colorado to see the aspen. Magnificent!

October 12

Sister Kay is here and I do so hope she is having a good time. Poor dear, she so hates her life in Kansas City. *[In comparison to Santa Fe, that is. She liked being near her son.]* Can't blame her. Boris is still preparing for his big expedition. You'd think he was going on a six-month safari to the North Pole. Such provisions and equipment! I can't sleep nights worrying about his going off alone and then dragging the Model A all the way back. However, there is nothing I can do since I can't go with him. Just hope all goes well.

October 15

Boris took off. God bless him.

October 16

6 P.M. It's snowing. I can't believe it. Weather has been ghastly ever since Boris left. It haunts me. Where is he and how is he managing? No word, of course. I wouldn't be too concerned except for the fact that he is rather helpless without being attached to the oxygen cylinders in back of the truck. Hoping that at the lower altitudes he won't be so dependent on it. He couldn't have picked a worse time—storms and cold all over. It must be terrible up North.

October 18

Yesterday A.M. Boris called from Sioux Falls. Truck had broken down. He was almost out of control, he was so upset and breathless. I was frantic to know what to do. Said he would get it fixed and head back. I didn't see how he could possibly make it. I called our dearest friend Bob Brodkey in Columbus, Ohio, and, after several calls, he informed me he had made reservations to fly up there and drive Boris back—I am sure at much inconvenience and expense.

I had asked Boris to call me last night and he did. Starter fixed and he was in fine fettle, breathing well, and had decided to push on. I called Bob to cancel all reservations. I am furious with Boris, of course, for putting all of us and himself through this, but you can't help admiring his spirit and guts with his terrible handicap and age. Hope all goes well from now on. He has decided not to try to bring the Model A back after all, but there are other things he wanted from up there, and also I am sure he wants to prove to himself that he can do it. What a guy!

October 24

Boris called from Corny. *[That is Cornucopia, Wisconsin, where his cabin was.]* He was at Gus's for supper. *[He was a neighbor.]* Weather horrible, cold and wet. The mud was so deep that he couldn't even drive in to the cabin. He hopes to be home next week. Dana and Betty arrive Friday, the thirty-first. So look forward to having them here.

October 27

Poor, dear Boris! Where is he? How is he? Have heard no more. He could hardly have picked a worse time. Snow, cold, and rain all over the country. The little wood stove and ceiling fan keep it nice and cozy back here. Thank God I have lots of wood. Carter and Reagan—not much choice, except that I guess Reagan is really the worst—dangerous situation. Dear old Anderson really doesn't have a chance, but I am going to vote for him.*

October 28

No news from Boris.

October 29

Boris called last night from Wichita, Kansas, tired but OK. Incredible! He expects to pull in sometime tomorrow. Cleaned house; did a laundry; made bread and cookies; carved a pumpkin. Sun has been out all day. Looks like a cold night.

---

*Jimmy Carter was defeated for reelection by Ronald Reagan, 1980. This race also included the strong independent candidacy of John Anderson (b. 1922), U.S. representative from Illinois, who ran as a centrist after losing the Republican primary to archconservative Reagan. Anderson won about 7 percent of the vote.

Epilogue

January 20, 2000

That unfortunate 1980 trip to Wisconsin was the last time Boris was able to travel, and it had a devastating effect on his already deteriorating health—coping as he did with the terrible weather and a broken-down truck, always connected to his oxygen. The next two years, which I would be happy to forget, were spent more in the hospital than out. Boris said often that the worse thing of all was the loss of dignity. Knowing him, I can imagine how utterly painful it was. I am sure that anyone with a knowledge of the progress of emphysema will understand. Boris died in April 1982 in his own room surrounded by his books, records, and tapes, in the house he put together, with the satisfaction that it had been preserved and knowing that his art, for which he lived, had attained recognition.

About a year before his death, we met Steve Kestrel and Cindi Kunselman through a mutual friend, George Carlson, who was showing his work in Santa Fe. George was a very well known sculptor whom Boris had known in Wisconsin. Steve had built a house for George somewhere up in the Midwest. He and Cindi were living just a few streets away, and the four of us (Steve and Boris, Cindi and I) immediately liked each other. That was the start of a beautiful, beautiful friendship. Cindi loved gardening, and she was a very free soul. Steve made furniture and built houses—that man can do anything with his hands—but he had always wanted to be a sculptor. He just never had a place to work or the money to buy tools. Steve made a wonderful crosscut saw for Boris's last Christmas, carving the handle out of wood. When Boris opened it he said, "This is not to be used. It should be hanging on the wall." So now it still hangs on the wall in the *zaguán*. Unfortunately, they got a job building a house up North somewhere so they were gone for most of the last year of Boris's life. It has always upset Steve very much that he missed that time with Boris and wasn't here when he died.

Afterward, they came back to Santa Fe, and Steve worked in Boris's empty shop, carving stone, molding waxes—creating from inside with feeling and meaning. He had all the tools and equipment he could possibly need—a lifetime's collection, really—and that is how he started being a sculptor. Eventually, they sold their house and moved into the front room here with their two big dogs, Mocha and Narse.

We had such a wonderful time together. A couple of passages in my journal express as well as I can my feelings at that time, which could have been so lonely:

> *September 20, 1982:* How grateful and lucky can I be? Steve and Cindi are a gift of the gods. They are working in the shop in exchange for doing work for me. I can go off and they stay with Chica and all is well. Dear friends.

> *November 20, 1982:* Can't imagine what my life would be without the closeness of Steve and Cindi. Their being in the shop, talking, walking, laughing with them. Having them here for dinner. Someone to plan for, cook for. How empty, lonesome, meaningless it would be. They are there if I need them. I hope I don't get dependent on them for I know they are free souls and may take off anytime. I know I must be prepared to accept this. However, Steve is getting into his stone carving and planning all kinds of things. Cindi constantly has jobs refinishing furniture. Chica adores having four-legged friends in Mocha and Narse. How can I be so lucky!

While they were here, Steve and Cindi helped me make one change to the house. I wanted to turn the added room that had been Boris's bedroom into a guest room. Since it was built as a storeroom originally, it had only one little window and no closet. Steve put in the pretty south window and built a closet. Later I had Archie put a ceiling and insulated roof onto the greenhouse *portal* and George Jackson *[my niece Karin's son]* made the removable plastic walls. Those were the last things I did outside of completely redoing all of the adobe walls from scratch in 1985 and continuing general maintenance.

Steve and Cindi were with me for a year and then they moved back to Fort Collins, where they were from. Steve has his own shop now and still works with many of Boris's tools. He is doing wonderfully well as a sculptor and is receiving nationwide recognition. It would be so satisfying for Boris to know that this admired young friend could use his shop and equipment to establish a career that carries on many of Boris's ideas with the same dedication and integrity. How proud he would be.

After Steve and Cindi left, Luis Tapia used the shop for five years. He got his reputation while he was here.

On July 14, 1984, I did a show for Boris up in the *sala*. I took all the furniture out except for the big table and hung his drawings on the walls. John Fleming brought down the beautiful big birds that were originally done for the American President Lines, and I borrowed a few other pieces from people in town. The room made a beautiful gallery. Four years later I did a book for Boris on his work, which I called *Greatness in the Commonplace.*

In October 1990, I married a dear, wonderful man, Eric Varney. Unfortunately, his death in December of the same year left me alone again—but not really, as I had Charlie, his dog, who was my constant companion for five years.

So here I am eighteen years after Boris's death still living at 518 Alto Street in Santa Fe at the age of eighty-five. Sweet old Charlie died about five years ago. I adopted Niña, a shelter dog, who was a devoted friend until her recent death. I still have "old faithful" Archie West to keep up the fences and roofs, to patch the mud walls, to paint and to plaster, and to keep up with the myriad of other chores that an old house requires. God bless him. I couldn't have kept things going without him. It is a great comfort to me that the Historic Santa Fe Foundation now owns the house and will preserve it. So life goes on—it hasn't been easy, but, God knows, it's never been dull.

215

Glossary

Adobe (Sp. from Arabic, "the brick"): Sun-dried brick consisting of clay, sand, water, and sometimes straw; widely used for thousands of years in arid parts of the world. Also refers to the mud from which bricks are made as well as the buildings constructed of them.

Arroyo (Sp., stream): A usually dry gully or gulch created by periodic drainage that is sometimes sufficiently heavy to sweep cars in its wake. In some states called a wash or dry wash.

Banco (Sp., bench): Traditionally constructed of adobe against a wall.

Canal, pl. *canales* (Sp., gutter): Roof drainspout traditionally constructed of a hollowed-out half log that projected through the parapet wall.

Chinches (Sp., bedbugs): Bedbugs.

Luminaria (Sp., altar lamp, festive light): Charlotte is speaking of the Christmas lighting generally called *farolitos* (Sp., little lanterns), which are candles set in sand in small, brown paper bags. The word *luminaria* is now usually reserved for small wood fires also set out on Christmas Eve.

Piñon (Sp., pine): Nut pine, one-needle pine (*Pinus monophylla*). Generally small, slow-growing pine tree. Provides edible nuts and fragrant burning firewood. Can live more than two hundred years.

Placita (Sp., little plaza): Open courtyard or patio. Traditional Hispanic buildings in New Mexico often grew by accretion, beginning with a single file of rooms to which others were added, creating an L, a U, or a complete square around a *placita,* without interior hallways.

Plaza (Sp., public square): Rectangular open space at the center of a town. Plazas were required by town planning ordinances first issued by the Spanish monarch in 1573.

Portal (Sp., hall, porch): Long porch with roof supported by vertical posts (traditionally peeled logs). Often placed around the interior of a *placita* and used as an external hall between rooms that each had an exterior door.

Sala (Sp., large room, hall): Traditionally, the largest and main room in a house, where visitors were received and most family life took place. Described in 1853 by W. W. H. Davis in *El Gringo* (1857): ". . . mattresses are folded up and placed around the room, next to the wall, which, being covered with blankets, make a pleasant seat and serve the place of sofas. . . . At night they are unrolled and spread out for beds."

Sopaipilla (Sp. dim. of *sopaipa,* fritter): Bread squares fried in deep fat that swell to form an inner pocket. Often eaten with honey.

Viga (Sp., beam, rafter): In traditional New Mexican Spanish building, generally peeled logs exposed on the interior and supporting a flat roof composed of branches, brush, and a thick layer of dirt. After 1846 lumber mills provided squared beams.

Zaguán (Sp., vestibule, hall): As described by W. W. H. Davis in *El Gringo* (1857): "A large door, called a zaguan, leads from the street into the *patio* or court-yard, into which the doors of the various rooms open. A portal, or . . . porch, runs around this court, and serves as a sheltered communication between different parts of the house."

Flora and Fauna

African gray: Parrot of the African rain forest. Said to be the master among parrots at reproducing human speech. Also very alert and relatively good tempered. Little differentiation in appearance between males and females. Both about thirteen inches long and light gray in color except for a squared, red tail and bare whitish face.

Aspen (*Populus tremuloides*): Tall, thin trees. Grow in dense stands on mountainsides northeast of Santa Fe. Rich green, fluttering leaves turn brilliant yellow in fall, presenting a panorama of the seasons from Charlotte's front window.

Asters, wild: Blue to purple blooms in the fall along roadsides and arroyos, often together with yellow chamisa. Have been used as a dye, a stimulant, and a medicine.

Carrion plant: Succulent of the *Asclepiad* (milkweed) family. The scent of brightly colored, star-shaped flowers mimics the stench of rotting flesh. Depends on flies for pollination.

Chamisa (rabbitbrush): Gray-green shrub. Abundant in upper Rio Grande valley. Pungent yellow flowers in fall yield a yellow dye, stems a green dye.

Chinese elm: Name often erroneously assigned to Siberian elm (*Ulnus pamila*), a nonnative, hardy, fast-growing tree, introduced to the area for shade. Great quantity of seeds a springtime nuisance. Deep-rooted seedlings sprout everywhere to the gardener's dismay. The true Chinese elm seeds in the fall.

Cholla: Name applied to various cacti of the genus *Opuntia*. Only cacti with spines covered with papery sheaths that can be bright and colorful, giving this cactus its distinctive appearance.

Cottonwood: Tree belonging to the willow family (*Salicaceae*), of the same genus (*Populus*) as the aspen tree. Grows along watercourses. Revered by Native Americans; for early settlers meant water, wood, shade. Stands of cottonwoods at lower altitudes in Santa Fe environs mark the presence of (sometimes intermittently) flowing water.

Gouldian finch: Five-inch bird, native to Australia. Said to be among the most vividly colored birds on earth. More difficult than other finches to care for. Sensitive to temperature, humidity, and stress of changes in living quarters.

Night-blooming cereus: Cactus native to deserts of southwestern United States and northern Mexico. Spectacular blooms last only one night. Called *Reina de la Noche* (Sp., queen of the night) in Mexico.

Painted lady butterflies (*Vanessa cardui*): Rosy brown butterflies with black-and-white spots. Emigrate north from Mexico's Sonoran Desert. Successive generations fly as far as Canada, over mountains as high as twelve thousand feet. In wet years populations can explode into spectacular migrations.

Russian olive: Small, thorny, many-branched tree with narrow silvery leaves. Introduced from Russia as shade and windbreak tree. Grows prolifically along watercourses above seven thousand feet.

Solomon's seal (*Smilacina stellata*): Also called Solomon's plume. Grows in shaded, damp areas. Often found along streams. Stems up to three feet high. Small, white, star-shaped flowers at the end of the stem in early summer; green berries with dark blue or reddish stripes. False Solomon's seal (or plume; *S. racemosa*) larger with branched flower clusters, red berries.

Tamarisk (salt cedar): Small, graceful, fast-growing tree. Masses of tiny, pink flowers in spring and summer. Native to Europe and Asia; introduced early twentieth century in United States by U.S. Department of Agriculture for use in erosion control, as windbreaks, and as ornamental trees. Dense thickets along waterways crowd out native plants.

Woodbine (Virginia creeper): Twining vine. Very hardy. Fragrant flowers, blue or red berries.

Yucca: Stiff-leaved, stemless or treelike succulent. Produces a tall stalk of white or purplish blossoms. Roots of some species used for soap. Soaptree yucca is New Mexico's state flower.

People and Places

Spiro T. Agnew (1918–1996): Lawyer, politician. U.S. vice president under Nixon, 1969–73.

Malcolm Alexander: Painter, sculptor. Born Detroit. Formal training in painting, southern California. To Taos, about 1959. Painted portraits and landscapes. Later turned to sculpture. Moved to Los Angeles, 1972.

The Babins, Victor Babin (1908–1972) and wife, Vitya Vronsky (1909–1992): Russian-born pianists; emigrated to the United States, 1937. Began coming to Santa Fe, late 1930s. Toured widely as duo pianists. Both taught at Cleveland Institute of Music; Victor the director from 1961 until his death.

Ernest Badynski (b. 1936): Sculptor. Born Chicago. Studied Illinois State University, Western New Mexico University. Taught art, jewelry, sculpture in Santa Fe public schools for twenty-five years.

Louis Wayne Ballard (b. 1931): Composer, musician, and educator. Born Quapaw Indian Reservation, Oklahoma, of Quapaw–Cherokee descent. Bachelor and master degrees in music, 1954, 1962. Music director (1962–65), director of performing arts (1965–69) Institute of American Indian Arts, Santa Fe. Director of music education curriculum, Bureau of Indian Affairs, Washington, D.C., 1969–79. Independent composer, Santa Fe, since 1979. Numerous awards and commissions. *Koshare,* a ballet on Hopi themes, premiered Barcelona, Spain.

Barn Gallery: At 831¾ Canyon Road.

Ambrose Bierce (1842, Ohio–1914? Mexico): American journalist, satirist, short-story writer. *The Devil's Dictionary* (1911), a volume of ironic definitions. Disappeared in Mexico during the revolution. *The Enlarged Devil's Dictionary,* edited by E. J. Hopkins, appeared in 1967.

Gertrude Duby Blom (1901–1993): Swiss-born journalist, photographer. Emigrated to Mexico to escape turmoil in Europe, 1940. Her photographs documented the traditional life of the Mayans and later the destruction of the Lacandón rain forest. Married archaeologist Frans Blom. Na Bolom, their home in a former cloister in San Cristóbal de las Casas, Chiapas, became a center for scientific study and community activism.

Boettcher School: Gilbertson created a steel-and-bronze bird mobile for the hallway of the Boettcher School for Crippled Children to symbolize the "independence and strength" of the students. School founded by Denver pioneer and successful entrepreneur Charles Boettcher (1852–1948), who came to the West from Germany in 1869. Established Boettcher Foundation for charitable activities, 1937, and the school, 1940.

Rafael Borrego House: At 724 Canyon Road. Later sold by OSFA with restrictive covenants to assure its preservation. Listed in the Foundation's Registry in 1981.

Edgar Britton (1901–1982): Sculptor, painter, printmaker. Born Nebraska. First studied dentistry. Art student of the painter Grant Wood. Painted murals under public works programs in the 1930s, including the U.S. Department of the Interior building, where he met Boris Gilbertson. Later career in Colorado Springs and Denver. In 1999 the Boulder Museum of Contemporary Art included his work in the exhibition "Vanguard Art in Colorado 1940–1970."

Cañones: Settlement seven miles west of Abiquiú, New Mexico.

George Carlson (b. 1940, Illinois): Sculptor. Trained at Chicago Art Institute and American Academy of Art in Chicago. Subjects include native peoples, horses, eagles, ballet dancers. Recipient of numerous awards.

Jimmy Carter (b. 1924): U.S. president, 1977–81. Born Georgia.

Cerrillos (Sp., little hills): Small village twenty miles south of Santa Fe. Named for nearby hills where turquoise was mined by Native Americans as well as lead and possibly silver by the Spanish. Boomtown growth followed new strikes of gold and silver-lead ores in 1879. Tiffany's of New York gained control of the turquoise mines in the late nineteenth century. Cerrillos residents in recent decades have fought subdivisions and renewed mining in the area.

Christian Brothers: The Christian Brothers are members of the Roman

Catholic institute of the Brothers of the Christian Schools founded by St. John Baptist de la Salle in France in 1684, and they are dedicated to education.

Contemporaries: Fine arts gallery at 418½ College Street (now Old Santa Fe Trail).

Randall Davey (1887–1964): Painter and teacher. Born East Orange, New Jersey. Studied architecture at Cornell; soon turned to painting. One of the youngest artists to exhibit in the groundbreaking Armory Show of 1913. Moved to New Mexico, 1919. Established home and studio in remodeled sawmill (Santa Fe's first, 1847) in the Santa Fe River canyon. Listed in the HSFF Registry, 1965.

Dressman's Flower Nook: Florist Frank Dressman. At 58½ Lincoln Avenue in 1960.

Thomas Harvey Dryce (1904–1984): Architect, painter. Born Dayton, Ohio. Educated Massachusetts Institute of Technology; École des Beaux-Arts, Fontainebleau, France.

Fremont Ellis (1897–1985): Painter. Born Montana. Trained as optometrist. Studied briefly Art Students League, New York City. Moved to Santa Fe, 1919. Member *Los Cinco Pintores* (The Five Painters), an exhibition group. Their five hand-built, early 1920s adobe homes on Camino del Monte Sol influenced development of the Santa Fe art colony and the Spanish–Pueblo Revival style architecture, which now predominates in Santa Fe.

Española: Small community on the Rio Grande twenty-five miles northwest of Santa Fe. Founded second half of nineteenth century. Grew as railhead of Denver and Rio Grande Railway after 1880. Today combines several older settlements within town limits.

Lewis E. ("Doc") Ewen (c. 1901–1992): Painter. Born Portland, Oregon. Studied at New York Fine and Applied Art School and New York School of Design. To Santa Fe, 1960. Career in graphic arts as designer, illustrator, commercial artist. Layout artist–illustrator for *New Mexico* magazine and for two years publisher of the *New Mexico Territorian,* a periodical devoted to New Mexico history.

Vivian Sloan Fiske (1900–1978): Painter, patron of the arts. Born Texas. Studied Broadmoor Art Academy, Colorado Springs, with Randall

Davey and in New York City with John Sloan (no known relation). Moved to New Mexico, 1938. Widow of Santa Fe doctor, Eugene W. Fiske.

La Fonda (Sp., the inn): In 1921 replaced the Exchange Hotel, Santa Fe's main hostelry in the days of the Santa Fe Trail. Added to the Fred Harvey chain, 1926. Enlarged 1929, 1950. Excellent example of an early Spanish–Pueblo Revival design. Said to be the oldest hotel site in the United States.

Ford Foundation: Philanthropic foundation established in 1936 with gifts and bequests from Henry Ford and his son, Edsel, for the general purpose of advancing human welfare. Chief concerns have been international affairs, communications, humanities and the arts, and, in later years, resources and the environment.

Marcelino García (1855–1929): Merchant, Democratic politician, owner of much Santa Fe property. Served as territorial auditor and in numerous Santa Fe county offices. Elected four terms Santa Fe City Council and was city treasurer. On first Santa Fe City Planning Board in 1912, which had as one objective "the preservation . . . of streets and properties . . . needed to preserve [Santa Fe's] character as the most ancient city in America."

Vicente García (1827–1889): Merchant, stock raiser, and politician. Served in Territorial House of Representatives and as its president. Son of Feliz García (1792–1872), an officer in the Mexican army and prominent Santa Fe citizen for whom Don Felix Street was named by his grandson, Marcelino García.

Greer Garson (c. 1904–1996); Irish-born, Academy Award–winning actress. Married in 1949 to independent oilman and philanthropist E. E. ("Buddy") Fogelson (1901–87), owner of the Forked Lightning Ranch near Pecos. In 1991 forty-five thousand acres, including the main house, were purchased for donation to the federal government to expand the Pecos National Monument.

Greer Garson Theater: This theater (1965), the Fogelson Library (1970), and the Greer Garson Communications Center and Studio (1989) attest to the generous benefactions of Garson and her husband, E. E. Fogelson, to the College of Santa Fe.

Leon Gaspard (1882–1964): Internationally known painter. Born Russia, studied in Odessa, Moscow, and Paris. Settled in Taos, 1919, where his home became a showplace. Known for studies of American Indians, Chinese, and Russian subjects and exotic colors.

Eric Gibberd (1897–1972): Painter. Born London, England. A leader in U.S. retail advertising before becoming a professional artist in 1952 with encouragement of his wife, former Pauline Seeberger Sowers. Exhibitions in Paris, London, Amsterdam, and Barcelona followed. Moved to Taos, 1954.

Eric Gilbertson: Deputy State Historic Preservation Officer and Director of the Vermont Division for Historic Preservation.

Warren ("Bud") Gilbertson (c. 1911–1954): Widely recognized authority on Asian ceramic technique. Studied pottery in Japan, 1939–41. Credited with introducing Japanese *raku* pottery techniques to the American public at a Chicago Art Institute exhibition. Moved to Santa Fe, 1951. Workshop, Valley Kilns, located 518 Alto Street, early 1950s. Died in automobile accident, 1954.

Vincent van Gogh (1853–1890): Postimpressionist painter. Born the Netherlands. His younger brother, Théo, was his confidant to whom he wrote revealing letters detailing the conflicts and aspirations of his troubled life.

Golden: Gold mining camp that grew into a small village briefly in the 1880s. Sixteen miles southwest of Cerrillos.

Una Hanbury (1904–1990): Sculptor. Born London, England. Educated Royal Academy of Fine Arts; also studied in Paris and Italy. Left England, 1944. Lived in Washington, D.C., twenty-five years. First traveled to Santa Fe, 1946. Settled there permanently, 1970. Best known for portrait busts of the famous, including Georgia O'Keeffe, Laura Gilpin, Rachel Carson, and Buckminster Fuller.

Peter Hurd (1904–1984): Painter, printmaker, illustrator. Born Roswell, New Mexico Territory. Apprenticed in studio of illustrator N. C. Wyeth and married his daughter, Henriette, also a painter. Resettled in New Mexico, 1930s. In 1967 his official portrait of Lyndon B. Johnson was rejected by the president.

Jémez Mountains: Range visible to the northwest in Santa Fe. Located

west of the Rio Grande and formed by volcanic upheavals that created the Valle Grande, a sixteen-mile-wide caldera that the mountains
surround. Named for the Jémez Pueblo.

Dr. Myra Ellen Jenkins (c. 1917–1993): Historian, archivist, teacher.
Doctorate in history, University of New Mexico, 1953. New Mexico
State Archivist and Historian. Leading expert on Indian lands and on
land grants. Served as both a member and chair of the HSFF Board
of Directors.

Lyndon Baines Johnson (1908–1973): U.S. president, 1963–69. His
administration initiated major social programs aimed at creating the
"Great Society," including Model Cities, but bore the brunt of national opposition to escalation of American participation in the Vietnam
War.

Bishop Everett Holland Jones: Pastor San Antonio, Texas, and then bishop of the Episcopal Diocese of West Texas and New Mexico. With his
wife, Helen, had a home in Santa Fe from around 1955 until around
1963. Boris Gilbertson on Bishop Jones: ". . . very intelligent, old
school, a real classicist. It is very flattering when people like that [enjoy
your work]—very quiet, very reserved, very keen." (Interview by
Sylvia G. Loomis, Archives of American Art, Smithsonian Institution,
Washington, D.C. [25 June 1964], 25).

Robert F. Kennedy (1925–1968): Lawyer, politician. Appointed U.S.
attorney general (1961–64) by his brother, President John F. Kennedy.
Elected U.S. senator from New York, 1964. Ran in the presidential
primaries of 1968 as a critic of the Vietnam War. Assassinated in Los
Angeles on the eve of winning the California primary, June 6, 1968,
just a few months after the death of Martin Luther King, Jr.

Martin Luther King, Jr. (1929–1968): Baptist minister and civil rights
leader. Led movement that successfully employed nonviolent tactics
to end legal segregation in the United States. His assassination on the
balcony of the Lorraine Motel in Memphis, Tennessee, was followed
by riots and disturbances in 130 American cities. Within a week of his
death, the Open Housing Act was passed by Congress.

King Ranch: In south Texas. One of the largest ranches in the world.
Established by Richard King (1825–1885), a steamboat captain, with

the purchase of a seventy-five-thousand-acre Spanish land grant known as Santa Gertrudis in 1852. Eventually more than a million acres. Santa Gertrudis breed of beef cattle developed early 1900s. Only true cattle breed developed in North America. Widely distributed throughout the United States and extensively exported.

Felix Labunski (1892–1979): Composer in Polish and Russian Romantic tradition, pianist, critic. Polish-born, trained Warsaw Conservatory and École Normale de Musique in Paris. To the United States, 1936. Taught Cincinnati College of Music, (subsequently merged with Cincinnati Conservatory of Music), 1945–64.

LaCerte: Theo B. LaCerte Carpenter Shop, home at 120 Mesa Verde.

Marjorie Lambert (b. 1910): Archaeologist, teacher. Curator at the Museum of New Mexico for more than thirty years.

Lamy: Small community fourteen miles southeast of Santa Fe. Railroad stop on the main line of the Atchison, Topeka, and Santa Fe Railway. Junction with spur line to Santa Fe.

Mario Larrinaga (1895–1979): Painter. Born Flores, Mexico. Thirty-five-year, much-awarded stage and screen career in set design and special effects (including the original *King Kong*, 1933). Also illustrator for major magazines. Moved to Taos, 1951.

Sylvia G. Loomis (c. 1906–1994): Administrator, teacher. To Santa Fe, c. 1950. Resident manager of El Zaguán, 1962–81. Editorial staff of *Landscape* magazine. Secretary of OSFA, HSFF, the Spanish Colonial Arts Society. For Archives of American Art interviewed artists who had worked for federal arts projects during the Great Depression. Archives of American Art: Founded 1954. Became a bureau of the Smithsonian Institution, 1970. More than thirteen million items encompassing American art from colonial times to the present. Oral history program throughout the country interviewing living artists and art world figures.

Loretto Academy: School for girls in Santa Fe (1859–1968), established by Sisters of Loretto. Property sold for commercial development, 1971. Buildings demolished except Loretto Chapel. Hotel Loretto built, 1973–75.

Los Alamos: Community twenty-four miles northwest of Santa Fe in the

Jémez Mountains. Los Alamos Ranch School (est. 1917) was taken over by the Manhattan Project of the U.S. Army in 1943 for the secret development of the atomic bomb. The successor, Los Alamos National Laboratory, is a premier research facility in the United States and is a major employer in north-central New Mexico.

Marion Love (1916–2000): Born Oswego, New York. To Santa Fe, 1943. Peter Krebbs her third husband. Founded *The Santa Fean Magazine* with Betty Bauer, 1972.

William T. Lumpkins (1909–2000): Architect, abstract watercolorist. Born on ranch near Clayton, New Mexico. Pioneer in passive solar, adobe design. Designed more than five hundred projects locally, including large commercial projects and more than seventy solar adobe homes. Practiced architecture in California, 1950–67.

Tommy (Thomas S.) Macaione (1907–1992): Painter, eccentric. Born New England to Sicilian immigrant parents. Trained as barber. To Santa Fe to paint, 1952. Familiar figure, with long, flowing white hair and beard, painting flowers out of doors. Menagerie of pets reached eighty-five. Write-in political campaigns for major offices on the platform of the Mutual Happiness Society. After his death Hillside Park, at Hillside Avenue and Paseo de Peralta, renamed for him. *El Diferente,* a bronze figure of him painting, was placed there.

Eugene J. McCarthy (b. 1916): U.S. senator, Minnesota. Outspoken critic of the Vietnam War after 1967. Challenged incumbent president Lyndon B. Johnson in 1968 presidential primaries with strong anti-war stand. His success in the New Hampshire primary caused Johnson to drop reelection bid. McCarthy eventually lost the nomination to Vice President Hubert H. Humphrey (1911–1978; vice president 1965–69), who had not run in the primaries.

Madrid: Former coal mining town twenty-four miles southwest of Santa Fe. Settled, nineteenth century. Company town of up to four thousand residents owned by Albuquerque and Cerrillos Coal Company, 1920–40. Entire town offered for sale with no takers, 1954. Revived as a tourist destination after buildings sold to individuals, beginning 1975.

Marberg Gallery: Located Southwest National Bank Building, 300 East

Main, El Paso, Texas. Director, Martha Schlusselberg. Exhibited work of contemporary artists.

Edward Marecak (1919–1993): Painter, lithographer. Trained Cleveland Institute of Art, Cranbrook Academy of Art, Colorado Springs Fine Arts Center. Exhibited Denver, New York, Beverly Hills, and Carmel but infrequently after 1960s. Taught art in Denver public schools twenty-five years. His work included in the Boulder Museum of Contemporary Art 1999 exhibition "Vanguard Art in Colorado."

María Martínez (1886–1980): Renowned Native American artist. Born San Ildefonso Pueblo. Major figure in the twentieth-century revitalization of pueblo pottery. With husband Julián Martínez revived technique of making distinctive black-on-black ware in 1918 by firing clay pots with dried horse manure. Numerous awards from around the world.

Guy de Maupassant (1850–1893): Naturalistic French writer. Best known for some three hundred short stories that greatly influenced the genre. Led an extravagant and dissolute life that ended in syphilitic madness.

André Maurois (Émile Herzog; 1885–1967): French novelist, essayist, popular historian. Wrote biographies of such authors as Percy Bysshe Shelley, Lord George Gordon Byron, Victor Hugo, George Sand, Honoré de Balzac, François-Marie Voltaire, and Marcel Proust.

New Canton Café, 125 West San Francisco Street. Established 1922; closed about 1975. For decades Santa Fe's only Chinese restaurant.

Richard M. Nixon (1913–1994): Lawyer, politician, author. U.S. president, 1969–74.

Don Peterson: News editor of the *New Mexican.* The *New Mexican:* the oldest newspaper in the state. First issues 1849–50. Begun again 1863. Published under several names, including *Santa Fe New Mexican.*

Aline Kilham Porter (1909–1991): Artist known for flower paintings. Born Brookline, Massachusetts. Lived in Santa Fe for forty-five years. Featured in major art shows in Santa Fe and New York.

Eliot Porter (1901–1990): Master photographer. Pioneer in color photography. Born Winnetka, Illinois. Studied chemical engineering and medicine at Harvard, where he taught for ten years. Left Harvard following successful 1938 exhibit of black-and-white photographs at Alfred Stieglitz's New York gallery. Moved to Tesuque, New Mexico, 1946. Produced two dozen books, probably more than any other photographer. *Eliot Porter's Southwest* (1986) features photographs taken from 1939 to 1965.

Preservation Hall: At 726 St. Peter Street, French Quarter, New Orleans. Tiny room with wood benches and a simple stage where old-time jazz musicians gather nightly to play original New Orleans–style jazz, providing a direct link to the jazz that evolved in New Orleans around the turn of the century. Also tour nationally and internationally.

Catherine Rayne (1909–1999): Born Maryland. Trained as registered nurse. To Santa Fe, about 1940. Friend and companion of Amelia Elizabeth White for thirty years. For many years director of the Garcia Street Club for children, founded by White. Managed White's estate until it was given to the School of American Research (SAR).

Rios Wood Yard: Family business at 324 Camino del Monte Sol. Begun by Jesus Rios (1901–1996), early 1940s. Continued by his children.

Nelson A. Rockefeller (1908–1979): Politician, philanthropist, art collector/connoisseur. Governor of New York, 1959–73. Vice president of the United States under President Gerald Ford (1974–77).

Norman Rockwell (1894–1978): Possibly America's most widely seen artist and most beloved. His nostalgic, humorous vignettes of American life appeared on more than three hundred *Saturday Evening Post* covers between 1916 and 1963. The fine arts establishment scorned his realism, accessibility, and middle-brow appeal—the "corny" sentimentality that Boris Gilbertson sought to avoid through the use of animal subjects. Reassessment has commenced with a comprehensive traveling exhibition of his work scheduled to conclude in 2002 at New York City's Guggenheim Museum, a citadel of modernist, nonrepresentational art.

Olive Rush (1873–1966): Painter in oil, watercolor, pastels, and fresco. Native of Indiana, studied in New York and Paris. Settled in Santa Fe, 1920. Early member of Santa Fe art colony. Her murals can be seen in Fray Angélico Chávez History Library and Southwest Room of La Fonda. Her garden a showplace behind her home and studio at 630 Canyon Road. The property now the Society of Friends Meetinghouse.

St. John's College: Four-year, private college. Founded 1964 southeast of Santa Fe. Offers the Great Books curriculum of its parent campus in Annapolis, Maryland, founded 1784. Saturday night movie series popular with townsfolk; especially important in the 1960s and 1970s, before Santa Fe's present wide selection of cinema.

St. Michael's College: Founded by the Christian Brothers as a boys' school, 1859. School building constructed on College Street (now Old Santa Fe Trail), 1878. Bill Lumpkins remodeled into a dormitory for St. Michael's High School. Split into College of Santa Fe and St. Michael's High School, 1965. Building acquired by the state of New Mexico to house state offices, 1965. Renamed Lamy Building.

San Ildefonso: Tewa-speaking pueblo, ten miles south of Española. Spanish mission built 1617. Named for seventh-century Archbishop of Toledo, Spain, Saint Ildephonsus.

Sangre de Cristo Mountains (Sp., Blood of Christ): Southernmost section of the Rocky Mountain chain, extending south from southern Colorado to Pecos, New Mexico. Santa Fe was founded in the early 1600s on the banks of the Santa Fe River, which originates in the Sangres northeast of the city.

Santa Fe Indian School: Established 1890 by the federal government as an off-reservation boarding school on a rural site on what is now Cerrillos Road. Closed in 1962 and succeeded on the site by the Institute of American Indian Arts. Returned to the original site under Indian control, 1981.

Santa Fe Opera: Founded by John Crosby (b. 1926) in 1956. Original open-air theater completed 1957 north of Santa Fe, 450 seats. Enlarged, 1965. Destroyed by fire, 1967. Rebuilt partially covered, 1968. Remodeled fully covered, 1998. Summer program features a yearly premier and always an opera by the German composer Richard Strauss.

Santa Fe Plaza: Center of Santa Fe life since early 1600s. Faced on the north by the Palace of the Governors, former New Mexico capitol building under Spain, Mexico, and the United States, and since 1909 a unit of the Museum of New Mexico.

Santo Domingo Pueblo: Pre-Spanish, Native American village on east bank of the Rio Grande, twenty-nine miles southwest of Santa Fe.

Jack Schaefer (1907–1991): Newspaperman turned Western writer. Had never been farther west than Ohio when his first Western, *Shane,* appeared, 1949. Film version, 1953, with Alan Ladd, Jean Arthur, Van Heflin, Jack Palance, and Brandon de Wilde, considered among the best Westerns ever made. Moved to small ranch near Cerrillos, 1954. Wrote some twenty novels. *Shane* voted the best Western of all time by the Western Writers of America, 1985.

Mrs. Ernest Thompson Seton (Julia M.; 1889–1974): Widow of E. T. Seton (1860–1946), the naturalist, artist, writer, founder of the Woodcraft League. Southeast of Santa Fe, 1930s, they established Seton Village and an "Indian Village" overlooked by their home. Here they taught "the Indian way of life." Mrs. Seton herself an author and lecturer on Native American subjects.

Seton Castle: The Setons' adobe home built mid-1930s. Grew to thirty rooms by 1945; forty-five by 1970. National Historic Landmark, 1965. In 1968 his widow gave much of his materials, which had filled the home, to Seton Memorial Library and Museum at Philmont Scout Ranch near Cimarron, New Mexico. Included were thirty-two hundred drawings, paintings, and sculptures; two thousand bird and mammal skins; thirty thousand books; and hundreds of Indian artifacts.

Eugenie Shonnard (1886–1978): Sculptor. Born Yonkers, New York. Studied New York Art Students League and in Paris with sculptor Auguste Rodin. Settled in Santa Fe, 1926. Her home and studio, at 1411 Paseo de Peralta, listed in the HSFF Registry, 1973. Conquistadora *reredos* (Sp., altar screen) in Rosario Chapel an example of her work.

Silva gang: Known as the "forty thieves." Led by Vicente Silva (1845–1893). Saloon keeper, Las Vegas, New Mexico. Responsible for a crime spree in the 1880s and 1890s that included murder, theft, and livestock rustling.

Marc Simmons (b. 1937): Independent historian. Author of numerous scholarly and popular books and articles on Southwest history, including a weekly newspaper column. Recipient of numerous awards, including the second highest given by the Spanish govern-ment. Lives north of Cerrillos in hand-built home without electrici-ty, telephone, or indoor plumbing.

Carlos A. Spiess: Spiess Roofing Service. At 710 Canyon Road.

Charles C. Stewart (b. 1922, Ohio): Sculptor, painter, teacher. Trained Toledo Museum, New York Art Students League. Began career in Taos, 1947. Opened his own gallery, 1949. Taught art and sculpture in Taos and in Tulsa, Oklahoma. Moved to Todos Santos in the Baja California peninsula of Mexico, 1986. Other artists followed; the village has become a noted art colony.

Igor Stravinsky (1882–1971): Russian-born composer, pianist, conductor. Married second wife Vera, 1940. Among the greatest twentieth-century composers. Ballet *The Rite of Spring* (1913) said to mark the beginning of the modernist movement in music. Lived in Paris after 1911. In the United States from beginning of World War II. Frequently in Santa Fe in the summer for productions of his work by the Santa Fe Opera, 1957–63.

Sweeney gymnasium: Santa Fe High School gymnasium, built around 1955. Converted to Sweeney Convention Center, 1979. Located West Marcy Street.

Chuzo Tamotzu (1891–1975): Painter in oil, watercolor, pen and ink. Born Japan. Settled in New York City, 1920. World War II combat artist with U.S. Army's Office of Strategic Services. Moved to Santa Fe, 1948.

Taos: Village fifty-four miles northeast of Santa Fe. Spanish settlement founded in 1617 near the Taos Pueblo on a plateau between the Rio Grande and the Sangre de Cristo Mountains. From about 1890, before Santa Fe, attracted a colony of artists and writers.

Luis Eligio Tapia (b. 1950, Santa Fe): Sculptor. Key role in the contem-porary renaissance of Hispanic art in the Southwest.

Truchas: Small Hispanic village located eighteen miles northeast of Española in the Sangre de Cristo foothills. Founded in eighteenth century.

Ermalee Udall: Wife of Stewart Udall, lawyer, politician, environmental-ist, author. Secretary of the Interior under President John F. Kennedy and President Lyndon B. Johnson, when major environmental laws were passed. Today their son, Tom Udall, represents northern New Mexico in the U.S. House of Representatives.

Van Soelen House: At this time Don Van Soelen and his wife, Valeria, owned the Juan José Prada House at 519 Canyon Road, directly west of El Zaguán. Van Soelen, a banker and the son of artist Theodore Van Soelen, is a former longtime member and chairman of the HSFF Board of Directors. The Prada House listed by the HSFF as worthy of preservation, 1962.

Alan C. Vedder (1912–1989): Born Massachusetts. To Santa Fe, early 1950s. Active board member of OSFA. One of three founders of the HSFF, 1961. Worked with E. Boyd, head of the Spanish Colonial Arts Department of the Museum of New Mexico, almost twenty years. With his wife, Ann Healy Vedder, largely responsible for reactivating the Spanish Colonial Arts Society, originally formed in the 1920s.

Donaciano Vigil (1802–1877): Soldier and politician. Served Mexican (1821–46) and U.S. governments (after 1846). As Secretary of the Department of New Mexico issued a proclamation of nonresistance in August 1846 to occupying American forces near onset of United States–Mexican War. Appointed secretary and acting governor in provisional American government. Elected to both the Territorial House and Legislative Council (Senate).

Juan Cristóbal Vigil (d. 1832): Soldier and politician. Santa Fe *alcalde* (Sp., civil official with executive, judicial, and legislative functions) and interpreter in the early days of the Santa Fe Trail.

Sallie R. Wagner (b. 1913, West Virginia): Trading post owner, author, community benefactor. Degree in anthropology, University of Chicago. With husband William Lippincott, operated a Navajo trading post, 1938–51. Settled in Santa Fe, 1953. Very active on behalf of cultural preservation and community service organizations. As a volunteer was the first to organize the Palace of the Governors photo collection.

Bernique Wallace (1923–1999): Painter known professionally as Bernique Longley. Born Chicago. Trained Chicago Art Institute; postgraduate fellowship travel in Mexico. Settled in Santa Fe, 1946. Three solo exhibitions at Santa Fe's Museum of Fine Arts.

Amelia Elizabeth White (1878–1972): Philanthropist. Born New York

City, daughter of writer and financier Horace White. Bryn Mawr College, 1901. To Santa Fe, 1921. A founder of the Indian Arts Fund, OSFA, and Laboratory of Anthropology—groups dedicated to the preservation of New Mexico's diverse cultural heritage. Her Garcia Street estate now the campus of SAR.

Dr. D. B. Witcher: Acoma Animal Hospital on Llano Street.

Helene Wurlitzer Foundation of New Mexico: Established in Taos, 1954. Provides housing, studio space without stipend for twelve artists per session in all media.

El Zaguán: At 545 Canyon Road. Nineteenth-century home of Santa Fe Trail merchant James L. Johnson. Owned by the HSFF since 1979. Contains HSFF offices and private apartments. Gardens and limited rooms open to the public during business hours.

Vera Zorina (Eva Brigitta Hartwig; b. 1917): Dancer, actress. Born Berlin. Ballet training in Berlin, London. Took a Russianized stage name as soloist with the Ballets Russes de Monte Carlo, 1934–36. Performed in many film musicals under contract with MGM, 1938–44. Married choreographer George Balanchine, 1938–46. Subsequently married Goddard Lieberson, president of Columbia Records. *Ashoka's Dream,* an opera by their son, the composer Peter Lieberson, was commissioned by the Santa Fe Opera, which staged the world premier in 1997.

For Further Reading

Bunting, Bainbridge. *Early Architecture in New Mexico.* Albuquerque: University of New Mexico Press, 1976.

Cobos, Rubén. *A Dictionary of New Mexico and Southern Colorado Spanish.* Santa Fe: Museum of New Mexico Press, 1983.

Davis, W. W. H. *El Gringo: New Mexico and Her People.* 1857. Lincoln: University of Nebraska Press, 1982.

Gilbertson, Boris. Interview by Sylvia G. Loomis. Archives of American Art. Smithsonian Institution. Washington, D.C., 25 June 1964.

Hall, Em. "Giant before the Surveyor-General: The Land Career of Donaciano Vigil." *Spanish and Mexican Land Grants in New Mexico and Colorado.* Eds. John R. and Christine M. Van Ness. Santa Fe: Center for Land Grant Studies, 1980.

Historic Santa Fe Foundation. *Old Santa Fe Today.* Albuquerque: University of New Mexico Press, 1991.

Hyer, Sally. *One House, One Voice, One Heart: Native American Education at the Santa Fe Indian School.* Santa Fe: Museum of New Mexico Press, 1990.

Iowa, Jerome. *Ageless Adobe.* Santa Fe: Sunstone Press, 1985.

La Farge, Oliver. *Santa Fe: The Autobiography of a Southwestern Town.* Norman: University of Oklahoma Press, 1959.

Lumpkins, William. *La Casa Adobe.* Santa Fe: Ancient City Press, 1961.

———. *Modern Spanish-Pueblo Homes.* Santa Fe: Western Plan Service, 1946.

Markovich, Nicholas C., Wolfgang F. E. Preiser, and Fred G. Sturm, eds. *Pueblo Style and Regional Architecture.* New York: Van Nostrand Reinhold, 1992.

Noble, David Grant, ed. *Santa Fe, History of an Ancient City.* Santa Fe: School of American Research, 1989.

Robertson, Edna, and Sarah Nestor. *Artists of the Canyons and Caminos: Santa Fe the Early Years.* 1976. Salt Lake City: Gibbs M. Smith, 1982.

Scott, Eleanor. *The First Twenty Years of the Santa Fe Opera.* Santa Fe: Sunstone Press, 1976.

Simmons, Marc. *Turquoise and Six-Guns: The Story of Cerrillos, New Mexico.* Santa Fe: Sunstone Press, 1974.

Stanley, F. *Giant in Lilliput: The Story of Donaciano Vigil.* Pampa, Tex.: Pampa Print Shop, 1963.

Tierney, Gail D. *Roadside Plants of Northern New Mexico.* Santa Fe: Lightning Tree, 1983.

Traugott, Joseph. *Pueblo Architecture and Modern Adobes: The Residential Designs of William Lumpkins.* Santa Fe: Museum of New Mexico Press, 1998.

Twitchell, Ralph Emerson. *The History of the Military Occupation of the Territory of New Mexico for 1846 to 1851 by the Government of the United States.* Denver: Smith-Brooks Company, 1909.

———. *Old Santa Fe: The Story of New Mexico's Ancient Capital.* 1925. Chicago: Rio Grande Press, 1963.

Vigil, Donaciano, Collection. State Records Center and Archives. Santa Fe, New Mexico.

Weigle, Marta, and Kyle Fiore. *Santa Fe and Taos: The Writer's Era, 1916–1941.* Santa Fe: Ancient City Press, 1982.

White, Charlotte. *Greatness in the Commonplace: The Art of Boris Gilbertson.* Santa Fe: Sunstone Press, 1988.

Wilson, Chris. *The Myth of Santa Fe: Creating a Modern Regional Tradition.* Albuquerque: University of New Mexico Press, 1997.